ART BRILES
LOOKING UP

ART BRILES

LOOKING UP

My Journey from
Tragedy to Triumph

NICK EATMAN

Foreword by Robert Griffin III

TRIUMPH
BOOKS

This book is available in quantity at special discounts for your group or organization. For further information, contact:

Triumph Books LLC
814 North Franklin Street
Chicago, IL 60610
(312) 337-0747
www.triumphbooks.com

Printed in the United States of America

ISBN: 978-1-60078-906-9
Book design and editorial production by Alex Lubertozzi

Photo Credits
Following page 132: (unnumbered page 1) photos courtesy of the Briles family; (page 2) all photos courtesy of the Briles family, except photo of Dennis and Art Briles, courtesy of the *Abilene Reporter-News*; (pages 3–5) photos courtesy of the Briles family; (page 6) photos of Kendal Briles and Art Briles courtesy of the Briles family; Glenn Odell photo courtesy of Ellen Skipper; photo of Art Briles and Jason Bragg courtesy of Sharon Bragg; (page 7) photos of the Briles children and family courtesy of the Briles family; Kendal Briles photo (playing quarterback) courtesy of Ellen Skipper; (page 8) photo of Kendal and Art Briles courtesy of the *Fort Worth Star-Telegram*; Can Fans photo courtesy of Ellen Skipper; Stephenville football team photo courtesy of AP Images.

Following page 212: (page 1) Kevin Kolb photo courtesy of AP Images; Wes Welker photo courtesy of Norvelle Kennedy, Texas Tech Athletics Communications; Donnie Avery photo courtesy of AP Images; (page 2) Art Briles photo courtesy of AP Images, Briles family photo courtesy of the Briles family; (page 3) photos of Branndon Stewart and Kelan Luker courtesy of Ellen Skipper; Robert Griffin III photo courtesy of Baylor Marketing & Communications; photos of Nick Florence and Casey Keenum courtesy of AP Images; (page 4) Art Briles photo courtesy of Baylor Marketing & Communications; first-round draft pick photos courtesy of AP Images; (page 5) photos courtesy of Baylor Marketing & Communications; (page 6) photo of Lovie Smith and Art Briles courtesy of AP Images; photos of Art Briles with Bob Simpson and Amos Lee courtesy of the Briles family; Alamo Bowl photo courtesy of AP Images; (page 7) Terrance Ganaway photo courtesy of James D. Smith; Kaz Kazadi photo courtesy of Baylor Marketing & Communications; photos of Kendall Wright and Ahmad Dixon courtesy of AP Images; (page 8) photo of Art Briles and Robert Griffin III courtesy of AP Images; Briles family photo courtesy of the Briles family; Baylor football team photo courtesy of Baylor Marketing & Communications.

Contents

Foreword

"WHEN THINGS ARE going bad, you've got to get good."

That's a phrase I've heard Coach Briles say numerous times, whether it's on the sideline, in the locker room at halftime, or even on the practice field. When things are looking bleak, coach always uses that phrase when trying to turn the tide of momentum. It's simple, but meaningful. He wants you to be accountable not only for your actions, but also for your surroundings.

As the quarterback of his teams at Baylor from 2008 to 2011, it was often my job to take charge and make sure things got turned around on the field. But Coach Briles wasn't always talking about the game of football. He wasn't just talking about avoiding a blitz, rolling to the side, and throwing a touchdown—turning a potential sack into a score. Sometimes he was talking about the game of life, a bigger picture altogether.

I know when we first stepped on the Baylor University campus in 2008, things weren't going well for the football program. He knew that, which is why he took the challenge. I knew it, too, and that's why I wanted to go with him. We thought that together, through hard work, desire, and drive, we could achieve great things.

I'm proud to say we did.

But it started with Coach Briles. He told me that, if I came to Baylor, I could be a starting quarterback in the Big 12. Not many schools were saying that back then. Some wanted me to play receiver. Some wanted me to be a safety. And some thought I had quarterback in my future, but down the road, with the proper development.

To Coach Briles, however, I wasn't just any quarterback. No, from the very beginning, I was *his* quarterback.

Even then, he had bigger dreams for me. He didn't just think I could play the position. He told me I had the potential to win a Heisman Trophy. He told me I could be a first-round draft pick in the NFL.

Like many things he says or does, Coach Briles was right. I put in a lot of long hours and worked hard. I had lofty goals for myself, but I also wanted to make sure I didn't disappoint my coach.

The journey that Coach Briles has taken in his life is an inspiration to all of us. He dealt with the most unthinkable tragedy for a college athlete—losing both parents at the age of 20 while they were en route to see him play. His life could've gone in a different direction, but he followed his father's footsteps into coaching. And I know I'm one of thousands of people in the world who are in a better place because of his decision.

Sometimes you just have that feeling about a person, a bond that is connected right away. When he was recruiting me to go to the University of Houston in his last season there, he told me how good I could be, and despite not knowing much about him and his history, I trusted Coach Briles. He made me a believer, and he made our entire team believers.

In doing so, we've been able to change the school's culture. The facilities are much nicer, including the building of a brand-new stadium, but the overall attitude and mindset that Baylor can succeed is different, as well. As a player, I take satisfaction in having played a part in that.

For me personally, Coach Briles is more than just my coach. He has a unique ability to bestow friendship without ever blurring the lines of player/ coach. He got on me when it was time for him to lead, but he also showed compassion and appreciation for all of his players.

While I've had some memorable moments as his quarterback, there have been special times in my life when it wasn't just about football. Yet Coach Briles was there.

When I competed in the 400-meter hurdles at the Olympic Trials in Oregon as an 18-year-old freshman, there was Coach Briles, who altered a summer vacation with his family to come watch me run.

When we went to New York City for the Heisman Trophy presentation, Coach Briles was there providing a calming influence on me. He found a way to get me to relax and kept me confident by saying: "You're going to win because you've played too well not to win it." Once again, he was right.

Attending the NFL Draft the following April, he was there sitting at our table with my family. He was as proud that day as he was when I won the Heisman. He understands that players dream of playing in the NFL, and for me to hear my name called as the No. 2 overall pick, he couldn't have been more ecstatic.

But it didn't stop there. The next season, in the middle of trying to get his team bowl-eligible again, coach made an effort to drive up to Dallas to watch us play on Thanksgiving. Seeing him on the field during the pregame warmups nearly made me cry on the spot. I got it together and had one of my better outings of the season, as we beat the Cowboys in a big game on national TV.

And when we played the Cowboys again up in Washington, D.C., a winner-take-all rematch for the division title and a trip to the playoffs, there he was again, on the sideline to see me and wish me luck. And don't forget that his daughter works for the Cowboys, too, so he has some split loyalties. But the way he hugged me and told me how proud he was, I know how much he wants me to succeed.

I've learned that if it's a big moment in life, Coach Briles is going to make the strongest effort possible to be there. Having already proven that every step of the way, it's never been more evident than right now. On or off the field, he's a winner.

But the reason Coach Briles is so successful is the very reason why he's not satisfied: his drive. I know he's working harder than ever to win next season and improve on the year before. That's the type of work ethic he instilled in us every day. He always wanted us to be better than the last season, or the last game, or even the last day of practice.

If you're not getting better, you're getting worse. Coach Briles has always believed that, and I know that's why he's even hungrier to succeed moving forward.

As I've gone off to further my career in the NFL, I now have other coaches in my life. And as Coach Briles continues to build his program at Baylor, he has other players who are first and foremost on his mind.

But he holds a special place in my life. Coach Briles is near and dear to my heart, and hopefully I'm near and dear to his. Wherever we are in our lives, he'll always be my friend. He'll always be my guy. And most importantly, he'll always be my coach.

—*Robert Griffin III*

Introduction

A BOOK BEING written about my life was the furthest thing from my mind because I love my everyday journey and really haven't reflected on my past. I still have so many unfulfilled dreams and goals. I am very grateful for all of the great moments in my life. Although I lost my immediate family, I have been blessed with a loving and supportive network of loved ones.

Since the day I lost my parents, my rock in my life has always been Jan. She continues to keep our family strong with love, courage, and kindness. She's an amazing wife, mother, grandmother, and friend.

We have been blessed with three kids, Jancy, Kendal, and Staley, and added two more family members in Sarah and Jeff. Our grandchildren, Jaytn and Kinley, keep us inspired to make tomorrow a better day.

I was approached a couple of times a few years ago by well-known authors. They made a couple of inquiries and did some "pilot" chapters, but I just didn't feel comfortable with the approach and timing. Nick is the guy I felt right about! I knew him as a family friend, and like all of us who were given that first chance, I wanted to allow him that opportunity.

The title *Looking Up* has multiple meanings in my life. I always try to keep a positive outlook, stay determined, and move forward at all times. I'm always feeling the need to accomplish more. In my life, I've always kept that underdog role where I feel like I'm looking up to achieve my goals, striving to be the best. And lastly, I'm constantly looking up to my mom and dad in the heavens, along with giving thanks to God for blessings.

There are countless mentors, friends, peers, and loved ones who have made my life's journey. To all of those who have had vision, faith, boldness—thank you for your care, love, inspiration, and influence. Relationships last, and I am fortunate to have many that will last forever.

Some of the real game-changers in my life include Bob Perry, who recently passed away, and Ken Bailey. Those two I met in Houston, and they supported and loved me through all my time at Houston and now at Baylor. I consider Bob Simpson a "foxhole friend for life." He's a man from Cisco, Texas, who understands and supports every need and situation. He's a bold and fearless leader and friend.

I have learned many life and leadership qualities from observing and conversing with these three trusted friends. The underlying common denominator is that they all care for me as a person above all else—as I do them.

I've worked in some great places with great people in my life. Right now, I couldn't ask for a better group around me than the "Baylor 7." The guys— Drayton McLane, John Eddie Williams, Bob Simpson, Jim Turner, Paul Foster, Clifton Robinson, and Walter Umphrey—have been nothing but supportive. I thank them for being proactive enough to jump-start the "Stadium on the Brazos" project that will define Baylor, Waco, and all of Central Texas for decades. I also want to thank Dary Stone for his bulldog drive and Jay Allison for our indoor facility. I'm truly grateful to represent a university that excels today, but plans for greatness tomorrow.

There are so many people who have helped me get to this point. I can't thank them all, but I hope everyone knows this journey is told out of humility, respect, and admiration for all whom I have had the pleasure of knowing, working with, and coaching.

What keeps me going more than anything is the young people I get to work with every day. As a coach, I am thankful and humbled every day to have the privilege to interact with today's youth and leaders of tomorrow. We are in good hands!

Each chapter of this book starts with some innovative quotes that have always inspired me and hopefully others. I've been known to use them once or twice on the practice field or a locker room or anywhere when the time meets the quote.

I am truly thankful and blessed to share my quotes, my stories, and my entire life through this book.

The most exciting aspect of all this is that I am more motivated and inspired now in my career because of my journey—a journey that feels more like the beginning than the end.

—Art Briles

ART BRILES
LOOKING UP

Prologue

WITH EACH FOOT forward, the light starts to get bigger and brighter. It's dark, it's loud, and it's exciting. The anticipation of each downward step is almost unbearable.

A 20-year-old sophomore wide receiver finds himself in a packed tunnel of teammates, just moments away from running out onto the field at the Cotton Bowl, one of the more sacred sports venues of its time. For a sports fanatic who grew up in West Texas, this is comparable to stepping onto the grounds of Yankee Stadium.

Finally, the Houston Cougars football team makes its way out of the tunnel and onto the field. Somewhere in the middle of those white jerseys is No. 5. That would be Art Briles, a reserve wide receiver who, like the rest of his teammates, is bursting with anticipation to play the SMU Mustangs on this mid-October day at the State Fairgrounds in Dallas.

The weather is overcast, but typical football weather for October. And the scene is even better as the Cougars are roaring into this game at 3–1, fresh off a win over Texas A&M two weeks earlier.

Everything is perfect for Briles. Now, if only he can just spot his mother and father in the grandstands. That's a pregame ritual between the son and his parents. Only this time, he hasn't located them yet.

Then again, this 75,000-seat stadium, albeit hardly full on this day, is big enough for anyone to get lost in. Briles can't really focus on it because, simply, there is a game to play and a team to beat.

That's exactly what the Cougars did that day. They disposed of SMU from start to finish, whipping the Mustangs 29–6. Briles played sparingly on offense and some special teams. At the very least, he was a contributor in a game his team controlled from the outset.

It was a good win, and a big win for a program looking to make a statement in its first season in the Southwest Conference.

As the game ended, Briles' excitement was tempered by the fact he still never found his parents up in the stands. They said they were driving in that day from Rule—a West Texas town near Abilene. But as the players trickled off the field, Briles had yet to spot them.

The players jogged up the tunnel with joy and laughter and a sense of pride. As the players all got to the top, they veered to the right toward the winning locker room. But as Briles went to follow them, there stood head coach Bill Yeoman. He wasn't smiling. He didn't seem happy. And he was waiting for Briles.

That's when Yeoman led the wide receiver into a small room inside the locker room, where he delivered the news that would change Art Briles' life forever.

His family never made it to the Cotton Bowl that Saturday afternoon. Involved in a tragic car accident about two hours outside of Dallas, his parents, Dennis and Wanda, were killed instantly at the scene, along with his aunt, Tottie, who had raised him like a grandmother.

Just like that, a 20-year-old football player was lost. His parents, his role models, his first real football coach, and the only grandmother he really knew, were gone. Devastated and demoralized, Briles didn't know where to turn, didn't know what to do. In a state of shock, he grabbed the helmet that he'd placed on the ground and walked into the locker room.

His teammates had just recorded one of the biggest wins of the season. Art Briles had just suffered the biggest loss imaginable.

December 18, 1999

There are only a few seconds remaining on the clock. It's a 10-point lead, and the anticipation is building with each moment here in the famous Astrodome in Houston. It's pretty much a formality at this point, but head coach Art Briles isn't premature about anything. He doesn't assume victory until the final seconds tick off.

But it's clear what is about to happen. At this point, his son, Kendal Briles, has done everything imaginable to get this win. Wearing the same No. 5 on his jersey that his dad wore, Kendal has run for three touchdowns as the starting quarterback. He's passed the ball all over the field for more than 200 yards, and as a safety, he's picked off two passes, including one in the final moments to give Stephenville High School the football back.

Now, all he needs out of Kendal is to make the easiest play of all—the kneel-down. Older Briles delivers the play. Younger Briles executes it, hands the ball to the official, and lets the celebration begin...again.

Stephenville 28, Port Neches-Grove 18.

This isn't just a Texas 4A State Championship for Coach Briles and the Stephenville Yellow Jackets. This is back-to-back state championships for the second time in the decade of the 1990s. Four state titles to a school and community that hadn't made the playoffs in the 37 years before he came on board in 1988.

He didn't just build a winner; this was a dynasty. And while the fourth one might seem like old hat, it's the sweetest for Briles, who grew up playing for his father in Rule, Texas. He quarterbacked the team of a small Texas town to a Class 1A state final game, although they came up just short, falling to a Big Sandy team led by Lovie Smith.

Now, it was Kendal who gave yet another state title to his father, who moved up to a new distinction with this latest victory.

You can't become the coach of Stephenville without being considered a good football coach. It takes a great team to win one state title, but to do it back-to-back, you probably need a great coach. But if it happens again, and now there are four state titles in one decade? Well, that good football coach, turned great football coach, has now become a legendary football coach.

December 10, 2011

If it was up to him, he'd be wearing a long-sleeve Dri-FIT athletic shirt and some comfortable wind pants. Usually, that's what you'd find Art Briles wearing on a Saturday afternoon, unless he's coaching a game. And even then, it's a pretty comfortable look for the head football coach of Baylor.

But today it's a sharp black tuxedo from Harold's in Houston, to go along with a shiny gold tie and Baylor pin above his right pocket. Briles has an assigned seat here in the second row of the ballroom, filled with some of the greatest college football legends of all-time. Players he grew up watching, such as John David Crow and Roger Staubach are up on the stage. Guys like Tony Dorsett, Jim Plunkett, and Archie Griffin were all players Briles admired.

This, however, wasn't about the guys on the stage, but more about the young man about to join them.

Briles sat on the second row here at the Downtown Athletic Club in New York City, the annual location of the Heisman Trophy presentation. His heart is beating like it's the third overtime of a bowl game. Instead, the regular season is over, but one of the biggest moments of his coaching career is about to take place.

Sitting directly in front of him is one Robert Griffin III, the quarterback of his Baylor Bears football team for the past four seasons and one of the most remarkable players he's ever coached. Griffin, who has now taken on the nationwide moniker of "RGIII" has led Baylor to five straight wins and a 9–3 record. He's the favorite to win the Heisman Trophy, even over preseason favorite Andrew Luck, a quarterback from Stanford.

Briles thinks Griffin will win. He knows he should win. Still, just like that state championship game back in 1999 in Houston, nothing is ever guaranteed.

Finally, the anticipation and suspense are over. The announcement is made, and Robert Griffin III is the 2011 winner of the Heisman Trophy. Blown away with excitement, all Briles can do is let out a surprised chuckle, although he knew and believed that Griffin would be standing there on that stage. And it's not a belief he concocted a few hours or days before the ceremony. Try about five years before when he recruited this lanky kid from Copperas Cove, Texas. When everyone else in the state thought he would be a wide receiver or safety, Briles had a vision.

Not only did he think Griffin would be a quarterback, or even just a great one, he thought he'd be a Heisman Trophy quarterback.

As RGIII accepted the trophy, Griffin displayed all of the traits Briles had bragged about for years. He was poised. He was mature. He showed personality, revealing his Superman socks he was wearing underneath his suit. He showed commitment and the sense of pride he had for his university, his team, his coaches, and his family and friends. Griffin delivered quite a message up on that stage in New York, a message that not only put Baylor University on the map, but caught the world by surprise.

Everyone except the man in the second row, wearing the black tux, the gold tie, and the huge smile.

1. Who Is Arthur Ray?

"Be who you are."

"DON'T LET THAT 'aw shucks' attitude fool you.... He's trying to beat you by 60."

That's how Arthur Ray Briles is seen by his first college quarterback, who just so happens to now be one of his colleagues. Kliff Kingsbury learned that lesson while playing under Art at Texas Tech, and fully expects the same attitude today when they compete against each other as rival Big 12 coaches.

Under the long-sleeved, Dri-FIT shirt, stylish sunglasses, and always-present ball cap, behind the smiles, laughs, and kidding around, lies a man who is eagerly looking to get any edge possible to win. Football games, a hand of cards, or even off the line at a stoplight in a residential area—whether there's a scoreboard or not, Briles knows who's winning.

As the head coach at Baylor, he's a busy man with people continuously tugging for his attention. But if he's got time for a little golf or even a board game with his family, having fun is fine, perhaps a close second. Art's intention, first and foremost, is to win.

And when it comes to his chosen profession, if you're not winning, you're losing.

Over the course of his life, Briles has faced challenges that tested more than just his competitive nature, but the very core of his fighting spirit. At the age of 20, he lost the only safety net he had ever known when his parents and aunt Tottie (who had been like a grandmother to him) were killed in a horrific car accident en route to one of his college football games in Dallas.

Does he carry any guilt?

"You bet I do," he said. "I definitely felt guilt about it and still do. One hundred percent."

While 37 years have passed since the tragedy, Art knows that feeling isn't going away. The loss is something he must carry with him. But he made a decision not long after the accident to live his life through the manner in which Dennis and Wanda Briles had raised him, with honor, pride, respect for others, an obligation to do and act right, and a burning desire to succeed.

His parents have been gone for nearly twice as long as he knew them, yet every day he pays respect to their legacy. Still, talking about his memories of the accident, or even how he continues to cope with the loss, is rare for him.

Briles doesn't want pity or charity. He doesn't want respect that isn't earned. He's a fair and honest man who abides by the rules, goes to church on Sunday when he can, and has genuine care for anyone who steps into his life.

He doesn't treat people the way he wants to be treated. He goes further. Ask a current player on the Baylor squad, a former standout at Stephenville High School in the early 1990s, or even an older colleague or coach, the opinions don't vary.

They'll all tell you how he has a knack for making people feel 10 feet tall. The coach knows how to push the right buttons, say the right thing, apply the right nickname, or assign the right chore. He makes sure the player, coach, trainer, equipment staffer, or anyone else he can help realizes that Art Briles is on his side.

If he knows you, he's a fan. And he'll be a fan until you cross him. And even then, you'll get the benefit of the doubt.

Not that he's always received the benefit of the doubt himself. He's had his share of fights, quarrels, and indifferences. From his childhood days to starring in high school football and track to becoming a Division I student-athlete to later forging a successful career as a football coach, Briles has learned from every experience along the way, both the good and bad.

He knows he can't please everyone. And he won't win every game or challenge before him. But that certainly won't stop him from trying.

"His positive outlook on life is incredible. It's raw and real," says youngest daughter Staley, who helps run the family-run yogurt shop, Oso's (Spanish for *bear*), located less than a mile from the Baylor campus in Waco. "He always sees the best in everyone. He has had everything taken away from him, so he strives every day to be his best and truly treats every day as a gift."

★   ★   ★

John Greeson is the Church of Christ pastor in Rule, Texas. He's in his late seventies and has known Art for more than 40 years. Ahmad Dixon is a

22-year-old senior at Baylor who grew up in Waco and surprised a lot of locals by signing with the hometown university. Bob Warner is a retired coach who taught Briles in elementary school and is playing golf to stay busy as he approaches 80. Jason Bragg was a star player at Stephenville in the early 1990s and helped Art win his first two state titles. Donnie Avery was an inner-city recruit at Houston who nearly quit school because he had trouble balancing class, football, and being a new father until his head coach convinced him not to give up. Avery is now a six-year NFL veteran.

Different people. Different backgrounds. Different cultures. Different relationships. Yet all of them say Briles is one of the most competitive human beings on the planet. In some way, some form, some fashion, through the years he has displayed the same consistent characteristic to his closest friends, mentors, teammates, and players.

As a football coach, having a competitive nature on the sideline is a given. In fact, Art rarely loses his cool anymore. There are always exceptions, but he's usually level-headed and stoic during even the most intense game situations.

These days, his will to win perhaps comes out more when away from the playing field, particularly on the golf course. Art doesn't necessarily crush the ball off the tee but has more of a smooth drive that glides, barely lifting 25 feet in the air. He's got a crafty short game, and his hand-eye coordination allows him to sink a few long putts here and there. He's a high-80s player, which is good enough to compete with just about everyone with whom he shares a round.

During a two-man scramble one Father's Day with Mike Lebby, who coached with him at Sweetwater and has remained a good friend to this day, the duo was actually winning the tournament midway through the back nine. Around the 15th hole, Art and Mike parked to hit their shots, and Mike went to the back of the cart to pull out a club. Art was in the middle of the fairway about to approach his ball when screeching brakes interrupted the quiet of the course, followed by Mike's loud screams. Art ran over quickly to see just what had happened.

A careless driver rammed Mike in between their carts, bringing the over-sized man to the ground. Mike was having trouble getting back to his feet and knew something was wrong with his knee, likely needing medical attention.

Art responded with the only questions he knew to ask.

"Dang, 'Lebb'…can we finish? Do you think we can still win this thing?" Art pleaded. "You've been playing your ass off. We've got to go win this thing."

And Mike tried to give it a go, but with no power in his legs, his shots started to falter, as did their hopes of winning. First place slipped away with Mike limping through the round. He eventually did need surgery to repair torn ligaments. To this day, Art is still disappointed they didn't win that Father's Day trophy.

A few years earlier, Art was playing in another two-man scramble with Mike Copeland, a longtime coach in Stephenville who was the only holdover from the previous staff when Briles got the job in 1988. Copeland was born with just one arm, but still manages to be extremely athletic. The last thing Copeland considers himself is handicapped, which is one of the things Art most admires about his longtime defensive coordinator.

The only handicap Copeland talks about involves his golf game. For years he was a 6-handicap and he can still play a competitive round now in his sixties.

But during a tournament in Stephenville one year in the late 1980s, they were just about to tee off when a female tournament official noticed Copeland and told him he could play from the ladies tees if he so desired. Although extremely offended, Copeland was used to that kind of reaction from strangers and kindly responded that he'd be fine and could play from the regular tee box like everyone else.

Art was shaking his head. What nerve. He couldn't believe…his playing partner would do such a thing.

"God almighty, Copeland. What are you doing? We would've won this thing."

But you don't have to be within earshot of Art Briles to know when he's ready to tee off on the golf course. He receives plenty of double takes from his attire alone. He'll wear his hat backward, have double wristbands on both arms over his long-sleeve shirts and wear Neumann football gloves that his receivers and defensive backs use in practices and games.

"People would look at him and say, 'Is this guy serious?'" Lebby said. "But he is always serious when it comes to playing golf or really anything competitive. He just wants to beat you. He takes everything seriously."

His competitive drive isn't always about playing sports, but also watching them. Before he became as well-known as he is now, Art got a rush out of getting into sporting events without paying. Whether in a side door at a basketball game, or the end gate on a football field, or maybe even an underground tunnel at a sports arena, Art would find his way into the game. The funny thing about it all is that, being a high-school coach and athletic director for many years, he could've likely gotten into anything he wanted to by simply showing a badge or his ID.

And it wasn't just sporting events, either. Once flying to Houston with coach Randy Clements for a coaches convention, the ever-impatient Briles thought the hotel shuttle that was supposed to pick them up was taking entirely too long. They could've called for a cab, but that would've been an unnecessary expense.

So Art waved down a man in a small pickup truck with a camper on the back. The man had just dropped off relatives at the airport and was somewhat surprised to have a complete stranger getting his attention. Art kindly asked the man if they could get a ride to the hotel, which was only about two miles down the road. The driver agreed but told them they'd have to get in the back of the truck.

So, wearing a dress shirt and slacks, Randy and Art climbed into the back, sitting on a spare tire as they bounced around holding their luggage in their hands.

Art looked over at Randy, who wasn't quite sure about this idea, but was going along for the ride.

"This is the type of stuff that drives my wife crazy!"

They made it to the hotel in a matter of minutes, shook hands with their unexpected chauffeur, and walked into the hotel.

"We saved time, for sure," Randy said. "We got our pants dirty…but we saved time."

★   ★   ★

Ask him his two favorite loves and undoubtedly family and football top the list—in that order. But what's third?

That's an easy one, actually. From his earliest memories of listening to Motown hits by the Temptations and Marvin Gaye while attending junior high in Abilene, to downloading a few of the new rap songs that his players work out to in the weight room, Art Briles is inspired by music. Always has been.

To this football coach's ears, music is more than just rhythmic noise. He appreciates the artistic talent involved, both in the musicians' skill to play instruments or sing vocally and, more importantly, in having the creativity to write the songs. Art doesn't just hear the music but listens to the lyrics. Even back when he was rocking out to Bob Dylan or Eric Clapton or especially Jimi Hendrix, Art always found a way to relate to the writing. In the late 1960s, he knew every word off the album from the latter's *Electric Ladyland*.

He uses music for inspiration but also to reminisce.

"I let music take me back sometimes," Art said. "It lets me remember what I was doing when I heard a particular song."

When Art got to Rule in the early 1970s, there weren't many FM stations in the remote region. But at night, he could pick up KOMA out of Oklahoma City. Just lying in bed, he would sometimes fall asleep listening to the likes of Stevie Wonder, Al Green, and Pink Floyd.

When he hauled hay as a summer job once in a while in high school, Art jammed to eight-tracks of Cream, Elton John, and Earth, Wind, & Fire, one of his favorite bands.

After Briles went off to college at Houston, he actually had some early aspirations of becoming a DJ, although his girlfriend and future wife, Jan, discouraged that idea. But living in the big city for the first time, Art and some of his teammates would work major concerts. That's how he was able to see Dylan, Willie Nelson, Joan Baez, Neil Young, Isaac Hayes, and Led Zeppelin.

The Beatles were on top of the charts throughout much of his youth, and like many of his peers, Art was no different in his admiration. He respected how they were able to evolve through their music, both culturally and lyrically.

In the early 1980s, when his coaching career really started to blossom and his family started to grow, as well, music didn't seem to play as big a role in his life. Coincidentally, Art wasn't really fond of '80s music either, but his interest picked back up as his kids got older and the music scene changed in the 1990s. He was a big fan of Creed, a band he saw live several times.

More recently, one of Art's favorite musicians has become Amos Lee, who has a classic sound of easy listening rock with a mixture of jazz and folk.

"He kind of throws me back to the Bob Dylan and Jimi Hendrix days, with the slow, soulful singers," Art says of Lee. "I've seen him six or seven times, and I've gotten to meet him. But I really like the old-school sound that you hear a lot today."

He even found a way to combine his love for music with his competitive nature. At Stephenville, he emphasized the importance of the weight room to not only strengthen his team physically and mentally, but to also build camaraderie between the players and coaches. Coach Briles would often crank up the radio during their workouts, a practice that wasn't taking place around other high school programs in that era. Art implemented lifting groups where the coaching staff would work out with the players, and he'd oftentimes see who could name the song on the radio first. "Who you got?" he'd ask when a new tune came on.

It was also very common for Art to be in the middle of a bench press and shout out, "Five, six, seven…Led Zeppelin…eight, nine, 10!"

One of his best players at Stephenville, all-state quarterback Kelan Luker, reminded Art of himself back in Rule. Luker knew he was a bit different than the rest of the players and didn't mind it. He was quirky at times and a little distant from his teammates. But he had a love for music that Art understood.

After leading Stephenville to a state title in 1998, when they set several passing and scoring records, Luker went to SMU for three seasons, but his heart just wasn't in football. He quit the sport to play bass guitar for the band Submersed, living his dream for seven years. He still recalls one of his favorite shows occurring in Houston, where he played in front of Briles and many of the current Houston coaches who had also been in Stephenville.

Whether he was listening to a famous recording artist worth a million bucks, or one of his former players bouncing around from gig to gig, Art just appreciated musicians and their ability to entertain.

★　★　★

One of the most common questions asked about Art Briles has nothing to do with football or his family or even music, for that matter. Of all things, what many fans want to know involves his attire.

It never fails, when Briles' name comes up, the question is raised: why does he always wear long sleeves?

The query is a valid one, too. Football isn't always played in the colder temperatures of November and December, and considering Art has never lived outside of the state of Texas, he knows all about the heat. But over the last decade or so, you can't find many, if any, pictures from his Houston or Baylor days when he's on the sideline or at a practice wearing short sleeves. Even if it's over 100 degrees at 3:30 in the afternoon, Coach Briles will likely be sporting a Dri-FIT long-sleeved shirt.

So what's the reason? The speculation has been humorous, ranging from the coach having multiple tattoos to scars or burns that he's trying to hide. His older brother, Eddie, has his own theory, though, after living with him for more than 16 years, remembering Art kept his front bedroom like a sauna.

"He's cold!" Eddie said. "He's wearing long sleeves because he's cold."

The real reason has more to do with wanting to sweat. While others would rather beat the heat, Art prefers to take his daily run in the middle of the afternoon. He would rather wear long sleeves and get in a good sweat.

And, more simply, he just prefers the look.

"It's really just a trend thing," Art said. "I've always liked sweatshirts and I love to sweat. The heat doesn't bother me. There's really no reason [for the long sleeves], other than I just feel more comfortable."

★   ★   ★

If Art Briles meets you once, he remembers you. If there's another meeting, he probably likes you. And if he likes you, you'll have a nickname.

More often than not, the choice stems from the last name. Among his quarterbacks, Case Keenum was "Kee-nom" to rhyme with *phenom*, Kevin Kolb was "Kabo," Kelan Luker was "Luke," and Kingsbury was simply "King." Former Stephenville wide receiver Jeffrey Thompson was tabbed "Tommy," and assistant coach Phillip Montgomery was naturally dubbed "Monty."

But Art was able to get creative with some nicknames. One of the nastiest, meanest, toughest players he ever coached at Stephenville was a country boy named Brad Smith, who admittedly tried to hurt his defensive opponents on every play. Art remains friend with Smith to this day and lists him with the same name he gave him 25 years ago: "Bad-S." When said fast enough, it's reminiscent of the badass attitude with which Smith played on the field.

At Baylor, long before the quarterback started using the catchy "RGIII," Robert Griffin was called "Cream" by Briles, who told him, "The cream always rises to the top." Receiver Kendall Wright liked his nickname of "BIC," as coach always told him he could be the Best In the Country.

His longtime assistant coach Randy Clements, after once making the mistake of telling Art he was an only child, got the name "Silk Sheets." Art would throw that out any time Clements might have had even the slightest complaint.

He gave catchy nicknames to other players and friends such as Curtis Lowery ("Big City"), Lanear Sampson ("Lenny Longchain"), Colin Shillinglaw ("Shack"), Wes Welker ("The Natural"), and Jason Smith ("Smooth").

Although he never coached Andre Ware, the two became friends when the 1989 Heisman Trophy winner would return to Houston while Art was the head coach, from 2003 to 2007. Simply put, Art started calling Ware "Trophy," a name that has since spread to his friends and family but originated from the coach. And when Baylor's Robert Griffin III won the Heisman in 2011, Ware called the coach and said, "Now you've got your own Trophy." But Coach Briles assured him that he'd always have the original nickname.

Art even has them for his kids. Oldest daughter Jancy was a standout basketball player in high school, prompting the nickname "Dr. J," which later was shortened to "Doc." Youngest daughter Staley is "Bubbs," while Kendal got an entirely new name on the practice field, getting called "Charlie" in an attempt to avoid signs of father-son favoritism. In return, Kendal would refer to his dad as "Roger" for the same reason.

While Art admits there is a method to the nicknaming madness, the practice actually stems from his father, Dennis. When they lived in Abilene, there was a rail-thin friend of Art's who often came over to the house. Barely more than 100 pounds, Dennis would jokingly call the boy "BC" for "Bone Crusher."

Today, Art recognizes the power of a nickname.

"It makes it more personal," he said. "You give someone a nickname, it shows you have an interest in them. You don't just know their name, but you know a little something else about them. Sometimes, I just go with what other people call them, but I've always liked giving nicknames. It just shows you care."

However, the admiration he has for his players, coaches, friends, and family comes from much more than any moniker or handle could ever convey.

Although he's still going to beat you by 60.

2. A Competitor Is Born

"It's not what you weigh...it's how you play."

IT WAS NEARLY 11:00 o'clock on a summer night at 1802 Glendale Road. There wasn't a lot going on this late, especially in Abilene, Texas, in 1967.

It might've been a slow night for some, but it was about to get rowdy for the "Sticking Group." This self-proclaimed handful of 11- and 12-year-olds were up to no good, just looking to go out and be a little mischievous.

It wasn't like they were going to get into a ton of trouble—maybe throw a few dirt clods at passing cars or toss some rocks over the railroad tracks. Nothing crazy or out of the ordinary for small-town, West Texas kids. The best part for most of them was just sneaking out of the house without their parents' permission.

But Art Briles wasn't really like the rest of the kids. He was different in many ways. His family was a little different, too.

So while his buddies, James and "Fitz," had all made their way out of their homes and over to the Briles house, young Art was ready for them but didn't share their excitement.

"They all snuck out of the house, but I would tell my dad when I was going out," Art said. "I just told him we were going to go out a little bit, and he'd let me go. And he'd stay up late and wait for us to get home."

For Art, Dennis Briles wasn't just his father. He was his coach and his friend. He taught him how to throw a football, with his hands just off the laces to toss the perfect spiral. He taught him to pitch with a windup. He taught him how to keep his elbow down while shooting jump shots in the yard.

And on this warm night in Abilene, he was teaching him how to be a man.

"It wasn't the same as the other kids," Art said. "It was really no big deal. We'd go out with boys and girls, and we'd just hang out and stay out late. We thought it was fun. But that's just the relationship I had with my parents. They trusted me."

Doing the right thing was something embedded into Art Briles' nature from as early as he could remember.

The son of a military father, Arthur Ray Briles was born on December 3, 1955, in Haskell, about 40 minutes north of Abilene. Dennis was actively serving in the Navy, once doing a tour aboard the USS *Hornet* during the Korean War as a parachute packer. But his military duties often left Wanda Briles at home by herself, tending to their newborn, along with young son Eddie, who was born just 19 months earlier.

When Dennis was home, however, he left no doubt who was in charge, and he did so without raising his voice too often. A burly man of about 6'2", 220 pounds, he was larger than life for Art and Eddie, who despite their closeness in age, weren't exactly two peas in a pod.

Art was interested in sports as early as he could remember, playing football, basketball, and baseball, as well as any other games the kids in the neighborhood had going. Eddie was more artistic. He participated in some sports here and there, but it wasn't a passion for him like it was for his younger brother.

Still, Art and Eddie learned early on not to cross Dennis and Wanda, who were also pretty opposite in both stature and demeanor. Dennis was quiet and reserved, dressed conservatively. Wanda was petite in her frame, but rather loud in her voice and her outfits. She loved to wear bold colors and big, dangly earrings.

Wanda smoked an occasional cigarette, while Dennis not only refrained, but also warned his sons about the long-term dangers of smoking. She went to bed early. Dennis was a night owl, reading the paper or working on puzzles, or in some cases, staying up to make sure Art made it home safe from running the streets in Abilene.

When he wasn't fulfilling his military obligations, Dennis was a civics teacher at a junior high in Abilene, where he also coached football, basketball, and track. With his college education having been paid for by the Navy, Dennis had previously finished up his degree at West Texas State (now West Texas A&M) in Canyon, Texas, where Art and Eddie actually lived in the dorm room with their parents as toddlers. Wanda eventually taught school, as well, but not before earning her degree long after her two boys were born. Both Eddie and Art can recall Wanda taking courses at nearby Hardin-Simmons University in Abilene to obtain her teacher's certificate.

With her late hours and Dennis either coaching late, grading papers, or sometimes working at a nearby grocery store for a few extra bucks, home-cooked meals were sometimes a rarity in the Briles home. Art and Eddie were often left to fend for themselves, resulting in TV dinners, pigs in a blanket, or maybe even a few packages of honey buns.

But Sundays were a big day for the family, typically starting out at Calvary Baptist Church in Abilene, where Art was baptized. If Dennis wasn't cooking steaks, the family would usually eat at Lavenders after church.

It wasn't always ideal, but they made it work as a happy family. Although the Briles family didn't have a lot of money, they always had enough. Dennis, Wanda, Eddie, and Art had their differences, but they were a close, tight-knit group who enjoyed each other's company. There was a common theme for all of them: plenty of love.

★ ★ ★

One of the earliest memories Art Briles has of growing up in Abilene wasn't even in Abilene, or Texas for that matter. When he thinks back to those early days of his life, he often recalls the long road trips he took to Colorado with Eddie and his grandparents, Bill and Elsie, whom the boys referred to as "Tottie."

Elsie was technically Art's aunt as Wanda's older sister of 25 years, but tragedy struck when Wanda was born as their mother died at childbirth, leaving Elsie to raise Wanda as her own.

Art and Eddie never saw Elsie as anything other than their grandmother. And they didn't call her anything other than Tottie. Art always referred to her as their "foster grandmother." Her husband, Bill, was an outdoorsman who loved to camp out, hunt, and fish.

To take breaks from the blistering Texas heat, Bill and Tottie would hitch up the trailer in the summers, load in Art and Eddie, and head off to Colorado for a few weeks at a time. Their trips would end up in various places such as Red River and Durango. That's where Art learned to not only fish, but also how to clean, skin, and cook them for meals. But there was always some down time for fun, which included swimming in the rivers and creeks and finding food to feed the chipmunks.

Sometimes, Tottie's sister Peggy would join the group on what became an annual trip. Board games and card games were often prominent. Even at the earliest of ages, Art didn't take losing well, even if it were a game of Wahoo. Bill and Tottie didn't have any children of their own, and obviously no grandkids per se. But for a couple of weeks out of the summer each year, they had both.

* * *

Like most brothers, especially two separated by only 19 months, Art and Eddie had to share quite a bit.

Sometimes it was big things, such as a bedroom when Art was three, the two brothers bunking together in the family's small two-bedroom, one-bath house in Kermit, a West Texas town just minutes from the New Mexico border.

Sharing clothes, toys, and sporting goods was also a given, although helping matters was the fact that Art and Eddie had different interests when it came to hobbies. If there was a comic book to be read, Eddie didn't typically have to fight Art for it. The same goes for a football or basketball. Eddie had little interest in playing those sports, especially as they got older.

But one thing they shared in common was a love for riding bikes. It started out innocently enough with standard bicycles and eventually escalated to mopeds and motorcycles.

And like everything else, Eddie realized at an early age that Art's competitive nature would surface regularly.

It was Christmas of 1959 in Kermit, and the boys were bursting with excitement to see what Santa Claus had brought to the Briles' home, where Eddie was a few months shy of his sixth birthday and Art had just turned four. After waiting rather impatiently, the brothers finally got to run into the living room to check out their loot, and there waiting for both of them were two bicycles—something neither of them had ever owned before.

One of them was a taller, banana-seat bike with high handlebars and made for speed. The other was accompanied with training wheels, obviously set for a beginner still learning how to balance and ride on his own.

But sure enough, what Dennis and Wanda intended to happen didn't exactly transpire. As soon as all of the presents were opened, hugs and kisses exchanged, and maybe some breakfast inhaled, the kids were off on their bikes.

Before Eddie could even make his way to what he thought was his new bike, Art was halfway down the street on the bigger model, popping wheelies and jumping the cracks in the sidewalk, even hopping up on the curb. Trailing way behind was Eddie, knees up over the handlebars of a bike with training wheels, still a little confused about this bike exchange.

"And once he got on that big bike, there was no getting him off of there," Eddie said. "That just became his bike. Even at that age, he had no fear."

Eventually, both of the boys would have bikes that would take them all over Abilene. During the summer, Art and Eddie would ride—sometimes once or twice a day—to the YMCA, where they would swim, play foosball and pool, and generally get into any mischief possible. Those bikes would also take them to Cobb Park and the steep hills on which they would go up and down. To rest, they would spend time playing in the storm drains.

While Art has always had a sense of humor, considered more of dry wit with an occasional zinger, Eddie is more of the prankster. Once, when Art was around 11 and riding his bike down the alley, headed toward the driveway, Eddie had the idea of trying to startle his younger brother. His plan was to throw a dart that would fly right in front of Art and hit the fence of the neighbor's yard. But Eddie's joke-intended dart ended up finding Art's stomach. Shocked and still confused as to what just happened, Art didn't understand why there is something sharp and pointy connected to his midsection.

"He was just looking at me like 'Why did you do that?'" Eddie recalled. "We pulled it out, and I remember talking to him about not telling on me. I asked him not to say anything, and he agreed. And then he went right in and told mama."

That was just another example of Art being a little quicker than anyone thought.

Their love for bikes would continue long into their teenage years. Art eventually rode a Yamaha YZ 80 when he was 13 and later a Honda CT90. Dennis would often load the motorcycles into a pickup truck and take them out to the country on the dirt roads. Once again, Eddie often found himself battling Art for the biggest and fastest of the motorcycles.

★   ★   ★

Art, at the age of five, was sitting in the front seat of a rental truck next to Dennis. It's probably one of the first memories he can recall of his life, as his family was making the move from Kermit to Abilene, where they lived in a smaller house on North 10th Street.

Whether he was playing football in the front yard with the older kids on the block or walking the tops of fence lines from house to house, Art found a way to stay busy. He was one of the class favorites at Johnston Elementary, having attended the first through third grades there.

Once the family moved to the house on Glendale, Art began meeting people he would call friends forever. Guys like Mike Cloud, Wayne Peel, and Ricky Stracener were all included in the crowd that would dub themselves the "Sticking Group." Art would hang out in Ricky's room listening to Jimi Hendrix, one of the many inspirational musicians who spoke to Art.

Most of those kids were a couple of years older than Art, and were even in the same class as Eddie. But athletically, Art fit right in, holding his own in the street games of kickball or football or anything else they could play and keep score at.

The Brileses lived just a few blocks away from Jane Long Elementary, where Art would make the 12- to 15-minute walk with his buddies every day.

At home, he never lacked for role models. His parents more than filled that need, and if he wasn't getting guidance from Dennis or Wanda, Bill and Tottie were there, as well. But as a young student at Jane Long Elementary, Art would come across yet another instrumental influence on his childhood. Bob Warner taught fifth and sixth grade at Long, having Art in his classroom for two years.

Back then, elementary coaches were similar to junior high and high school coaches, where they would field specific teams for football, basketball, and track. Teaching much more than just a regular P.E. class, Warner spotted Art's physical prowess right away.

"Back in those days, the fifth- and sixth-grade teachers were the coaches," Warner recalled. "It wasn't like what they have today. We had a full sports program. It really got everyone involved."

Warner was in charge of the standard fitness test that had to be passed by all students. The test included various activities, such as running, jumping, pull-ups, push-ups, and other agility requirements.

Taking those agility tests were some of the first times that Art discovered the importance of the monkey bars. While he was no stranger to swinging around carelessly on a playground, when it became part of a school-organized test, Art not only realized how advanced he was, but he also recognized the importance the exercises were to upper-body strength.

There was only one person who performed that test any better than Art—Coach Warner.

Even as an 11-year-old who frequently used "yes sir" and "no sir" responses and always respected his elders, Art didn't shy away from competition, no matter the opponent.

When Coach Warner would demonstrate to the kids how to use the parallel bars, there was Art, trying to keep pace, movement for movement. While he couldn't flip around with the same grace, or perhaps couldn't hold himself up for as long, Art was pushing his physical limits.

Needless to say, he didn't have any problems passing those standard fitness tests. And when it came to the more popular sports, Art was Warner's best athlete, as well—not only in those years, but also in all of Warner's 13 years as an elementary coach.

"He just did everything really well," Warner said. "He was the top dog on the track team. He was just an outstanding athlete and student. In football, he was the quarterback. Just a real, sharp, smart guy. If you were picking people you expected to succeed in life, he would be one you would choose. Even back when he was 11 or 12 years old."

★ ★ ★

When it came to athletic excellence, Art Briles didn't just outshine his classroom peers, he would often dominate the neighborhood, which included many kids from older grades, some even older than his brother Eddie.

No, Art wasn't the tallest by any means and might have been one of the skinniest in the group. So what made this rail-thin boy any different from the rest?

"Speed…I could run," Art said. "That's one thing I learned early on was that I was a lot faster than the other kids. We used to race all the time, and you knew who could run fast. I was always one of the fastest."

And it wasn't just a few young kids sprinting down through the neighborhood streets.

"City track meets were a big deal in Abilene back then," Art said. "I can remember being in the third grade at Johnston Elementary. We ran probably 50 meters or so, and I won the race. It's one of the first ones I can remember winning. That was a big deal. When you're not the biggest kid, you want to be the fastest. I would say I usually finished first or second most of the time. I got beat. I lost some races. But I remember being up there first or second most of the time."

Like most kids, especially in the 1960s, Art didn't shy away from any sport, especially the ones you could play out in the street. It was easy for the guys to grab a football and throw it around. Or play stickball or baseball. And they'd often find a hoop to shoot baskets.

A natural athlete, Art stuck to the basic sports and wasn't exposed to what he described as "country club" activities like tennis or golf. Over time, he learned how to play both, but stuck to what he knew best.

Football and track were his favorites because he could utilize his speed. In the third grade, Art played on his first organized football team, where he was the quarterback, a position he played through his days at Jane Long Elementary and then at Mann Middle School. Art can still recall some battles with rival Madison.

"We went to Mann, which fed into Abilene High. And the kids at Madison went to Abilene Cooper. It was a big-time rivalry in Abilene and still is. But you could feel it in junior high, too."

★　★　★

It doesn't matter the size of the town, Friday nights in Texas are a big deal. They always have been and probably always will be because of high school football.

As long as he could remember, Art Briles spent his Friday nights at Shotwell Stadium in Abilene. They sat on the same side every week, although the home team would rotate back and forth between Abilene and Abilene Cooper High Schools. But it didn't matter who was playing, the Briles would be in attendance. Sometimes the entire family would join, but most of the time it was just Dennis and Art.

Early on, Art spent many games playing catch with his friends in the end zone or under the grandstands. When the games were over, he and his buddies would often go onto the field to be close to the players. Maybe it was a high-five, a slap on their shoulder pads, or occasionally carrying a helmet, but the big thing for Art was to collect chinstraps from the players. Art's bedroom had dozens of sweaty, yellowed chinstraps thumbtacked to his wall.

But as he got a little older—probably around 12 or 13—Briles started to sit for the entire game with his father. More importantly, he started to appreciate the game the way his father did.

With limited TV exposure, Briles kept up with the pro and college game from a distance, but at that age, he didn't need look very far for admiration. He rooted for guys like Don Brown or a running back named James Jones, who played at Abilene High. Jack Mildren was a standout quarterback at Abilene Cooper before he became an All-American at Oklahoma and eventually lieutenant governor of Oklahoma in 1990. One of his fondest memories is sitting with his dad in the stands for a 1969 playoff matchup between eventual state champion Wichita Falls High School and Abilene High in a game that was played in 15-degree weather. Like always, they stayed until the *bitter* end.

Football was turning into Art Briles' biggest passion, but he didn't limit his respect to just the gridiron. Dennis and Art loved all sports, and they'd make their way to the basketball gym on a weekly basis.

"I'll never forget going to a game at Abilene High, and they were good, really good," Art said. "And I remember they played Crane. I can see their bus pulling up, and it said 'Crane Golden Canes.' They had a player named Tommy Jones in 1969. Tommy Jones came in there and scored about 65 points in the Reagan County Tournament. And that's before the three-point line. I don't think Crane even won the game, but I can just see Tommy Jones in that gym scoring."

While his mind and heart were focused on playing football, even at an early age, Art was developing an eye for talent.

3. Learning the Rule

"You can't make a slow guy fast."

HE DIDN'T WANT to be there. Art Briles made that pretty clear from the start.

While he was always respectful and tried to understand his parents' decision to move to the town of Rule, Texas, populated with roughly 1,000 people, he didn't exactly have to like it. So he didn't at first.

To Dennis Briles, getting the job at Rule wasn't just an opportunity to become a head coach for *any* team. This was a homecoming for the man who graduated in the Bobcats' Class of 1950. Wanda Briles was also an alumna of Rule, 1952. One of Dennis' good friends growing up was Ed Fouts, whose presence on the school board certainly didn't hurt Dennis' chances of getting hired. He took the job as the football coach and then was asked to also assume principal duties just before the first week of classes.

But this wasn't just about Dennis, a man who had never been described as selfish. He looked out for the best interest of his family and his children. In 1970 Dennis knew he'd be welcomed with open arms. More importantly, he knew his family would thrive in the town, most known for its two cotton gins.

Not that his son agreed. Make no mistake, Art was living in Rule physically, but his heart was still in Abilene. As a superior athlete, the 14-year-old didn't see any light at the end of the tunnel. Still to this day, he calls it a "devastating time" in his life. He was established in Abilene. While it might not have been Dallas or Houston, the city was a booming metropolis in comparison to Rule.

What Art had no way of knowing when Dennis and Wanda moved the family into the tiny agriculture town just 60 miles north of Abilene, was how much change Rule would see over the next 40 years.

Art thought Rule was dried up, a rustic settlement with no hope and no future. As it turned out, they moved there during one of the town's most exciting eras, both in the community and with the school's athletics. Now Art would actually play a major role in the latter success, but at the time, none of that really mattered to a young teenager who didn't exactly understand the reasoning behind family decisions like this one.

When the Briles first settled into Rule, the town was already starting to decline. Rule was probably at its peak in the early 1960s. The town had five grocery stores, six service stations, two lumberyards, and two pharmacies. There were three restaurants, including a 24-hour diner called the Bluebonnet Café that stayed open through the 1990s.

Halliburton, one of the largest oilfield service companies in the nation, had offices in Rule and employed 27 families alone. Rule had two stores each that dealt in dry goods and electronics, as well as one that sold furniture. For years, a main attraction in Rule was its drive-in theater just outside the city limits, but it also had a walk-in movie house downtown. And at one point, Rule had three domino halls.

Today, Rule has a bank and a convenient store. There is a Tex-Mex restaurant nearby, the latest of many short-lived businesses that simply cannot survive in a town that has just over 650 residents. For any kind of civilization, residents of Rule have to either drive to Haskell or Stamford, or possibly Abilene for a wider selection of food, shopping, and entertainment.

Lavon Beakley, who worked in Rule for 33 years—13 as principal and 20 as the superintendent—moved to the area in 1957 and still lives there today after having retired from the school district in 1990.

"We had two main sources of employment back then: agriculture and oil," Beakley said. "Agriculture got to the point where if you didn't have more than two to three acres, you just couldn't afford to do it. And the oil around here played out. But not too long after we moved here, we just lost the infrastructure. The oilmen would move to Abilene or Snyder or even Midland and Odessa. We just lost a little more of the town each year."

Whether Rule was on its way up or down in 1970, Art wasn't about to call it home.

★ ★ ★

The Briles family moved to 707 Union Avenue, right off one of the two main streets in town. The three-bedroom home was by no means extravagant but certainly provided everything they needed. Both Eddie, who was entering his junior year of high school, and Art had their own rooms. And that proved to be a blessing for the elder sibling, mainly because of the temperature difference. Art had the front bedroom, which always absorbed more heat.

"He kept that door closed all the time, and it would get so hot in there," Eddie recalled. "You'd open the door, and it would take your breath away. He just liked it that way. He was never bothered by the heat. So he didn't have to worry about me going into his room."

The two brothers had their occasional quarrels but nothing major. And with both of them now transplanted in a new spot, they gravitated to their common interests more than ever. One of those similarities involved motorcycles, a recreation that was still a bit rare for the residents of Rule. You hardly ever saw anyone riding around on them, much less high school kids.

Art described himself as an "outcast" from the very beginning at Rule. While the school was tiny by any definition—about 40 to 60 students per grade—some of the boys already had their cliques and let him know right away that he wasn't welcome.

"I got into a few fights early on," Art said. "I had some issues with the guys, away from school at a party or something. It's part of growing up. It helped me later. I started to find out that you could depend on yourself. You've got to stand your ground and protect your thoughts and values. But I was an outsider, no question."

Of course, the animosity shown by the boys in Rule was the exact opposite of the attention he received from the fairer sex. Art came in with shaggy hair, a city-boy attitude, and drove a motorcycle. Needless to say, the girls in Rule flocked to him soon after he arrived.

Though not everyone. Jan Allison was about to be an eighth-grader, but still hung around the same group. While some of her older friends let their attraction for the new boy in town be known, Jan was more reserved. She had some interest but wasn't about to show it. Yet she was there the day Art let the girls take turns riding on the back of his motorcycle.

"That was a *big* deal," Jan said. "I just remember getting to ride with him and being alone for a little bit."

For more than a year, nothing really materialized between the two. Art was getting plenty of interest from other girls in the school, and Jan, who was one of the top cheerleaders on the squad, wasn't about to chase.

"I think the reason he liked me is because all the girls were crazy about him, and I really just ignored him," she said. "I just played it cool. I was into him like the others were, but I didn't show it. And I think that made him like me more."

Nothing got too serious that first year, but by the time he was a sophomore, there was a definite attraction. He started stopping by her house more frequently to simply visit in the living room or outside on the porch.

On February 11, 1972, they decided to officially "go steady." And it's a date both of them still celebrate to this day.

★ ★ ★

Whether it was Art's relationship with Jan, his athletic ability, or a combination of both, he started to fit in more around town. He also hit it off with Larry Barbee, who grew up in Rule and was considered one of the area's best athletes, even as a freshman. Art and Larry ran around together for four years in high school, occasionally dabbling in a little mischief.

One summer day, two policemen showed up at the doorstep of Fouts, who lived a quarter-mile down the road from the Briles home. The officers tracked a complaint at Stamford Lake that his registered boat had been driven recklessly, disturbing nearby fishermen.

Fouts talked his way out of a ticket, telling them the truth that he hadn't been to the lake in months, and his children were way too small to take it out. A few days later, he found out Art and Larry had commandeered the boat one afternoon without his permission.

But that's probably the extent of the trouble you can get into in Rule. With his dad serving as his football coach and the principal of the school, pushing the envelope too much wasn't a great idea for Art, anyway.

And there really wasn't a lot of time for misbehaving. Art kept himself busy with sports. During the school year there was football, basketball, and track, and then he would play club baseball in Haskell over the summer.

As a natural athlete, he was good in everything. Basketball wasn't his best sport; he was more of defensive hustler who was big enough to play the post and grab rebounds. In baseball, he had a nice arm and could handle just about any position, including pitcher.

Not surprisingly, his two loves were for football and track, which allowed him to do what he did best: run.

As a freshman on the football team, Art saw action sparingly in his dad's first season as head coach. Although he was more of a scout-team player, he occasionally got in the games as a reserve running back or safety.

Back in 1970 high school classifications in Texas were 5A, 4A, 3A, 2A, and Class A. And then there was Class B, which included the tiniest of towns, such as Rule. At that time, Class B football did not have a championship game, so the furthest a school could advance in the playoffs was to regionals, which Rule did during that first season, playing Sundown on Thanksgiving Day in Childress. The Bobcats of Rule lost, but the ride was magnificent with even brighter days expected ahead.

Dennis' only real assistant during his time in Rule was Jasper Wilson, a fiery coach whose demeanor often served as the perfect complement to Dennis' mild-mannered style. Wilson was the head track coach and led the school to victory at the Class B state meet in 1971 with Art running on the sprint relay team as a freshman.

By his sophomore year, Art had started to develop into an even bigger force athletically, especially in football. He played a variety of positions, but mostly halfback, making quite an impression. In the 1971 season opener, Rule blasted Aspermont 28–6 as Art caught touchdown passes of 20 and 30 yards, along with a two-point conversion. The next week, his 45-yard score ignited Rule to an 18–0 win over Knox City.

Actually, Art wasn't the only Briles on the team, as Eddie spent his senior season in uniform, the older brother admitting that was "pretty much the extent of it." On the other hand, Art continued to have his share of clutch moments, including a decisive two-point conversion catch in the fourth quarter to beat Throckmorton 14–13 to keep the Bobcats undefeated at 6–0. The next week they went to 7–0 after a 20–12 win over Roby that saw him break a 12–12 tie with another two-point conversion grab in the fourth, which was followed by a game-clinching 30-yard touchdown catch moments later.

But the Bobcats' dreams of a magical season ended with a 26–20 loss to Newcastle in the ninth game of the season. Newcastle earned the playoff berth and eventually advanced to regionals. After a meaningless, yet impressive 61–6 thrashing of Rochester in the season finale, in which Art caught three touchdown passes of 15, 17, and 65 yards, the Bobcats' season came to an end with a 9–1 record. Art was one of three sophomores named to the Class 2-B All-District team.

While Rule was coming up short in football, that wasn't the case in track. With Art running the 100 and 220 meters, as well as the sprint relay, the school successfully defended its Class B title in Austin, winning state once again. Art finished second in both the 100 and 220, and was part of a mile-relay team that finished fifth.

Two years after arriving, Art wasn't just fitting in at Rule; he was now shining as one of the top 10th grade athletes in the greater Abilene region, also known as "the Big Country."

★ ★ ★

Heading into 1972, Art's junior season, Rule's football team was starting to get some statewide respect. The Bobcats received 14 of 17 first-place votes and were picked No. 1 in the preseason rankings for Class B, which now allowed teams past the regional round and awarded a state championship.

Just like that, they had a target on their chests, especially Art, who took over as the team's quarterback. Dennis ran mainly an I-back offense, but with his son's mobility, included some run-pass options. While the system wouldn't be considered innovative compared to today's spread-out passing styles that are now popular in high school, college, and even somewhat in the pros, in the early 1970s, when most teams were running the wishbone attack, Rule's offense was considered unique.

Paired with senior tailback Don Hisey, the Bobcats had quite the backfield, proving so early on by whipping Class A rival Aspermont 38–6. Hisey scored three touchdowns in the game while Art added two more, including a 78-yard jaunt in the fourth.

Art's third-quarter touchdown pass to Jesse Macias lifted the Bobcats past Knox City 12–7, before he exploded for three touchdowns and 111 rushing yards in a 25–3 win over Munday.

Rule continued to dominate and was 7–0 heading into a home game with Throckmorton, a team the Bobcats edged by a single point the year before. And when this rematch was scoreless at the half, fear of their undefeated season coming to an end trickled through the home grandstand. But Rule exploded in the third quarter with two quick touchdowns thanks to a scoring pass from Art and an interception return by his good buddy, Barbee. The Bobcats cruised to an 8–0 record with a 28–0 victory and then followed that up the next week by beating Rochester 45–6 as Barbee, Hisey, and Art all surpassed 100 yards rushing.

That set up Rule's 9–0 squad for a showdown against Chillicothe and the right to advance to the playoffs with a perfect record.

Having posted an 18–1 mark over the last two seasons, confidence wasn't a problem for the Bobcats…unless they had too much of it. On a cold and rainy night on the Eagles' home field, Rule took a 7–0 lead into halftime, where Dennis put his team back on the school bus to get out of the rain since Chillicothe didn't have a closed-off dressing room.

"He told us right then on the bus, 'This team can beat you. You better take care of business,'" Art said. "But I didn't think there was any way they could beat us."

Dennis was right. Chillicothe did beat Rule, scoring twice in the second half to win 14–7.

"I learned right then and there that you better respect every opponent," Art said. "Regardless of the situation, you can lose anytime."

The result of that game created a three-way tie atop the Class 5-B standings among Rule, Chillicothe, and Throckmorton, who had all beaten each other en route to 3–1 district records. That led to a coin toss, won by the Eagles, who just like that, advanced to the area round.

To this day, Art says that 1972 team was probably the best he ever played on. Town leader John Greeson, who has served as pastor at the local Church of Christ for 46 years and drove the team bus for many, as well, said Rule took an emotional hit with that defeat.

"I don't know of any greater disappointment when it comes to athletics," Greeson said. "We shouldn't have been beaten by Chillicothe. We really thought we had a great team that year. It was a tough, tough loss."

Greeson said there has been plenty of fun bus rides home. That one from Chillicothe was one of the worst. For the second straight year, the Bobcats were 9–1. For the second straight year, the playoffs began with Rule on the outside looking in.

4. Senior Run

*"The only one who remembers who
got second is the one who got it."*

FOR ALL OF its different communities, cultures, and traditions, there is one thing about Texas that is always consistent, especially in early August.

It's hot.

From Corpus Christi to Amarillo, El Paso to Texarkana, just trying to keep cool is a state pastime. And that goes for morning, noon, and night. Running outside to get the mail can be hazardous.

Now imagine wearing full pads and conducting a two-hour football practice. And then doing it again. Even a football-lover such as Art Briles doesn't exactly love two-a-days in August, where triple-digit temperatures are the norm.

So in 1973, the final Sunday before the start of Rule's grueling preseason workouts, a group of football players planned to take advantage of a recent storm that produced an abnormal amount of heavy rain, causing the nearby Brazos River to flood its banks.

Two or three truckloads of students—mostly football players who were a few days away from becoming seniors—had planned to float the river on inner tubes, but only four of them were brave enough to try. Of course, Art was among the daring, along with friends Larry Barbee, Hal Hunt, and Eugene Lee.

The starting point was about 13 miles away in Saegertown, an even smaller settlement that actually fed into the Rule school district. When the group got in the water, they could sense this might not be the best of ideas. Determined, the four classmates tied the tubes together and set sail anyway, only to discover 50 yards downstream that the roaring rapids were too treacherous to keep everyone together.

"Once we got in there, it was a lot worse than we ever expected," Art recalled. "It was something we wanted to do, but it got dangerously rough—just a scary situation."

At certain spots in the river, the highline power wires that usually ran overhead were actually three to four feet below water. The intense rapids caused Art to flip backward and hang on for dear life.

When the group came up to the bridge in Rule, it was packed with spectators who were checking out the abnormally high water levels. Some had also heard about these crazy kids who had found themselves on a ride more frightening than that of any old water park. At the bridge, a few people tossed ropes down in an effort to help, which Art even thought at the time was strange because had they been able to grab them, the force of the river's impact might have dragged even more into harm's way.

As the foursome continued to coast down the muddy river, the waves finally weakened to the point where all four could paddle to the side and climb back on shore, drawing a few cheers but mostly sighs of relief.

When word spread around town of the incident, some of the body surfers wound up getting in trouble at home.

"I don't think my parents were that upset," Art recalled. "They just were happy that I was okay."

And for a moment or two floating down that river, even Art wasn't so sure he would be okay. After that harrowing experience, entering two-a-days the following Monday suddenly didn't seem so dreadful.

★ ★ ★

There was irony in Art and his three friends spending the final day before the first practice floating down the Brazos River. That's the very place Dennis Briles was going to send the team during certain points of the two-a-day workouts.

Behind the practice field at Rule High School was a trail that led to a fork in the Brazos. Normally, it wasn't a long haul for the players, but the trek could seem like a marathon when Dennis would surprise them in the middle of practice by telling them to run to the river. That wasn't exactly the "water break" the players had in mind.

But Dennis was trying to build toughness and character. Every ounce of emphasis Art Briles currently applies to a conditioning program stems from his father and the days they would have to do unconventional rope drills or climb monkey bars, or just knock out a set of regular pull-ups. Dennis was big on building upper-body strength, having to use your arms and shoulders to pull your entire body weight. That's something at which Art was always good, dating back to early elementary school, but mainly because Dennis had him doing those particular exercises since he was about five.

While Dennis was considered a soft-spoken man with only the occasional tantrum or flare-up, he surrounded himself with contrasting personalities, both at work and at home. Assistant coach Jasper Wilson was more of the butt-kicker in practice. If a player had trouble focusing or wasn't giving full effort, Wilson had no problems being the enforcer, especially when it came to conditioning.

"That's something me and Dennis agreed on," Wilson said. "I ended up coaching 41 years, and I thought my kids were going to be in better condition than our opponent. Dennis felt the same way."

They simply had different methods of getting there.

The same occurred at home, too. Dennis and Wanda shared completely different personalities. She was petite in size, but made up for it with her voice. While Wanda always gave words of encouragement, she had no problem speaking her mind when the moment struck. Once at a basketball game that Dennis was coaching, a mother of one of the players had an issue with the way things were going. After a few verbal attacks on her husband, Wanda stood up, grabbed her fancy purse and whacked her right on top of the head in the middle of the bleachers, even stopping the action on the court momentarily.

Some of the friends who knew her called her a "spitfire" or a "feisty booger," but Wanda had the caring heart necessary for any teacher. In fact, she drove 12 miles out in the country every day to home-school Wes Kittley, who missed his entire eighth-grade year because of a detached retina. Wes was a freshman when his brother Rob and Art were seniors.

"I developed a close bond with Wanda that year because I couldn't really do anything," said Wes, who is currently the head track and field coach at Texas Tech. "She helped me get through the eighth grade. It was a difficult time in my life, and she was fabulous. I appreciate her so much."

While some of her personality traits were more apparent than others, the same could be said for Dennis, especially when it came to coaching. All of his friends and colleagues from that time speak of his superstitions and how they oftentimes affected his ability to focus.

If the Bobcats beat Aspermont one week while he wore a white shirt and blue cap, he made sure that was the exact attire the next week. Whatever flavor of bubblegum he was chewing that night had to be repeated.

If the team went a certain route or on a specific highway to a game one year, he made sure bus driver John Greeson had them go the exact way again.

During the 1973 season, Greeson's five-year-old son, Leon, would often make the trips at Dennis' request. The head coach was always family-oriented, and he knew Leon getting to ride with his dad driving the bus was a fun experience for both of them. But it turned into more than just a nice gesture the night Leon wasn't with his father when the bus pulled up to take the team to a playoff game in Jacksboro.

"Well, let's get the team loaded up, and when we drive by your house, stop the bus, and I'll go in there and get him," Dennis told Greeson, who was also a local pastor.

If Leon couldn't go to the games, he made sure to sit on the front steps of the house as the busses rolled out of town to give a wave to his daddy and his football heroes. But this time, the bus stopped and Dennis got out, trying to convince his mother to allow the youngster to make the trip.

"But she wouldn't let him go," Greeson said. "And it worried Dennis all night long. He just knew because Leon wasn't there, we were going to lose. We ended up winning, but he was so worried. He wanted the same exact thing every time."

★   ★   ★

After the 1972 season ended in such disappointing fashion, losing first to Chillicothe in the final game and then the subsequent coin toss to break a three-way district tie, Rule had only two main goals heading into 1973 campaign: be perfect and stay perfect. Getting close obviously didn't matter as the Bobcats were coming off a pair of 9–1 efforts, only to miss the playoffs both years.

"We entered that season with a bitter taste in our mouths," Art said. "The way we lost the year before, and to have two straight 9–1 teams and not make the playoffs…we just felt like it was our turn."

And it seemed as if Dennis had the type of squad to make a run, considering his son was one of seven players with three years of varsity experience. Rule was ranked No. 4 in the state in Class B heading into the season, which began once again with Class A Aspermont.

Art scored the first touchdown of the season on a quarterback sneak as the Bobcats held on for a 14–6 win. He had two more touchdowns in a 29–6 romp over Knox City and then really showed what he could do against Munday, accounting for 28 points in Rule's 29–0 win. Art rushed for two scores, passed for two more, and even caught a two-point conversion from teammate Steve Anders.

Rule went to 4–0 after a 26–0 win over Jayton, thanks to Art's 85 yards rushing and two touchdowns. (Art's first grandchild was named after the town of Jayton. During many road trips to Lubbock over the years, the family drove through Jayton, and Art's son Kendal always admired the name. So in 2009 Kendal and wife Sarah tabbed their firstborn Jaytn, leaving the *o* out.)

The statement game of the season occurred on October 12 in a clash between two of the best Class B teams in the state. Rule was ranked No. 2, while Loraine entered the game at No. 6. Both sides featured a great collection of talent and usually finished 1-2 in the state track meet every year.

What it turned into was the Art Briles Show. The senior quarterback scored touchdowns early, late, and a few in between as Rule dominated 69–34. The Bobcats jumped out to a 34–6 lead in the first quarter and never looked back.

The game was a huge contrast in styles as Loraine passed for 336 yards to just 85 for Rule. But the Bobcats were dominant on the ground, rushing for 545 yards, including 202 by Art, and held Loraine to only 63 rushing yards in the process. Briles scored on the final play, scrambling 43 yards to the end zone, pushing the combined score for the game to over 100 points at the final gun.

"For a non-district game, that was about as big as it gets," Art remembered. "They were also one of the fastest teams we played because they had great athletes. There were just a lot of fast people on the field."

While Art was the star for Rule, Loraine receiver Michael Jones showcased his speed, catching a 59-yard touchdown pass in the second quarter. Briles and

Jones had raced against each other in track several times, and while football took precedent over everything else, especially during the season, the rivalry between the two was prevalent and was something folks in the Big Country were looking forward to in the spring.

After beating a ranked team so handily, Rule once again had high hopes for the football season heading into district play. While the Bobcats had been running over teams thus far, Art switched gears against Rochester in the district opener. He rushed for 143 yards in the first half, then passed for a season-high 196 in the second as his team easily won 42–0. That would be the first of three straight shutouts, as Rule whipped Newcastle 47–0 and then handed Throckmorton a 29–0 defeat. Art threw just one pass in the latter game, but rushed for 114 yards, including a 95-yarder in the first quarter.

Rule went to 9–0 and remained No. 2 in the state behind Big Sandy, an East Texas town filled with college-bound stars. Although it appeared a showdown between the two was looming, the Bobcats didn't dare look past the regular season, considering the heartbreak the town had already suffered.

For the second straight year, the district title came down to a matchup against Chillicothe with Rule trying to get into the playoffs for the first time in three seasons. In 1972 the Eagles ruined the Bobcats' dreams with an upset in the finale. But it didn't take long to find out that this year would be a different story.

Rob Kittley scored on the second play of the game as Rule jumped out to a 35–0 lead after the first quarter and a 50–0 advantage at the half. Art scored a touchdown in three different ways: with a 12-yard run, an 11-yard touchdown to Steve Anders, and a 35-yard interception return in the third quarter. Overall, Rule dominated from start to finish in a 64–3 victory. The Bobcats were in the playoffs.

With the regular season in the books, the awards started flowing in. Art was a unanimous all-district selection at quarterback, having ranked second in the greater Abilene area with 98 points scored, which included 15 rushing touchdowns. And he was running his father's offense to perfection. Dennis was quoted in the Abilene paper, saying, "I call the plays, but Art usually knows what I want to call."

Whoever made the calls in the playoff opener was right on point. With the game held in Haskell, Art scored the first three touchdowns against Rising Star and finished with four total in a 45–6 rout.

The Bobcats moved on to the quarterfinals in Jacksboro, where they dismantled Prosper, 21–0. On the first touchdown of the game, Rule had a fourth-and-goal, but Dennis didn't like the way his team was lined up after breaking the huddle. Calling a timeout, he told Art that since the defensive ends were forcing everything back to the middle, take the ball wide and get around the edge. It was wide open, and Art basically walked in for an easy touchdown in what turned out to be an easy win.

The Bobcats lost a coin flip before their semifinal matchup with No. 3–ranked Motley County. Dennis wanted the game in nearby Stamford, but instead they traveled 140 miles to Floydada, where Rule had its toughest test of the season in a game between two 12–0 squads.

Art took some vicious hits and suffered two cracked ribs in the first half, but his 25-yard touchdown pass to Barbee gave his team a 14–0 lead. But that's all the scoring the Bobcats could muster, meaning they had to win the game defensively. After a late Motley County score with 2:39 to play, Rule stopped Matadors quarterback Steve Stevens on the 1-yard line for what would've been a game-tying two-point conversion. Instead, the Bobcats held on for a 14–12 win and were headed to the finals.

The collision course that seemed inevitable all season long was finally here: Big Sandy and Rule with the state title on the line.

★   ★   ★

Anyone who followed Class B football in 1973 should've known these two teams would square off at the end. However, Big Sandy appeared to be in a class by itself.

Both teams had 13–0 records, but the Wildcats weren't just beating opponents; they were mauling them. Just how dominant were the Wildcats? They weren't even yielding a point per game heading into the finals, having allowed just 12 points total on the season, and only three in the playoffs. On the flip side, Big Sandy had eight games scoring at least 40 points, including two complete mismatches earlier in the year when they won 84–0 and 92–0.

Big Sandy had some horses in the stable. Guys like Bobby Mitchell, a running back who went to Texas A&M, as well as a freshman defensive tackle named David Overstreet, who later suited up for Oklahoma and then became a first-round pick of the Miami Dolphins. The Wildcats' middle linebacker was a player named Lovie Smith, an eventual All-American at Tulsa University. He would go on to coach 17 seasons in the NFL, including nine as the head coach of the Chicago Bears.

"They had a ton of talent," Art said of Big Sandy. "We weren't afraid of them going into the game. We were confident because we had never lost either. But they had a lot of great athletes. You just don't see that many great players on one team in Class B."

The game was played in Weatherford on one of the coldest nights of the year. Rule superintendent Lavon Beakley usually worked the gate, collecting money. Not long after the tickets were sold and distributed, he spent the rest of the night close to a trash barrel with a burning fire to keep warm.

As both teams took the field, Rule assistant coach Jasper Wilson was standing near the 50-yard line when he was approached by receiver Larry Barbee, who pointed toward the Wildcats.

"Coach, look over there. I think we might be in trouble."

And Rule was in trouble. As great as the Bobcats had been all season, they were no match for a Big Sandy squad that steamrolled its way to the final with a combination of speed and power. And in this game, they had too much of both. To make matters worse, Rule had lost its starting center two weeks earlier to injury. "Overstreet ate our ass up," Art said.

Art played the game with cracked ribs. Having trouble breathing, much less barking out the signals, he was bottled up by a too-fast, too-strong Big Sandy defense. Rule's best chance to make it a game occurred in the second quarter, trailing 6–0 with a second-and-one from the Wildcats' 8-yard line. But three straight runs were stopped for loss, and Rule never got any closer.

Big Sandy kept the pressure on all game, taking away a 25–0 victory, its 11th shutout of the season. That marked the first of a three-year run of dominance for the Wildcats, who went 41–0–1 and claimed three straight Class B state titles.

After the game, Art was asked by *Abilene Reporter-News* writer Bill Hart about facing the staunch defense.

"Big Sandy just got after us. That's all there is to it. They didn't hit any harder than we did. They just knew where to hit."

From the press box, Hart recalled being disappointed in the Rule fans for exiting the stands early with about 2:30 left to play and their team down 19–0. What he didn't realize until later was that they weren't leaving the stadium, but instead were going down to form two lines for the players to walk through from the field to the locker room. The fans had been on quite a ride themselves and wanted to honor the players and coaches who had made it possible.

Following the game, as Art was getting out of the shower, he recalled seeing Big Sandy head coach Jim Norman in the locker room, shaking hands with the coaches and a few players. His team had dominated pretty much everyone en route to the title, but he told the Rule players what a great team they had and how proud they should be.

To this day, Art said he's never seen or heard of an opposing head coach entering the locker room following a game. "But he did it with class. It wasn't disrespectful at all."

Just like that, the 1973 football season was over, and Rule had come up short yet again. The previous two years, they failed to even make the playoffs. This time around, they were one victory away from winning it all. Regardless, losing hurt just the same for Art, who always believed missing out on the postseason the previous two years hampered his team in the end.

"It was our first playoff run, and I think we were happy just being in the game," he said. "I think, had we gone to the playoffs our sophomore and junior years, it would've given us a different perspective. We felt like it was a good season by doing what we did. And that hurt us. You have to approach the playoffs in a very mature manner. Happy teams don't win…determined teams do."

Three days later, many of the players were in the gym as basketball season was finally able to start. After resting for about a week to let his ribs heal, Art made it to the court soon afterward. Yet that wasn't the "other" sport he had on his mind.

★　★　★

If Big Sandy and Rule were on a well-known collision course in football, Art Briles and Michael Jones were on another in track.

They were two of the fastest runners in the entire state, not just in Class B. During the Tarleton Relays in Stephenville that March, Art won the 100 yards in Division I with a time of 10.1 seconds. The winners from the bigger schools of Division II, III, and IV all won the same race at 10.2. A few weeks later in the Redskin Relays in Comanche, Art took the 100, 220, and anchored Rule to a first-place finish in the mile relay.

Meanwhile, Jones was winning his share of races in other events. Loraine was about 80 miles southwest of Rule near Sweetwater, so they were considered to be in different regions of the state, although their proximity often landed Briles and Jones at the same meets.

After Jones beat Briles in the 220 at the 1973 state meet in Austin, Art was looking for revenge. Every time they raced in 1974, he came out victorious, both in the individual races and in the relays with Rule vs. Loraine.

At the Rolling Plains Relays in Jayton, Briles bested Jones in the 100 and 220, taking first in both events. In the mile relay, Rule broke the Class B record with a time of 3:32.9, besting a two-year-old mark of 3:34, set by Loraine.

Shortly thereafter, Jones made headlines by running a 21.6 in the 220 to win the Lubbock Regional. The next week, on the same track at the state-qualifying meet, Art ran a 21.4, adding even more fuel to the brewing fire. But looking back, racing just a few days before the state final probably turned out to be a hindrance.

When the showdown finally arrived in Austin, Jones edged Art in the 100 yards, running a 9.9 to Art's 10-flat. In the 220, Art knew he was in trouble when he drew his lane assignments, getting the always-dreaded Lane 1. At that distance, the ideal lanes are 5 and 6, with less curve around the track. The inside lanes have a sharper turn, which sometimes makes running with a smooth stride harder.

In the end, Jones took first place in a photo finish, beating Art by 0.1 seconds with a winning time of 21.8.

"That was devastating to me. It's hounded me for decades," Art said. "I felt like I should've won. I had been faster than him all year. I was the favorite, and I beat him every time. But I knew Lane 1 was tough. It's a bad lane, and you clearly have to be better to win. It still bothers me. I still feel it today."

For the third straight year, Art finished second. And while he did have the mile relay to prepare for, he said that was a good enough reason for him to skip out on the award ceremony for the 220 yards.

"I didn't go there to get second."

As a team, Rule did what it set out to do. Thanks to a state-record time of 3:22.1 that lasted for 16 years, the Bobcats were able to win the Class B title for the third time in four years.

Actually, they did need some help from the camera. While Rule defeated the favorites from Danbury by a full three seconds, it appeared initially that the

Panthers finished second, which would've given them enough team points to claim the overall title. Fortunately, a second look from the photo-finish camera showed the anchor from Wortham had come back to place second, which took a few points away from Danbury's score. It was just enough to give Rule a 54–53 overall edge to claim the title.

After the meet, the team celebrated at the Rio Motel in Austin, an economical destination for the low-budgeted school. But the motel still had a pool, as freshman runner Wes Kittley soon found out. Excited that Wes was able to run the third leg of the mile relay and hold his own, Art picked up the fully clothed freshman and chunked him into the water for a celebratory dip.

As heartbroken as he was in not winning the individual events, Briles still put on a show. His 33 overall points were the most by any athlete in any classification at that state meet that year. Still, while the overall team title was an accomplishment, coming up short to Jones left a familiar, bitter taste in his mouth again.

★　★　★

Art's final high school sporting event was back on the football field once again. The Oil Bowl is an annual all-star game played in Wichita Falls, pitting the top athletes from Oklahoma and Texas against each other. While the game has taken a backseat lately to many other all-star affairs around the state, the Oil Bowl was much more prominent in 1974, and therefore, small-school players had trouble getting invited.

And Briles wasn't initially selected. But when a certain running back from Tyler backed out of the game, Art was the late addition. It prompted a headline in the Wichita Falls *Times Record News* that stated, "Art Briles Takes Over for Earl."

That would be Earl Campbell, the future Heisman Trophy winner at Texas and NFL superstar. In fact, a few weeks earlier, Art and Campbell were teammates in the Texas High School game in Houston. But now in Wichita Falls, Art was replacing him.

Briles was the only Class B player on his state's roster and primarily played defense. Like most of these events, the Oil Bowl started out light-hearted, with players getting interviewed on the sidelines during the game. But sporting events usually get competitive near the end, and this one was no different.

Early in the third quarter, Briles told a sideline reporter he would get an interception before the game was over. And sure enough, with Texas leading 20–13 in the final minute, he snagged an Oklahoma pass in the end zone, preserving the win for his team.

"I had a good time out there," Art told a reporter after the game. "Of course, you only have a good time when you win."

And with that, Art's high school career was a wrap. In his four years at Rule, he was labeled many things, from a halfback to a safety to a small forward to the coach's kid to the quarterback to captain, sprinter, anchor, and leader.

Albeit just an all-star game in Wichita Falls, Art Briles proved once again that the tag "winner" definitely needed to be included in that lengthy list of distinctions, as well.

5. H-Town Bound

"Believe in you."

EARLY DURING HIS senior season at Rule, Art Briles was sitting in his 12th grade English class when the topic of college and the future came up. Many of his peers had their plans all figured out; others had no clue.

Art was somewhere in the middle. He certainly didn't know for sure what he was going to do, but he had at least narrowed down some options.

"I was either going to get a football scholarship or join the Marines."

Those two routes seemed best. Obviously, he wanted to pursue football, the game he loved and learned from his father, Dennis. If he couldn't, then going into the service was the next-best strategy. Maybe there was a huge unknown element with either path, but there was also a common link—both would get him out of Rule.

As it turns out, his senior season, both in football and track, produced enough highlights and newspaper headlines to garner some attention. While Dennis wanted him to go to Texas Tech, the Red Raiders didn't offer him a scholarship.

That's when Dennis got on the horn and phoned a former coaching colleague from his days in Abilene. Don Todd worked with Dennis at Franklin Junior High about 12 years earlier, and the two had stayed in touch, although technology didn't warrant frequent communication, especially between coaches with busy schedules.

But Dennis kept up with Todd, who was now the defensive coordinator at the University of Houston and was one of the main recruiters on the Cougars staff. After a quick call, Dennis sent over some highlights for review.

"I didn't have to look at a full reel. I knew this guy could play college football," Todd said. "I called his dad right away and told him we were really interested in him and we'd like him to make a visit and see how he liked it."

While Dennis wanted Todd to be directly involved in the recruiting of Art, the Houston coach already had about a dozen recruits he was trying to sign.

So he had to pass it off to another Houston assistant, Larry French, who then took over Art's recruiting.

As long as Houston was interested, there wasn't much to see or discuss. When the Cougars offered him a scholarship to play quarterback, it was a win-win-win situation.

Dennis wanted his son to play college football. Art wanted to play quarterback. And he wanted to get far way from Rule, both geographically and culturally. So the University of Houston was a perfect spot for all three…at least in the beginning.

Art had track scholarship offers to the University of Texas and Tulsa. Other than Houston, his opportunities to play football included Southwest Texas State (now Texas State) and Arkansas. The chance to stay in Texas and go to a big city were the final determining factors.

He also liked where the football program at the University of Houston was headed. Bill Yeoman had finished his 12th year as the Cougars head coach. Despite being without a conference and playing as an independent, Houston was starting to make some noise. When Art joined the team, the Cougars were coming off a Bluebonnet Bowl win and a No. 9 ranking in the Associated Press poll to end the 1973 season.

To start the 1974 campaign, the school announced it would be joining the Southwest Conference and would play a full SWC schedule in 1976, the first year the Cougars could compete for a championship. Being a part of something new was a big attraction for Art.

"Houston just had a lot things that I really liked," he recalled. "It was really a great time to be at a place where everything was underappreciated. People viewed Houston as an independent [that] didn't have a home. I liked that. I could sense that we had a drive to prove people wrong and become a family. We wanted to show we were a valid commodity to be dealt with. I liked being a part of something fresh and new, something no one had any idea how it would turn out."

★   ★   ★

When Art went off to college in the fall of 1974, he left behind a town of approximately 1,000 people. He arrived in a city with about 2 million. The university's student body was then approaching 30,000 students, so even being on campus was a culture shock for Art, who thought Abilene was a big city until he landed in Houston, which had the highest population in Texas at the time and still does with more than 2.1 million.

Art indeed began his collegiate career as a quarterback, although that didn't last long. His recruiting class also included Danny Davis, who went on to become a three-year starter for the Cougars. Art spent a few early practices with the passers, but it wasn't long before he started doubling up as a receiver—for obvious reasons.

Davis actually knew of "a guy named Art Briles" whom he had seen a few months earlier in Austin at the state track meet. Surely this 145-pound kid with the scraggly hair wasn't the same one.

"Art was the fastest guy on the whole team," Davis said. "He wasn't used to playing receiver, but if there's one thing about him, he could really run. We used to always watch him at practice. Me and my buddies would say, 'Whew, that's the fastest white boy we've ever seen.'"

Yeoman also saw Art's speed right away, but he wasn't sure exactly where to use him. In one of his first practices as a true freshman, Art was serving as the scout-team quarterback when the play broke down. He decided to take off, ran right past a linebacker and split two starting safeties on his sprint to the end zone. Yeoman looked over at Coach Todd and said, "Even faster than I thought."

But with Davis in the fold, along with Bubba McGallion, Houston had depth at quarterback. And the same could be said for the receivers, which already featured established standouts such as Elmo Wright and Don Bass. To this day, Art calls Bass the "best athlete I've ever played with or coached."

Ultimately, the Cougars decided to redshirt Briles as a true freshman. But back then, NCAA rules allowed redshirting players to have a limited role on the varsity team, as well. So while he did redshirt in 1974, giving him four more years of eligibility following the season, Art was one of five freshmen who traveled with the team. He didn't play much, but the Cougars found a way to occasionally take advantage of his speed to cover kicks and punts on special teams.

Still not sure where to play him, Yeoman had Art practicing with both the quarterbacks and receivers. And that was fine with him, considering he was used to playing different positions. He started as a halfback in Rule before switching to quarterback his last two years, and even then he would sometimes line up at receiver, such as on two-point conversions.

Art rarely came off the field during his days with the Bobcats, so once he got to college, *where* he played was the least of his concerns.

In 1974 most university programs had a freshman team, which allowed anyone who didn't get in the game the previous week to play. Normally the squad was made up of those who were redshirted, but there were a few upper-classmen in the games, as well.

Similar to a junior varsity schedule in high school, the freshman games in college would also take place on Thursday nights. Not every school had a freshman team, and with Houston still playing an independent schedule, its matchups didn't always correspond with those of the varsity that weekend. Houston's freshmen played against Texas Tech, SMU, and Rice.

The one at SMU that year helped shape Art's life forever. Against the Mustangs, he was dominant in the first half, catching five passes before the break, where Houston trailed by a touchdown.

It didn't matter that only a few hundred fans were in the stands. To Art, this was college football. If they're keeping score, then it matters. So after a few months of being the quiet, reserved freshman just trying to fit in, he decided to speak up in the locker room that Thursday night.

"Guys, I've got something to say.... Hey, I came to U of H because I wanted to be a winner. I wanted to prove something to somebody and do things other people didn't think I could do."

Not sure how that would be received, Art was relieved to see a few head-nods from his teammates. They perked up and were listening. So he kept going. He continued with a rant about "competing, fighting, and working together" in what sounded like typical coaching rhetoric. But he wasn't a coach. He wasn't even 19 years of age. Some of the players on that team were 21 or 22, yet he wasn't afraid to say what needed to be said. Houston rallied in the second half to win the game, but Art remembers the halftime even more.

"Everyone was really paying attention and really responsive," Art said. "I can remember exactly where I was sitting and I was thinking, *Hey, maybe I've got a knack for this…maybe this is what I'm meant to be."*

★ ★ ★

Heading into his second year at Houston, Art Briles was now officially a wide receiver. The coaching staff liked what they saw in Danny Davis and figured

Art's best chance to contribute would come from catching the ball instead of throwing it. Considering that his blazing speed rivaled that of any player on the team at any position, the move just made sense.

During two-a-day practices before the season, Art displayed that speed, along with good hands and a football IQ that comes from being a coach's son.

Just a few weeks earlier, he had moved into the Moody Towers dormitory on campus. His roommate was Bubba McGallion, the second-team quarterback behind Davis, and McGallion made sure to get the ball to Art, who consistently made plays in practice against the first-team defense. He would get a few reps with the starters, but Art had mostly solidified a spot on the second unit. As a redshirt freshman, that was more than acceptable. He knew he would not only travel to road games again, but he was also expecting to have a formidable role in the offense.

Unfortunately, on the last scrimmage of two-a-days in late August, Art broke his wrist in two places. He needed surgery, a procedure that would end his season. Before the 1975 campaign even got started, Briles was done.

After redshirting in '74, he now was a medical redshirt for '75, which still left him with four years of eligibility. But he wasn't thinking that far ahead. All Art ever wanted to do was get in the game. He played only sparingly as a freshman, and now he'd have to wait another full calendar year before he would take another snap. On top of that, having to wear a cast for two months was annoying.

It was a frustrating year for Art, who was now without the two passions of his life: football and Jan. She had decided to go to Texas Tech in Lubbock, just two hours away from Rule. Despite their distance and the difficultly in routinely communicating, the couple continued to date. They cherished holidays and any other chance to visit. Phone calls were seldom, but they would both write letters back and forth when they had the time—something of which Art now had more than he ever wanted. But just like he did in the locker room of the freshman game at SMU, he started gravitating toward coaching.

One day, he finally got up the nerve to ask Yeoman if he could sit in with the staff and review film. Surprised by the request, Yeoman obliged and allowed him in the coaches' locker room where he'd watch as the old 16mm movies played up on the wall. Sometimes Art would be alone but usually he would sit there with the assistants. He even recalls a couple of one-on-one film sessions with Yeoman, who was known for his offensive mind.

"I remember he wasn't ever watching the offense. He was watching defenses," Briles said. "He watched the way the defensive end was lining up or what the linebacker was doing on this play. Right then and there, I learned it was more than just lining up and beating your guy. When I figured out it was a very intellectual game, that really appealed to me."

To this day, Yeoman says Art Briles is the only player he ever had who asked to watch film with the coaches.

★　★　★

In 1976 Art was determined to change the course of the previous two years. Not only was he healthy again, but he also felt much more confident in the system, thanks to his film sessions with Coach Yeoman and his staff.

That experience showed from the very start of the preseason practices. He ran crisp routes, caught the ball well, and hadn't lost any of his speed. If anything, the college weight program had made him an even more explosive runner. More than anything, though, his knowledge of the offense was a notch ahead of even some of the starters.

"I felt really good about that year. I figured I would play a lot, and maybe even start," Art said.

While he was excited about his role, the entire program had a sense of exhilaration as the Cougars entered their first season in the Southwest Conference. Just like the entire team, looking to make its mark and prove its worth, Art had the same feeling individually. The time had come to show what he could do.

Houston started the 1976 season with Baylor in Waco, where the Cougars sent a statement to the rest of the conference. Houston whipped the Bears 23–5 in a game that saw Art in on several snaps. His grasp of the offense and understanding of the plays was beneficial to the coaches, who trusted him when sending in the calls from the sideline. He did that in a rotation with other receivers and occasionally had a few passes thrown his way.

The Cougars ran into a brick wall at Florida the next week, taking it on the chin, 49–14, from the Southeastern Conference power. But any thoughts of a hangover ended the following Saturday in the home opener against No. 9 ranked Texas A&M. Getting his first start, Art played most of the offensive snaps against the Aggies, who might have underestimated the conference newcomers.

"They used me to block and to do some things that other guys wouldn't commit to doing with an eager attitude," Briles said. "I wanted to get on the field, and I'd do whatever it took to get out there."

Art caught two passes as Houston rolled to a 21–10 victory, giving the Cougars a 2–0 start in SWC action.

He played even more in a 50–7 win over West Texas State (now West Texas A&M, located in Canyon, Texas), which improved the Cougars to 3–1 overall. But late in the game, Art limped off the field for a play, knowing something was wrong with his left knee. He tried to run it off, but the pain and discomfort were overwhelming.

All of a sudden, Art found himself in a tough situation. He had waited so long to play that he didn't want to risk anything by sitting out because of injury. He tried to fight through it, hoping it was nothing and that the aching would subside eventually.

In the back of his my mind, though, he knew something was terribly wrong. His leg was stiff and unable to bend.

Heading into the SMU matchup, Art knew he wouldn't be able to practice as normal. The team trainers had picked up on his injury and were giving him treatment, which forced him to miss crucial practice reps. As the game grew closer, he knew he wouldn't play a lot.

And that was extremely disappointing, considering his parents, Dennis and Wanda, had planned on traveling to Dallas for the game. Because of his injury, Art didn't really want them to come. Although he missed them dearly, he didn't think they should make the drive if he wasn't going to see much, if any, action.

But Dennis and Wanda were just too eager to see their son, who had told them how much playing time he had been receiving the past few weeks. They couldn't wait to see him again.

So on the Wednesday before the game, Dennis called up Coach Todd and asked if it was too late to get a few tickets, requesting three or four. That afternoon, Todd put six in an envelope and overnighted them to Rule.

The tickets arrived on Thursday. Wanda called Art on Friday and relayed how excited they were to be able to check out No. 5 in action and visit with him—even if it was just for the 30 minutes after the game before the players got on the bus.

Art knew his parents were coming and would probably bring along Tottie, his "foster grandmother." Maybe Dennis' friend, Ed Fouts, would tag along, and while there was hope that Jan could make the game, she was throwing a wedding shower for her good friend, Jamie Barbee, at her house in Rule.

Art hung up the phone feeling better about the situation. Sure, he might not play much, but that wasn't the point. So many times in the last two years he had walked off the field in Houston with no parents or family in the stands, no one calling out his name or coming over to hug him.

He realized how much he missed that feeling. All of a sudden, he was now excited about the trip to Dallas—to see the people who loved him the most.

6. October 16, 1976

"Pain has a memory"

AS THE PRINCIPAL of a high school and a retired football coach, Dennis Briles more than believed in punctuality. If you weren't five or 10 minutes early, you were late. And that mentality was for simple proceedings such as going to class or a doctor's appointment.

But driving four hours to Dallas for a football game was a much bigger occasion, so he made sure they rolled out of Rule, Texas, in plenty of time to arrive at the Cotton Bowl, get their seats, and then hopefully find a way to visit with their son.

For Dennis, trips like this were the exact reason he decided to stop coaching. He remained principal of the school and had also become the mayor of Rule. But he wanted less on his plate so they could drive around to see their son on the field.

Dennis and Wanda had circled this game on their calendar for months. They took Tottie, Wanda's sister who had raised her from childbirth and was like a grandmother to Art and his brother.

With six tickets sent to him from Coach Todd, Dennis asked around to try and fill up the car. He checked with good friend Ed Fouts, who agreed to go. Dennis also called over to Jan's mother, Helen Allison, to see if she was interested. As it turned out, Jan was in town that weekend, coming in from Texas Tech, but was hosting a wedding shower for her friend, Jamie Barbee, the younger sister of Art's good friend and former teammate, Larry.

So Jan had to decline, although she desperately wanted to see her boyfriend, whom she missed profoundly. At the last minute, Fouts then had to back out, as well, citing a few chores that needed to be done around the farm.

So around 7:00 AM on Saturday, Dennis, Wanda, and Tottie pulled their beige Ford LTD out of the driveway and headed east toward Dallas, leaving plenty of time to make it there before the 2:00 PM kickoff.

It was a cloudy day throughout North Texas, having rained some in Dallas, although there hadn't been a drop around the Rule and Abilene area.

With Dennis driving and Wanda alongside in the passenger seat, Tottie sat in the back, although at age 66, her hearing wasn't the best anymore. Coupled with a car traveling at least 55 mph, it's likely Elsie spent most of her trip leaning forward in order to chime into the conversation.

All three were excited, not just to see Art, but to also go to a prestigious sporting event at a stadium that was already considered a treasured landmark.

★   ★   ★

A little more than an hour into the trip, about 12 miles outside of Graham, their car was approaching a hill on Highway 380 near Newcastle. Out of nowhere, a water truck that was attempting to pass another truck veered into the Briles' lane and struck their vehicle. With his vision limited because of the steep incline, Dennis never had a chance to swerve, the car simply no match against the larger, overpowering truck.

The two vehicles collided head on. Dennis, Wanda, and Tottie were killed instantly. The driver of the truck was not seriously injured, only going to the hospital with a broken arm.

Police officials got in touch with Dennis' brother Dalton, who lived in nearby Throckmorton, to come to the scene and identify the bodies. From there, they were able to formulate an official report that listed the time of the accident at 8:06 AM and apparently stated that the driver of the truck, reported in the *Abilene Reporter-News* as being 25-year-old Lowry Ero. While there was speculation that the driver of the truck was racing on the highway, no charges were ever filed.

With Art and his teammates more than two hours away in Dallas, the horrific news started to slowly spread back west, toward Rule.

Eddie Briles, a registered nurse, had just finished a long night shift when he first got wind of the accident. His wife, Teresa, fielded a call from her sister, who was working at the popular café in Rule where many of the locals gathered on Saturday mornings. That's when the county undertaker, Lance Pinkard, showed up to inform some of the town's residents of the news, and to try to round up a few volunteers to help pick up the bodies.

"You just can't believe it's true," Eddie recalled. "You never think that stuff happens to you. I just remember trying to figure out what was going on. But it never really sinks in."

Eddie got on the phone, hoping this was a mistake. Hoping somehow, some way this was not happening to him. He called the local police, and they had no information for him. Finally, he got hold of his great aunt, Mary Place, and found out that the authorities had contacted her, as well. She told Eddie the news was true.

The oldest son of Dennis and Wanda Briles was in shock as he hung up. The nightmare was a reality. Now, he had to find out how to tell his little brother, who he knew was only a few hours away from kickoff in Dallas.

Bad news can spread fast in a small town. Everyone knows everyone as it is, but these were three prominent people in the community. In a single moment, the town's mayor and school principal/former football coach, along with the special education teacher and the sweet lady from the dry goods store…were all gone.

It's an incident people from Rule will never forget. Wes Kittley, then a high school senior at Rule, was working at the Swofford Exxon in Saegertown, fixing flats and pumping gas, when someone rolled up and talked of the accident.

Larry Barbee was home that weekend from a semester at West Texas State in Canyon. His mother came to his room to tell him.

Jan remembered getting ready for the shower, held at the Allison house, when the word came in. Her mother, Helen, was dear friends with so many people in the community, and still is today. Together, they were preparing for the bridal festivities and also planning to celebrate a birthday for her husband, Jan's father, Wallace. Obviously the news changed not only the day, but also the town. Forever.

"We were all so sad because we knew the only reason he quit coaching was because he wanted to follow Art and his career and wanted more time to watch him," said Kittley, whose family down the line was related to Tottie. "It was just a sad deal. Everyone was heartbroken."

Superintendent Lavon Beakley, who was notified by the undertaker, as well, became responsible for telling many of the other community members, including Church of Christ pastor John Greeson and Dennis' good friend, Fouts.

With advice from those three elders, Eddie tried to determine how to tell Art. A phone number for the Cougars' locker room in the Cotton Bowl was somehow tracked down, and a member from the grieving community in Rule informed Houston head coach Bill Yeoman of the tragedy. Now, Yeoman and his staff had to decide how and when to tell Art that his parents had passed.

★ ★ ★

Houston defensive coordinator Don Todd rarely traveled with the team on road games. Being one of the Cougars' lead recruiters, he often left Houston on Thursday to visit a few prep players or perhaps a high school or two, and would then take in a Friday night game before meeting up with the team on Saturday morning. There were times when Todd cut it close and didn't reach the locker room until a few minutes before kickoff.

Against SMU, Todd managed to arrive around noon, driving his rental car close to Houston's locker room. He quickly dressed and made it out on the field for warm-ups, where he noticed Art being extremely vocal and encouraging. He was clapping, yelling, hollering—just getting his team fired up for a big game against a traditionally good opponent.

When the Cougars went back to their locker room for final preparations, Todd saw a highway patrolmen talking to one of the equipment managers, who then looked over at the coach and pointed in his direction.

"I remember thinking I probably parked my car in the wrong spot or something," Todd said. "But he came over and asked me to step outside."

On the floorboard of the mangled vehicle, rescuers found the envelope Todd had mailed to Dennis just two days earlier. The tickets were inside with a message that allowed police to make the connection to the Cotton Bowl, where they informed Todd. He then called for Yeoman to step outside. Just moments earlier, the head coach had gotten off the phone with the representatives from Rule, telling him the same news.

Kickoff was less than 30 minutes away. Where in the coaching handbook did it say how to handle this?

"That's one of the worst days I've ever had as a coach," Yeoman said. "You just don't know what to do. I knew what a great relationship Art had with his folks. We talked about it. I thought of about 50 different answers but we decided to wait to tell him."

As the team filed back onto the field for the start of the game, only a handful of coaches were aware. Back in Rule, many of his family and friends had been informed, as well. To Art, all he knew was the game was about to start and he hadn't been able to find his parents in the stands just yet.

★ ★ ★

In the years that followed the worst day of his life, Art Briles has continued to keep those heartbreaking hours close to the vest. He never forgets and always revisits what happened. Yet he rarely talks about it, if ever.

His three children certainly know of the story but can't recall their father speaking about the tragedy more than once or twice, and never in full detail.

None of his close friends can remember Art opening up to them. Even Jan, who has been with him every step of the way since that dreadful moment, says Art has chosen not to bring up the day he lost his parents.

Nearly four decades later, talking about October 16, 1976 is still unimaginably difficult for Art Briles:

> The last time I talked to my mother was in the hotel room Friday night before the game. She was telling me her, dad, and [Tottie] were coming over tomorrow. When I talked to my mom, they said Jan might come. She was having a bridal shower for someone at her house that Saturday on the 16th. That's the reason she didn't come. She didn't think she could get through in time to make it.
>
> When I talked to Mom, everything seemed well. I was excited about seeing them in the stands tomorrow. I had already suffered my ACL injury and I was just hanging on through the season. I knew I wouldn't play much. If I had any time, it'd be late in the game.
>
> They wanted to come, anyway. I told Mom, 'I'm not going to play. Don't worry about it. We'll just get on the plane and head back.' I wouldn't be able to hang around much, anyway. But they wanted to come.
>
> I think it was probably a 2:00 o'clock kickoff. It was a cloudy day and it had rained some that morning. I remember warming up. I always

liked being on the road even though there weren't a lot of fans. When we got to the Cotton Bowl, I remember looking up in the stadium to the parents' section, and I didn't see my mom and dad. Usually, she'd always holler, and I'd wave and acknowledge her and Dad. But I didn't see them in pregame.

I went into the locker room and remember running back out. I remember being on the sideline and looking up there right before game time. Once again, I'm not seeing Mom and Dad. I was thinking something like, *Well, I don't know, maybe they're not up there or gotten there yet.* I really didn't know because I knew Dad would've been right there at the open of the game, with a chance to wave hello.

So the game went along and it was the same thing at halftime. I looked up there; they weren't in the parents' section. No Mom and Dad. I can remember thinking, *This is weird.... Something strange is going on.* I kind of remember, seems like it was a radio guy, Bill Worrell, who covered Houston games, gravitating toward me in the second half. I'd be on the sideline watching the game, and he was around. I actually got into the game in the third quarter or fourth. I think I had one catch near the end. But I do know we won the game pretty convincingly.

Coming off the field, I remember looking up once again and not seeing Mom and Dad. At that point, I had a suspicion something just wasn't right. As we're walking up the tunnel, someone grabbed me. I couldn't tell you who it was, an assistant coach maybe, but I remember coming up the tunnel and getting to the top just before the dressing room when someone said, "Coach Yeoman wants to visit with you."

I can remember walking in the dressing room, and they led me back to a little side room. Then it was just Coach Yeoman. Coach Larry French, I think, was in there, too. Honestly, I'm not sure who all was in there; everything was just a shock.

I walked in that room and shut the door. I can remember thinking, *Something is really wrong. This is really bad. I don't know what it is. It's not good.* I wondered if it had something to do with me or football or whatever. Honestly, at that time it didn't dawn on me that it was anything about my parents.

I had my pads on. I sat down. Coach Yeoman said to me: "Art, there's been an accident."

Right then, I knew. Like a ton of bricks hit me right in the face. I just knew exactly what was going on. I remember saying, "This isn't my mom and dad?"

He said, "Yes."

I asked, "Are they okay?"

He said, "No, Art." He told me they had perished, along with my foster grandmother. I just remember saying, "No, this can't really be happening." And, of course, everything just goes into a daze. You just go in a daze and float outside of your body for a period of time. I can remember Coach Yeoman saying, "I'm sorry to tell you this and deliver this news."

They had known before the game; it had happened in the morning. I think somebody made the decision to wait until afterward. This was a time when there were no cell phones, no Internet. I don't know how many people at U of H knew, but not many. A few coaches, the radio guy, trainers maybe.

As I tried to collect myself, I knew this was a life-changing moment. I can remember walking back into the dressing room. I'm sure 15 minutes had elapsed, in that timeframe, and we had just won a big Southwest Conference game, but I can remember the dressing room being silent. I walked back through there, and everyone was silent. I went over to my locker and some of the players started coming over and saying, "Art we're so sorry." There was a lot of love and support from the players on the team.

I think that's what I appreciate about the team concept so much today. People are there for each other. A team is there for each other. Certainly my coaches, my teammates, and people who were associated with me, they certainly pulled me through those dire times.

I took a shower, got dressed, and they said, "We'll get you to Abilene tonight; there's a car there to pick you up." They pulled Paul Humphreys, a good friend and captain, our starting middle linebacker and an All-SWC player. Paul said he'd come with me, and we got in a car outside the dressing room. We got to the airport and flew on a small plane to Abilene. Again, it was just a blur.

We landed in Abilene around 9:00 or 9:30. There was a carload of people there. Ed Fouts, my brother Eddie, Jimmy Lisle [a high school friend], and then Paul and I all got in the car. It was a 60-mile drive back to Rule at night. When we got to the house, I really just wanted a little me-time. Ever since I had found out, I'd been around people. As soon as I got to the house, there were people at the house: friends, immense family, my mother and dad's friends. I just remember going back to my bedroom and just sitting there on the bed thinking, *I can't believe this has happened.*

Jan was back in town from school at Tech. She had a bridal shower that day. It was great to see her that night. Jan has always been a rock in my life, without question. She's the inspiration and stability that has allowed me to be a strong person. She was strong for me that night. I'll always remember that.

7. Now What?

"Starting at the bottom—Looking up!"

IF ONLY IT were a dream.

Although Art Briles likely didn't sleep a wink, he arose on the morning of October 17 wishing he had simply endured the worst of nightmares. But the number of people at his house offering support and sympathy was proof enough that he was indeed living in a horrific reality.

All sorts of thoughts and questions were entering Art's mind.

What now?

Why me?

Why did they even come when I told them I wouldn't play much?

When are we having the funeral?

How could this happen?

What do I have to wear to it?

Should I even go back to school?

How do I tell these people I don't want to visit right now?

What do we do with the house?

How could this happen?

How could this happen?

How could this happen?

Art had nothing but questions. And, he had no answers for anything or anyone. All he wanted to do was lie in his bed and feel sorry for himself. He never liked being the center of attention, especially for something like this.

Communities like Rule pull together in such tragedies. While the comfort was appreciated, the constant care was overwhelming, especially for a 20-year-old who didn't know how to react to losing the only safety net he'd ever known.

On Sunday, he went with Eddie to the cemetery located just two blocks from their house, which sat right between two cotton fields. Later that afternoon, the brothers rode to Haskell, where a department store opened its doors to let them both buy suits for the funeral.

Haskell is only nine miles east of Rule, but on that Sunday, the trip felt an hour long for Art and Eddie. They barely drove over 40 miles per hour and wouldn't dare let the car close to the middle of the road, traveling most of the way on the right shoulder of the highway, making sure to steer clear from head-on traffic. Just 24 hours earlier, they forever lost their parents and grandmother because of a deadly head-on accident, so they weren't going to take any chances.

Art remembered going with Eddie and other family members to pick out a tombstone, but he didn't have much opinion. He was there physically, but still in just a daze.

Because of Eddie's work and Art being in school, the turnaround for the funeral was quick. Paul Humphreys went back to Houston on Monday morning for class, missing the memorial service that afternoon.

No church in Rule had room for a three-person funeral, so the family held the service in the high school gymnasium, which could accommodate 450 people. The gym was packed with folks sitting in the aisles and standing in the corners of the bleachers. Three closed caskets rested in the middle of the wooden floor.

Dennis' casket was draped in blue and white carnations for the school colors of Rule. Wanda's was covered with red carnations, one of her favorite colors, while Tottie had bronze mums placed on her casket. Preachers from both the Baptist church and Church of Christ spoke, telling stories of the town's fallen friends. Dressed in their new suits, Art and Eddie remained stoic during the entire service.

As one of the pallbearers, Ed Fouts remembered both boys keeping their composure during what had to be a horrendous ordeal for both.

"Eddie did a really good job of handling everything as the older brother," Fouts said. "Art was a lot quieter. He really didn't want anything to do with anything. I think he really felt guilty."

Fouts was one of those who rode with Art on the way home from the airport the day of the accident and remembered the discussion during the drive centered on anything but what had happened. Art talked about the football season and school. He was quiet, his thoughts obviously tormented. Even right then he didn't know what to say about the tragedy.

After the service, while heading toward the grave site, Art had a long talk with Church of Christ pastor John Greeson. As they were walking, Art stopped the preacher and said to him, "Please tell me God didn't do this to my mother and daddy."

Startled, yet fully understanding the pain the young man felt, Greeson responded, "God didn't do it. It was an accident, son. A terrible accident."

Art thanked Greeson for helping him see it that way and then asked, "When is this all going to end?"

To this day, Greeson always thought he was referring to the pain and suffering. Never described as a patient person, Art remembered asking the question, but more in a literal sense. He was simply talking about the service. The emotional strain had taken its toll. Art was ready to go home.

★   ★   ★

After the funeral on Monday, Art made his way back to Houston. As if his mind hadn't been racing before, now the college junior—albeit a redshirt freshman on the field—was wondering just what he wanted to do with his life.

He loved football, but it also reminded him of his father. And he wasn't playing, anyway, because of a knee issue that doctors and trainers couldn't fully evaluate. Getting an MRI wasn't as procedural as it is today, so Art limped around, trying to fight through the injury.

"I went back to Houston and started trying to rebound, restructure, and refocus," Briles said. "I had to figure out what I wanted to do. I felt like I had no safety net."

Art rejoined his teammates, who didn't know how to act around him. Clearly, he wasn't interested in discussing the matter with anyone. Then again, acting normal was hard for people like Bubba McGallion, his roommate at the time, or Gary Drake, who had not only developed a close friendship with Art but had taken him home to his parents' house in Port Arthur for holidays when he didn't have enough time to get back to Rule. So while Art was feeling a different kind of pain, his teammates were hurting along with him.

That was evident in the following game, a home contest against Arkansas, which was ranked 15th in the Associated Press poll, one spot behind the surging Cougars, who had moved up to 14th that week. Played at Rice Stadium,

Arkansas won 14–7. To a man, every player from that Houston locker room as well as the coaching staff would say the accident had a lingering impact.

"Arkansas was a good team," quarterback Danny Davis said, "but we went into that game with heavy hearts. We were affected all week in practice and didn't play together in that game. I remember some of the leaders of the team standing up after the game. We said we're not going out this way. We decided right then to rally, and that propelled us the rest of the year. We didn't lose another game."

With Art barely getting any playing time, Houston continued to roll through the Southwest Conference. A 49–21 win over TCU set the Cougars up for three straight road games to finish conference play. They waxed Texas 30–0 in Austin, then edged Texas Tech 27–19 in Lubbock before a crosstown win over Rice, 42–20, that gave the Cougars their first-ever SWC title.

In its inaugural season, Houston had shocked the conference, earning a trip to the Cotton Bowl. And yes, that meant another visit to the Fairgrounds in Dallas for Art Briles.

"It kind of felt like returning to the scene of the crime," Art recalled. "It didn't happen there, but all of those feelings came back again. It was eerie going back and rekindling the emotions of everything. Just walking down the tunnel and being in the locker rooms…it was hard."

Individually, the return was overwhelming for Art. As a team, the Cougars had a job to do. Ranked No. 6 in the country, Houston knocked off fourth-ranked Maryland 30–21 on a cold, wet New Year's Day.

Art's brother Eddie, along with Fouts, made the trip over to Dallas for the game. Not only did he have to travel in bad weather, but he was headed to the same exact destination, on the same exact route, that killed his parents just 11 weeks earlier.

"We didn't even think about that," Eddie said. "If we did, I don't remember. You just block it out and do what you have to do. We wanted to see Art and see how he was doing, so we went."

As he walked up the Cotton Bowl tunnel, Art again felt uncertain. The concern about his parents that developed in his mind during that SMU game turned out to be valid. This time, he was unsure about his future with the team and in football altogether.

Just as before, his intuition was spot-on. Like the rest of his teammates, Art removed his shoulder pads as he sat at his locker after the game. He would never put them on again.

* * *

Figuring out exactly what was wrong with his knee took precedence as soon as the season ended. The team doctors decided to do exploratory surgery, with Art thinking he was getting a simple scope. He woke up hours later with a cast from his thigh to his shin. What the doctors found was a torn anterior cruciate ligament (ACL). The reconstructive operation and rehabilitation afterward back in 1976 weren't nearly as advanced as they are today, where athletes have shown the ability to return to full strength in as little as seven to eight months.

Back then, a torn ACL was potentially career ending. And for a player who was already contemplating leaving the team for a needed change of scenery, Art's injury was just one more reason to walk away. He stayed through that spring semester, but his close friends started to get the hint that he wasn't coming back.

Back in Rule, Eddie and his family relocated to his parents' house to take care of loose ends. While that was a necessary move that Art understood, he was uneasy about returning to what he used to call home. Now, it was his brother's home, and Art felt uncomfortable.

Consequently, he always gravitated to Jan's house. He wanted to see her, but her parents, Helen and Wallace, had also become like mother and father figures to him. He enjoyed Helen's cooking, especially her homemade buttermilk pie, as well as the man-to-man talks he would have on the porch with Wallace. Without coming on too strong, the Allisons did their best to welcome Art into their household. Deep down, they both knew he and their daughter had something special and it was likely just a matter of time before their relationship became official.

One weekend in the spring, Art was visiting Jan when the phone rang at the Allison household. Oddly enough, the call was for Art. On the other end was coach Don Todd, who had heard that Art was considering leaving school at the end of the semester. Todd offered him the chance to return to the Cougars and become a student-coach. From their film sessions, the staff knew how much Art understood the game.

Coaching was a developing passion in his life, and he also cherished the opportunity to get his foot in the door on the collegiate level. But in the end, Art needed to get away from Houston. "I didn't want to be known as the guy whose parents died in a car wreck," he said. "I just needed a new start, a new environment."

He also needed to be around a different kind of support group, so naturally he transferred to Texas Tech, both to be with Jan and his friends from Rule and the surrounding areas. When the semester ended, Art didn't have any sappy endings. He didn't even say good-bye to some of his teammates. He packed his bags and headed home with no plans of ever returning.

★   ★   ★

When he showed up at Tech in the fall of 1977, Art had a much different mentality about school than he did three years earlier in Houston. Getting his degree was suddenly first and foremost on his mind. Coaching was now on his radar, and the quicker he could get done and get started with the next chapter of his life, the better off he would be.

Art developed some lifelong friends in Lubbock, hooking up with a group of guys who also played high school football. They weren't talented enough to compete in college, but there were still some good athletes in the bunch. So they decided to form an intramural team, calling themselves the "No-Ifs." While he was slowly recovering from his knee surgery that first year, Art was at full strength in 1978.

Playing with buddies Tim Tanner, Rusty Erwin, and Jackie Young, Art led the No-Ifs to a stellar season of flag football, going undefeated without yielding a single point. But not long after the schedule ended, intramural officials informed the team about a school policy prohibiting players who had lettered in any Southwest Conference sport. Since Art earned a letter in football at Houston, the No-Ifs were stripped of their title, which went to the runners-up.

Along with going to school, Art also earned a few bucks with a job at the TG&Y warehouse, where for two summers he drove a forklift and was a stocker, unloading trucks.

Work, school, and being with Jan all helped ease the transition. He still went to high school games on Friday nights, especially the smaller-school matchups that played in the Lubbock area, and he would also catch pro and college action on TV. But he never went to a game at Tech, even when Houston returned to Lubbock during the 1978 season.

He was just a frustrated ex-athlete who couldn't bring himself to attend a game in which he thought he should be playing. High school contests were fine, especially since he would sit in the stands and break down the plays schematically. But he wanted no part of the college game.

Of course, the best part about being in Lubbock was getting to see Jan on a daily basis. The two had maintained their relationship for three years while he was in Houston, and their love only blossomed when they finally lived in the same town again. The couple picked out rings in early December, and Art proposed on Christmas 1977, with an engagement ring Jan still wears today. The two were married at the First Baptist Church back in Rule on June 8, 1978, a little more than six years after they first began going steady.

Jan knew all along they were destined to be together. Likewise, Art said he never envisioned himself with anyone else.

He had married his high school sweetheart. She had been there cheering him on from the sidelines when he was a star at Rule. She had been there emotionally during some tough times in Houston. And she had been there right by his side the night his world turned upside down.

But his marriage to Jan only somewhat eased the void from losing his parents. He still missed them dearly:

> When they passed away, I knew I could take two paths. As ignorant as it sounds, if I wanted to be an alcoholic and bury myself in pity, I could do that. Or I could take a stand and move forward and live for my mother and father, to make them proud and to carry on all the good things they bestowed upon me.
>
> Thankfully, they made me a strong enough individual to make the right choice, and that's what I dedicated myself to and still do today. Mom and Dad did a great job of raising me and making me independent, and at the same time gave me faith to believe in God and believe in myself. If you do things right and do it long enough, good things will happen.

After all the bad he had endured over the previous three years, the time had come for some good. Marrying Jan was a start. Graduating from Tech was the next step. Now it was time to take another—one that his parents, especially his father, knew plenty about.

8. Following the Footsteps

"Play fun, not happy."

BY THE TIME he'd started his final classes at Texas Tech, Art Briles knew what direction he wanted to take his life.

Playing football was over, even his flag football career didn't last long, so the next-best thing would have to do. And the way he saw it, coaching was his true calling.

His dad was a successful junior high and high school coach, and Art was thinking and acting like a coach, as well, even long before he'd hung up his cleats. Whether he was studying film with Coach Yeoman's staff at Houston, giving halftime speeches on the Cougars' freshman team, or just dissecting trends and philosophies from the stands at a high school game in Lubbock, Art realized he had the makeup to become a coach.

And what better way to make his parents proud, especially his father, than to follow in the footsteps of Dennis.

Art Briles wanted to be a coach. Now was the time to make it happen.

Nearing graduation in the summer of 1979, Art found himself in a class that required group partners. One of them was a lady named Sharon Jones, who over those few weeks came to know Art and his career choice. As it turned out, her husband was the head coach of Class A Sundown, a small town located about 45 miles west of Lubbock and less than that from the New Mexico border. Sundown is as "West Texas" as it gets.

But at that point, Art didn't care where he started, even if it was out in the middle of nowhere. He drove over and interviewed with Gary Jones, the head coach of the Roughnecks, and immediately got the job, earning $19,000 a year. Just days after graduating in August, Art moved with Jan into a small two-bedroom house in Sundown.

And just like his father did at Rule, Art found himself coaching—everything. Class A schools in 1979 had limited resources, so he coached running backs, defensive backs, and helped with special teams. He also coached JV basketball, men's and women's golf and, of course, track and field. And, it didn't end there. He was responsible for the laundry, washing, and folding the uniforms, painting the chalk on the fields, and even driving a few busses when needed.

But he loved it.

"As long as you're staying busy and doing what you love, it's never work. It was more of an adventure," said Art, who at 23, wasn't much older than the seniors at the school.

On the field, Sundown struggled to score. In their seven losses, the Roughnecks totaled only 26 points combined, suffering through three shutouts. They did manage to win two games, even taking out some frustration against Whiteface with a 63–9 victory.

While Art is as competitive as the next guy, he was too excited about being a coach to let the losses bother him. And once the football season was over, he quickly moved on to another sport. In fact, his fondest memory about his first high school stop has nothing to do with football. Junior women's golfer Sabra Srader won the 1980 Class A individual golf championship in Austin.

"I used to tell her the greatest job I ever did was not telling her what to do," Art said of Srader, who lettered in golf three years at Texas Tech. "She really was a good golfer."

That accomplishment for Sundown was one of Art's last at the school. As much as he enjoyed the work and appreciated the opportunity to get his feet wet, he yearned for something bigger.

★　★　★

In the summer of 1980, Art and Jan welcomed their first child to the family. Jancy was born on June 16 in Abilene, just a few weeks after they moved to the town of Sweetwater, the second stop on Art's journey up the coaching ranks.

Art saw an opening for a running backs coach at the 4A school near Abilene. Sweetwater had a new coach in W. T. Stapler, who surprised many in the coaching ranks by leaving an established program at Conroe, just north of Houston, to lead the Mustangs, who hadn't made the playoffs in 15 years and were coming off a 1–9 season in 1979.

Stapler was told Sweetwater was a "graveyard for coaches" and his closest friends and colleagues warned him not to go. Still, he was ready to move on from Conroe and was looking for a fresh start.

A few years earlier, Stapler needed to fill a position on his Tigers staff. He fielded a phone call from a friend, Larry French, a former Houston assistant coach who not only recruited Art when he was at Rule High School but was also in the room with Coach Yeoman when Art was told about his parents' accident.

French called Stapler up and advised him, "W.T., of the coaches I've ever coached, there's only one I'd ever tell you is a can't-miss coach, and it's Bubba McGallion. He's looking for a job."

Stapler hired McGallion, the former quarterback at Houston and a roommate of Art's in 1975–1976, and said French "wasn't fibbing…Bubba was the real deal."

So in 1980 Stapler needed some help filling out his new staff, which was a bit harder to do in Sweetwater, considering the program's lack of success in recent years. But while searching to find more young coaching talent, he got another unexpected call from French.

"W.T., I lied to you one time. I told you there's only one kid I'd ever recommend as a can't-miss coach. There's another one."

"Oh, really, who is he?"

"Art Briles."

Stapler knew the name because of Art's previous success at the state track meets. He also knew he had signed with Houston, but that was about the extent of it. Still, because of French's strong recommendation and how well things had worked out with McGallion, Stapler didn't hesitate.

"Larry, you call him and tell him he's got a job."

Right away, Stapler's presence proved to be invaluable for Sweetwater, which enjoyed its first winning season since 1971 with a 6–4 record. Art coached a running back named Gerald Todd, who rushed for about 900 yards that season but never scored a touchdown. With his failure to reach the end zone, Todd was dubbed "EZ Todd" by Art. Even back then he had a way of relating to his players in a fun-filled way, while also motivating them.

The 1980–1981 school year was also when Sweetwater introduced a powerlifting team, thanks to Art's persistence. After several conversations with Stapler, Art asked him if he could take a few students to a competition during school hours.

Stapler's first thought was maybe they just wanted a day off from school, but after a meeting with the principal, Stapler agreed to let Art enter the group. Now his own curiosity was up, though, so without telling Art, he decided to get in the car and check out this powerlifting "stuff" his young running backs coach had been talking about.

"I get in there and I see Art with every kid…he's working his butt off," Stapler recalled. "He's trying to win the title. He was working. He didn't take a day off."

What Art liked about powerlifting was the benefits it provided for football.

"It really kept the players active through the winter months," he said. "It gave smaller guys a chance to compete and get involved in their own class. If you weighed 114 pounds, you're just as important as a guy who weighs 285. Everybody has a chance to compete. So if you weren't in basketball or track, it was a good sport to get into. And then, when football came around, they were stronger and ready for the season."

One day in 1981 Art was in the weight room, shouting encouragement to some of the players when he first met a newly hired assistant named Mike Lebby, who was brought on board to coach basketball and freshman football. Later he would move up to the varsity full-time as a defensive line coach. Immediately, Lebby and Art hit it off as great friends. They shared the same competitive drive and had similar interests off the field. Not long after Lebby arrived in Sweetwater, their two families would get together away from work for cookouts or other gatherings.

Lebby remembered seeing how enthusiastic Art was that day in the weight room. He thought it was a bit strange to be that intense during an off-season workout. He would soon realize that was only a glimpse at the intensity Art had boiling inside.

★ ★ ★

With the help of a good, young staff that included Briles and Lebby, Stapler made Sweetwater's Mustang Bowl the place to be on Friday nights in the fall.

But Monday nights brought some intense battles, as well. In what became a tradition for many years, the Sweetwater coaches would take on local businessmen in pickup basketball games that were supposedly friendly.

One particular night in the off-season saw the action become extremely physical with bodies banging on every rebound. After a loose ball, the game stopped suddenly when one guy fell to the floor, surrounded by a pool of blood. Art was not involved in the play but hurried over to see what had happened.

Turns out it was the mayor of Sweetwater, Rick Rhodes, who had taken an elbow to the face and was now down on his back, holding the ball in one hand and his bloodied nose in the other.

Never one to stop in the middle of a good sweat and worried that losing a man would uneven the teams and possibly halt the game completely, Art leaned down and snatched the ball from the injured player.

"Get up. There's nothing wrong with you. Let's go."

Of course, Rhodes actually became a good friend of Art's. Still, the situation proved that if he wasn't afraid to speak his mind to the town's mayor, he'd have no problem subjecting his players on the team to much worse.

Once during a district game against San Angelo Lake View, Sweetwater's running backs were having a hard time hanging onto the ball, thanks to cold, wet, muddy conditions. Art didn't care much for excuses and so made a promise to the entire backfield during a sideline timeout.

"Don't worry about anything. Just do your job and take care of your responsibilities. If you don't, then we'll make some changes and we'll get someone in here who can do it for you."

The fumbles and missed assignments continued, although Sweetwater managed to win 7–0. But the following Monday, the starting running back and fullback were both replaced in the lineup. Message received.

One of the running backs who felt a connection with Coach Briles was Danny Williams, considered a top athlete on the team. He was big for a running back at 6'2", 225 pounds, but was gifted and graceful in the open field. However, in 1980 Williams wasn't really sure how much he enjoyed football. Yes, he was good at the game, but previous experiences with coaches in middle school had left a sour taste in his mouth.

"Being a black kid and living in West Texas could be hard," Williams said. "We experienced our share of prejudice and racism. As a kid, growing up in Sweetwater, I had a coach who belittled me on the field because of the color of my skin. That was my first slap in the face of racism. At the time, I didn't have much respect for coaches."

Enter Art Briles, who at the age of 24 was still a young buck himself. He was only a few years removed from college, where he regularly interacted with African American teammates and students. Whether it was his love for all kinds of music, his general laid-back nature, or possibly the fact that he could outrun just about everyone around him, Art always got along with black athletes. And it was no different as a coach. In fact, some of the Sweetwater players even referred to him as "Brother Briles."

Williams wasn't alone in thinking Art was someone he could trust, both as a coach and a friend.

★ ★ ★

Sweetwater followed up Stapler and Briles' first season with another winning campaign in 1981. The Mustangs finished with a 6–4 record, although after a 4–0 start, the year ended in disappointing fashion as they lost four out of their final six to miss the playoffs yet again.

The postseason drought continued in 1982, with Sweetwater losing to Lake View in its final game to finish 7–3. However, progress was definitely being made by Stapler's bunch. The Mustangs hadn't enjoyed three straight winning seasons since a four-year run from 1957 to 1960.

But Art wasn't just enjoying success as the varsity running backs coach. He was having a blast with the ninth grade B team that he coached alongside Harvey Oaxaca. The two were allowed to be somewhat unconventional in their coaching methods, so they took advantage, running unorthodox formations with various trick plays.

They created a kickoff return called the "roving quail" where the initial returner would get the ball and turn his back to the kicking team. He would then be surrounded by a host of teammates, who all appeared to receive the ball before scurrying off in an attempt to create enough confusion that the actual ball carrier could break free for a big gain. Sometimes the huddle would move in tandem to pick up yardage before the handoff to one player.

Art was able to try out a few new ideas at Sweetwater, which traditionally ran the wishbone. During some spring practices he had the offense spread out, running a no-back alignment with five receivers. He didn't have specific plays, but just wanted to give the kids a break from the norm.

Call it foreshadowing or just plain fun, but Art was in the early stages of developing his own unique game plan.

Meanwhile at home, the Briles family was starting to increase. Jancy was walking and talking at two when her little brother Kendal was born in November 10, 1982. So far, things were falling right into place for Art, who had a loving and supportive wife in Jan, and now a daughter and a son. Career-wise, he was in his late twenties and doing the thing he loved the most.

Heading into 1983, Sweetwater, behind a four-year starter at quarterback in Scott Richardson, reeled off six straight wins to open the season. In reality, though, the strength of the team was the underclassmen, as six sophomores started and more than a dozen had prominent roles.

One of those was a defensive back named Mike Welch, who was perhaps the smartest, most instinctual player on the roster. He saw action on both sides of the ball and helped on special teams. But Art was bothered by Welch's workout habits, which sparked the nickname "Light Man." The young star might not have been the best practice player, but when the lights came on, he was ready to go.

The lights were on one night at Fort Stockton in a game that was tied at the half. Just before the start of the third quarter, Coach Briles went up to Welch as he was heading out to the field for the kickoff.

"The lights are shining bright tonight...just take it back 100 'Welchy.'"

Sure enough, he caught the ball just inside the goal line and took off on a dazzling touchdown that gave the Mustangs the lead in an eventual 21–14 win.

But Sweetwater would miss the playoffs once more after a heartbreaking 36–34 loss to Lake View, ending its season at 7–2–1 and on the outside looking in. While it proved to be Briles' final year in Sweetwater, the sophomore-laden team in 1983 proved to be something special after all, as Stapler led the Mustangs to a Class 4A state title in 1985.

Ironically enough, that same year Art Briles would be knocking on the door of his own state title.

9. Spread 'Em Out

"A desperate man is a dangerous man."

AFTER FIVE YEARS as an assistant coach, including the last four in Sweetwater, Art Briles finally had his own team.

He landed his first head-coaching job in Hamlin, a Class 2A school at the time, located just 45 miles northwest of Abilene and only about 40 miles from Art's hometown of Rule. Although W.T. Stapler, a Hamlin graduate, hated to see him leave his Sweetwater staff, he not only recommended the young coach, but referred Art just as Art had been referred to him by Larry French four years earlier.

"I told [Hamlin] he was a can't-miss coach," Stapler said. "And every time I've ever been asked about Art, that's the only thing I've ever said—he's a can't-miss coach."

Unlike Sundown or Sweetwater, or even Rule when he was a player, Hamlin was unique in its playoff success before he was hired in 1984. The Pied Pipers had advanced three rounds deep in the playoffs the previous year with a 12–1 record, so Art knew he was inheriting some talent.

"The thing I loved about Hamlin is we had a great mixture of kids," he said. "It was about a third/third/third of whites, Hispanics, and African Americans. We had some great athletes, but it was a really tough community. If you could just get them to the games on Friday nights, you'd have a chance to win every game."

In Art's time at Hamlin, they just about did.

Before his first season even started at Hamlin, he made big changes to the program, adding a powerlifting team, an off-season regimen, and a new weight room. When the season began, Hamlin might have had a first-year head coach, but it certainly didn't play like an inexperienced team. In fact, the Pipers won six games that were decided by a touchdown or less.

Art's head-coaching debut was a rout as Hamlin rolled past Baird 41–6. That set the tone for the Pipers, who stayed perfect the entire regular season.

A close shave did come against Haskell, which was located just 10 minutes away from Art's hometown of Rule. Haskell tailback Robert Ivey, who later went on to become a successful high school coach in his own right, was a load for the Pipers to bring down all night.

With Hamlin leading 15–14 in the final seconds, the Indians were knocking on the door. But Pipers linebacker Mitch Hall—a gritty, undersized defender—stepped into the hole and stuffed Ivey for no gain on fourth-and-inches, allowing Hamlin to run out the clock.

More close games occurred in the playoffs, but the team kept rolling, beating Morton 19–14, Eldorado 20–13, and White Deer 12–9. The Pipers were a perfect 13–0, and Art Briles was unbeaten as a head coach.

Hamlin's quarterfinal matchup against Panhandle High School featured two undefeated squads squaring off in Childress. With just a few thousand fans in the stands, which was a nice-sized crowd for the Class 2A playoffs, the game changed Art Briles' coaching philosophy forever, as he explained:

> At that time, we were running split-back veer and running the ball a lot. We had good people—just had some guys who could run around. We had a good quarterback and a really good defense.
>
> My philosophy was to put the better linemen on defense and try to find an offensive lineman and coach them up. We put better skill people back in the secondary as opposed to on offense. So we did a good job defensively, and we were good enough offensively to be productive and win games.
>
> The Panhandle game was 7–7 in the third quarter. Back then, we didn't have sudden death on ties. We went to penetrations and first downs. So we're tied 7–7 and running the split-back veer. They're running a split defense. What they were doing was manning up in the secondary.
>
> It was me and [assistants] Boe Smith, Hal Porter, Jerry Gooch, and Larry Morehead. We really had no people in the press box, so it took me a while, about three quarters, to figure out what they were doing from a defensive standpoint. But I finally figured out we could run what we called a Pro Set—tight end, flanker, split 2 back—and get them to man up in the secondary. That would get our left halfback lined up on a linebacker and we could run a 12-veer throwback. We thought we

could get that down the middle of the field for a potential touchdown. That's what we were going to do when we got the ball back.

So we punted on the final play of the third quarter…and never touched the ball again the rest of the game. They kept it the entire fourth quarter. To my knowledge, that's never happened in the state of Texas. I'm sure that's a state record that we're on the wrong side of. We lost the game on possessions and first downs and they moved on. It was a great year for the 1985 [team].

What that game taught me was that if we were going to have a chance to win a state championship, we had to spread the ball out and do some no-back, one-back, and shotgun formations. Because I knew, by being in the playoffs, we were going to come up against people better than us, that had equal or better talent. What we needed to have was an edge.

★   ★   ★

In 1985 Hamlin started using an offense that was rather foreign around the state of Texas. Better yet, it was foreign to most defensive coordinators.

"We started going no-back, spreading the ball, spreading the formations," Briles said. "We wanted to use the entire field. We were trying to create a little more flow offensively, which we did."

But Hamlin could get away with trying out new offensive schemes and formations that season, mainly because of a stingy defense that didn't allow an opponent to reach double-digits in scoring until the playoffs.

Using Coach Briles' creative game-planning, led by quarterback Michael Howerton and running back Coy McGee, the offense exploded, averaging 41.6 points per game. Overall, the Pipers outscored its opposition in the regular season 416–26.

One of Art's most memorable games that year occurred against Stamford. Only a few hours after Art had chalked the sidelines himself—one of his many duties despite being the head coach—Hamlin's Piper Stadium was packed with fans to witness a 31–6 win over the Bulldogs, who were expected to give the Pipers a tough game.

In the playoffs, the team steamrolled Morton, McCamey, and Memphis to reach the quarterfinal round, where they played Abernathy in Lubbock, which was essentially a road game for the Pipers. Abernathy had three players who later suited up for Division I programs, but the Pipers held strong and rose to the challenge for a 23–12 victory, sending Hamlin to the state semifinals for the first time in school history.

Awaiting them in Abilene were the Electra Tigers, another 14–0 team that had manhandled opposing teams on its way to the semifinals. Up to that point, Electra's lowest margin of victory all year was an impressive 20 points, which occurred in a 20–0 win over Seymour earlier in the season.

Located just 27 miles northwest of Wichita Falls, Electra had started to garner some media coverage from the bigger city's *Times Record News*. Longtime sports columnist Nick Gholson has been at the paper for more than 40 years and puts the 1985 Electra squad in a class by itself.

"I've said forever that that Electra team was pound-for-pound the best team I've ever seen from our area," Gholson said. "They could've beaten a few 4A and 5A teams that year."

On an icy, snowy night in Abilene, Electra overpowered Hamlin behind workhorse running back Charles Lott for a 35–19 win. The Tigers led 28–0 and 35–7, but the final 16-point margin of victory was the closest any team came to beating Electra all year. In the finals the next week, Electra posted another 16-point triumph, beating Groveton 29–13 for the school's first and only state championship.

For the first time in two seasons, Briles' Pied Pipers had actually lost a game. Still, there was little shame in the defeat. Art told reporters afterward, "They're awesome. They could win a lot of games in a lot of classifications. I don't feel too bad losing to a team like that."

While it was a tough loss for Hamlin, they were about to endure an even bigger one.

★   ★   ★

After two seasons and a 27–1–1 record with the Pied Pipers, Briles was ready for yet another challenge—emphasis on the word *challenge*.

With a desire to work in a different region of the state, he accepted a head-coaching position at Georgetown High School north of Austin, a 4A school at the time that was about to move up to 5A. More than 65 coaches applied for the job, but Briles won out in the end. It didn't hurt that Sweetwater had captured the Class 4A championship in 1985, with Georgetown's athletics director, K.Y. Owens, telling reporters after the hiring, "He helped build that championship." Coupled with the Pipers' consecutive playoff runs, he was once again a good fit.

But he left behind some heartbroken folks in Hamlin, including members of the football team. Not long after Art made the jump, a few of his former players got together to write an open letter to the editor, which ran on February 12, 1986, in the *Georgetown Weekly*:

> We would like to introduce you to our coach, Art Briles. Before he was chosen to be our coach, we wondered just how horrible things would be having an entirely new coaching staff to deal with.
>
> We wondered how much he would make us run, how much weight-lifting we would do, and how badly he would chew us out when we messed up.
>
> We really wanted a "dream coach," one that would run with us, one that would lift weights with us, and one that told us how to improve, not how poorly we played.
>
> They always say, "Be careful what you ask for, because you may get it." Well, we did.
>
> For the past two years, we have lived this dream. We had a coach that worked out with us, one that made us want to play football more than anything else. And one that took us further than we had ever been before.
>
> Unfortunately, we forget that all dreamers finally wake up. On January 21, 1986, we did.
>
> Please take good care of him and give him all the love and support that we would if he were still here. We promise you will like him. If not, send him back.
>
> Oh, and one other thing…remember that nobody gets too much heaven anymore, so make the most of every moment you have with him. He's destined for bigger and better things than we can imagine, but at least we had him first!

★ ★ ★

Moving up the ranks calls for a bigger salary. While Art knew he had his work cut out for him with a struggling Georgetown program that was below average in 4A, much less 5A, he was now making $42,000 a year—living in Georgetown, Texas, in 1986. Art and Jan also welcomed their third child, Staley, who was born soon after the couple moved from Hamlin. In fact, both Jancy and Kendal had the chickenpox at the time of Staley's birth and were not allowed into the hospital room to greet their baby sister.

Art actually was in the middle of a meet-and-greet with the parents of the football players when he was notified that Jan's water had broken and it was time to head to the hospital.

Just as he did at his previous two stops, Art helped rebuild the strength program, and not long after he was hired, a local Georgetown family donated brand new equipment for a revamped weight room. But for all the weights Coach Briles had them pumping, the Eagles were still a small team that didn't have the ability to line up and play smash-mouth football with its opponents, especially in district play.

Life was good at home with a growing family; the job, however, was a struggle. The Eagles were simply outmatched, facing stiff competition against the likes of Temple, Waco, Killeen, and Copperas Cove.

"Even though we expanded the offense some at Hamlin, when I got to Georgetown, I had to be even more innovative because of the mismatches we were faced with on the field," Briles said. "We started doing unbalanced sets with the offensive linemen. We had a lot of four-receiver sets with no backs and a lot of motion. We ran some quarterback option, too. All of it started mostly out of necessity, just trying to spread out the field."

In 1986 Georgetown's signature win came against Copperas Cove, coached at the time by Hal Mumme, who later became head coach at the University of Kentucky, and is currently the offensive coordinator at Southern Methodist. The Eagles won the game 21–20 on a controversial missed field goal by the Bulldogs.

"I think if you asked Coach Mumme today if it was good or not, he'd say 'good.' I think I'd have a hard time disagreeing with him," Art said. "But our kids fought hard. It was a big win for us."

A few weeks later, Art's imagination and trickery nearly pulled off another huge upset, this time over Waco High, a team that was extremely talented and picked to go deep in the playoffs. He knew his team was outmatched and figured this would be the right time to experiment.

That's when Coach Briles introduced Waller-Ball. The goal was to simply have the players "waller around on offense." The plan was to run one play a minute.

At that time in Texas high school football, the officials started the play clock by hand, waiting until the ball was set. Art told the offensive lineman to lay on the ground and when the umpire asked them if they were all right to say, "Yes sir, I'm fine." The goal was to keep the clock moving to limit the scoring and try to steal the game at the end.

And that's nearly what happened. Georgetown came up short on a late touchdown attempt in the final minutes and lost 19–14.

The following year, 1987, was marked by a scary on-field incident that involved Georgetown safety Corey Jackson, who was hit in the head and suffered an aneurysm, forcing him to go to the hospital for immediate surgery.

"It was a real numbing effect. I remember walking out on the field and seeing his eyes roll back in his head," Art remembered. "It was really scary and numbing for me as a young coach. It really taught me that these kids are precious. It's just kids playing a game. You never need to lose sight of that."

In his first two years at Georgetown, the Eagles were just 4–15–1. The Briles family liked the community, and Art enjoyed the people he worked under: athletics director Owens and superintendent Jack Frost.

But he wasn't sure about the direction the school was headed competitively. Moving up to 5A was quite a jump, and after producing just four wins in two years, he wasn't sure the situation was workable. Art began looking for other opportunities.

Passed over after he interviewed for the head-coaching job in Snyder, Art heard about another 4A opening available in Stephenville, a town about which he knew very little.

Likewise, Stephenville didn't know much about Briles. In fact, the high school's prime candidate for the job in 1988 was W.T. Stapler, who had left Sweetwater for Boswell and then landed in Andrews. He wasn't keen on moving again, but made sure to drop Art's name to Stephenville superintendent Ben Gilbert.

Initially, his back-to-back two-win seasons at Georgetown didn't generate much excitement, but Marlon Lewis, who was on the hiring board at

Stephenville, coached with K.Y. Owens at Brady High School and decided to reach out to see about this Mr. Briles. If anything, Stapler was well respected, so if he insisted Art was indeed a "can't-miss," they had to at least do some research.

As the story goes, Owens told Lewis that Art was the best coach he'd ever been around and cited his ability to relate to kids. Obviously, Georgetown didn't want to lose Art, but Owens wasn't about to lie.

So Gilbert called Art around Christmastime in 1987. The Briles family was en route to Rule when they made a stop near Stephenville at a Holiday Inn. The meeting was short but productive. The Yellow Jackets had the man they were looking for. Art Briles had the job he was looking for.

And just like that, the next chapter in his life began.

10. Culture Change

"Three Fs...Fast, Fearless, and Fhysical"

THERE IS AN old adage that ripples through smaller towns, particularly in Texas, that says the pulse of the community is usually pretty consistent with the state of its football team.

If the local high school is successful, winning games, competing with the top rivals in the surrounding areas and especially making the playoffs, then there's a good chance the town considers itself in good shape, too.

In the late 1980s Stephenville wasn't doing so well.

Oh, economically the sleepy dairy town located about 70 miles southwest of Fort Worth was doing just fine in 1987; milk prices were actually at their highest levels of the decade. But as a football-starved community, Stephenville was rock bottom.

Not since 1952 had Stephenville High School reached the playoffs, although granted, it was a time and age when only one team per district advanced to the postseason. In the 1990s, that number went up to two and eventually three while Art was in Stephenville. Today, most districts, even those with only five or six teams, will take four to the playoffs.

Still, whether using the old rules or the current setup, not many Stephenville teams would've ever made the postseason. Since that last playoff appearance in 1952, the Yellow Jackets had gone through nine coaching changes.

In 1984 Stephenville suffered through an 0–10 season. Imagine a town that doesn't have much else besides the high school going through an entire calendar year without a single victory. The local coffee shops and the water-cooler talk around the offices had little, if any, positive spin—even during the season.

Three years later, things weren't much better, the team posting a 4–6 record in 1987. It was time to move on from coach Joe Loudermilk, Art Briles being the man hired to take over. The town knew as much about their team's new leader as he knew about them—very little.

But that was actually attractive to both sides; sometimes the unknown can be as exciting as it is scary. For Coach Briles, he was just happy to get on a more level playing field than he had been on in Georgetown. For the people of Stephenville, they didn't see their football program as even remotely equal to any of their regular opponents—particularly the one that mattered most: Brownwood.

That was the team Stephenville always strived to better, but for more than a quarter of a century, it wasn't close. The Yellow Jackets hadn't beaten their rivals from Brownwood—about 60 miles south of Stephenville—since 1963.

So in 1988, when Briles came on board, winning state titles wasn't exactly on the radar for the folks in Stephenville when getting to the playoffs was still seen as a far-fetched goal. Right then, just being respectable was good enough.

★ ★ ★

Before Art could even really get started on the field, changes were necessary within the football program. As with all new head coaching hires, assistants need to be added and replaced.

That was one of the first duties on Art's to-do list, and although never a fun job, the responsibility goes with the territory. Assistant coaches know the drill, especially if their head coach has already been let go. Not long after Art stepped in as the boss, he started bringing in assistants to interview. Almost none of them, however, were retained.

It was clear that a change in culture was needed. Holdovers, and anything else associated with the "old way," were not necessary.

Art did make one exception, though. Defensive assistant Mike Copeland had to sit and stew for a few days wondering about his future, but he eventually got the call into the head coach's office and was told he would be remaining on the staff.

Copeland, who was born with one arm, is considered a Stephenville lifer. He graduated at Division II Tarleton State in Stephenville, before then joining the Yellow Jackets coaching staff in 1969. Never one to use his birth defect as a crutch, Copeland stayed athletic. He plays just about every recreational sport possible and can easily hang with the group in golf, basketball, and anything else.

Copeland knew of Briles because he regularly worked the state track meets in Austin. He even saw him run as a member of Rule's state championship teams. But as a coach, Copeland didn't know much about Art, who was also unfamiliar with the current Stephenville assistants.

"Well, I checked up on Mike and found out he was a passionate coach," Art said. "He was inspiring, too. We all have a story, but that to me was something I really gravitated to. For him to be able to do everything he does, that was inspiring to me. I also knew he was a damn good football coach, and he certainly was."

If that wasn't enough, Coach Copeland recalled having a couple of other "aces in the hole" during that time—two sons in the program. His oldest, Matt, was the current quarterback of the squad, while the younger Mitch was in the sixth grade but already had the build and physique of a future stud on the gridiron.

Not long after learning he would be kept on the staff, Copeland invited his new boss over to the house for dinner. Art's family had yet to make the move from Georgetown, so the early days at the office were rather lonely for the new head coach.

Art accepted the offer and went over to the Copeland residence for dinner, which was followed by a friendly game of Ping-Pong. At least that was the intention. It was right then and there that Copeland found out what kind of fierce competitor he was now working for.

"I thumped him around pretty good, and he didn't like that," Copeland said.

Art then returned the invitation and asked both Mike and his wife Becky out to his house. Not sure where this was going, they accepted and headed over to Briles' new home, which didn't have much in the way of furniture at the time. But there was a basketball goal in the driveway, and that's exactly what Art had in mind. To even the score after the Ping-Pong match, Art took on Copeland in another "friendly" game of hoops. With just one arm, basketball wasn't the easiest of sports for Copeland to master, but like everything else, he gave it his best shot. Art got his revenge with a victory.

Right then, both coaches found out a little bit about each other. The head coach knew he had a defensive coordinator who would battle and compete despite long odds and unfortunate circumstances, and do so with success.

The defensive coordinator learned that if losing hurt his head coach that bad in a basement or a driveway, he knew losing on the football field would be deemed unacceptable. Based on the mindset from previous years—both within the program and the community—Copeland knew right then that Stephenville had the right man for the job.

★ ★ ★

Changing a culture starts long before a team actually takes the field. The players who returned to the football program in the 1988 off-season saw a noticeable difference right away.

And it had nothing to do with Xs and Os, playbooks, schemes, or personnel.

The most obvious change when Coach Briles took over came in the weight room. Regardless of what they knew or were accustomed to beforehand, the boys were about to work harder and longer than ever before.

The ones who couldn't keep up would be left behind. The ones who embraced it learned how to push themselves to heights they never realized, survived.

But the players weren't the only ones doing the work. One of Briles' unique trademarks that remains a rarity today is the way the entire coaching staff works out with the team. Art would assign each assistant coach with a lifting group, based on weight/performance and endurance.

Without a doubt, Art was right in the middle of it all. In fact, his competitive nature was most noticeable when in the weight room.

One of the early examples of Art's dedication for conditioning occurred in a spring lifting session just a few weeks after he arrived in Stephenville. The story has since become legendary and has likely been passed around several times with a few variations, but Coach Briles does recall a particular day in the weight room when a pair of upperclass linemen—two of the biggest players on the team—were flexing their muscles after a bench-press workout.

The bar had about 225 pounds on it, meaning two plates of 45 pounds on each side, along with the 45-pound bar.

Either to make a point, show these kids who was in charge, to flex his own muscles, or perhaps all of the above, Art chuckled at both of the players. He grabbed two more plates of 45 pounds, increasing the setup to 315. He got down on the bench, without a spotter, and did 10 reps—not only more weight, but more reps than any player was currently lifting.

While typically a place of yelling, screaming, grunts, and cheers, the weight room was replaced by silence. Coach got up, smiled at both players, and said,

"If I'm the strongest guy in here, we've got a problem…I think y'all have got some work to do."

★   ★   ★

The players in the off-season-conditioning program quickly found out something about Coach Briles' new workout plan—it didn't always involve actual weights. In fact, some of the toughest drills and exercises the players did had nothing to do with a barbell or bench.

One rainy day in the spring of 1988, Coach introduced his players to the parallel bars, or monkey bars, that were located in the indoor workout facility. A place known as the "Green Room," it featured a turf field where the team often practiced to beat the heat or escape foul weather.

On this day, it was all about the monkey bars, hanging 10 feet off the ground, forcing most of the players to stand on a box in order to reach them.

Linebacker Keith Graham, who was entering his sophomore season, recalled the workout: "We got up on the box and then the monkey bars, and nobody could really do it. We were skipping some drills. We were awful. That first day, we all ended up with dime- and quarter-sized blisters on our hands. We were bleeding profusely all day trying to hold a pen and everything else. It was a mess."

The phone was definitely ringing all night at the Briles house. Art fielded several calls from parents, some of them very upset with the type of work being asked of their kids during the off-season, a time that had typically been more laid back.

The next morning, the players were chatting among themselves and wondering what would be on the agenda for the day's workout. The consensus was that the high volume of calls and complaints ought to have given them a break from having to get on the monkey bars again.

Moments later, Coach Briles gathered all of the boys in the Green Room and walked them over to a 16′ x 16′ garage door that led out to the parking lot. Just in front of the door was an oversized cardboard box.

The coach yanked down on the chain to lift the door up, revealing about 20 to 30 of the kids' parents, including several who had made phone calls the previous night.

"Guys, I know you're hurting," Coach Briles told his blistered players as he pointed to the box on the floor, "but here's a pair of workout gloves...or there's your mom and dad. But make your decision right now because we're going to close this door and go back to work."

The athletes didn't know what to think. Many of them were surprised their parents were out there during work and school hours. Some of them weren't sure if they were supposed to go or not. Sure enough, there were some players who walked out the door and didn't return.

"I think that was one of those huge turning points," Graham said. "If you weren't here to make the cut, then get on right now. Some of them got on right then...and that's a good thing."

The brave ones who stayed, put on their gloves, and fought through the workout, which was designed to increase and improve upper-body strength.

And, along the way, it improved some mental toughness, as well.

★   ★   ★

The coaching staff had plenty of changes. The weight-room schedule was vastly different. Now it was time to see if the product had improved, as well. The only way to officially find that out was to take the field.

The Art Briles era kicked off in early September 1988, when the Yellow Jackets matched up against the Graham Steers, which had been Stephenville's season-opening opponent the previous 10 years.

Most of the games had been relatively even battles, but the Jackets defeated Graham in 1987 by a score of 21–7, so a win in Coach Briles' debut was expected.

Needless to say, a 9–7 loss to the Steers brought fears of another long season, especially considering starting quarterback Matt Copeland was lost for the year with a broken collarbone. If that first game didn't provide a gloomy enough mentality, the next two certainly did. Springtown blanked Stephenville 48–0, and Sweetwater, a team Art coached as an assistant four years earlier, smashed the Jackets 34–7.

Despite the team perhaps being overmatched, that game provided some early examples of Coach Briles and some of his players refusing to quit. Just a sophomore at the time, Graham went toe-to-toe with Sweetwater's stud, Kenneth Norman, a top-rated tailback in the state who later played professional baseball in the Minnesota Twins organization. On one play late in the third quarter, Norman was returning a punt and collided head-on with Graham, right in front of Briles and the Stephenville bench. Both players went straight to their backs, clearly dazed. Norman got up and gingerly headed to the sideline, but Graham stayed down, knocked out silly. Coach Briles picked up his player, got him to his feet, and simply said, "Nice hit, Graham." Somehow, the sophomore made it back out on the field and finished the game.

While rules and regulations regarding concussions are entirely different today, earning a coach's respect with determination and a will to succeed hasn't changed. From that moment on, Briles has always called Graham one of the toughest players he's ever coached.

With an 0–3 start, it wasn't too early for people around Stephenville to wonder about Briles' future. Not that he had a short leash, but with three losses, including two blowouts, there was a definite "here we go again" rumbling around the community.

Things brightened up the following week in Crowley. And Stephenville can thank a rather hefty-sized marching band as a possible contributor. The Yellow Jackets got off the bus in Crowley and immediately went to the dressing room to put on their pants, undershirts, and helmets for a routine warm-up on the field. Most of the coaches were still inside and were surprised to see the entire team heading back into the locker room.

In a miscommunication, the Crowley band, which had an abnormally large enrollment of about 300 members, was set to practice at the same time and marched their way onto the field to prepare for the weekly halftime show. Coach Briles had a hard enough time swallowing three straight defeats by a combined 77 points. Now his players were getting pushed off the field by tuba players?

By the time the coaches and players straightened things out, it was nearly time for Crowley's team to take the field. So Stephenville trekked back outside to get ready for the game. But it wasn't forgotten.

While Coach Briles isn't known for emotional pregame speeches that include a ton of yelling and coach-speak, he did make sure his players wouldn't be disrespected. "No band is going to kick us off the field," he told them. "It doesn't matter who it is, we're going to earn people's respect."

Three hours later, they earned more than that, whipping Crowley 51–7 for Art Briles' first win at Stephenville. It was the start of three straight victories as the Yellow Jackets turned an 0–3 record into a 3–3 mark by also beating Breckenridge (31–0) and Granbury (45–12). Stephenville was suddenly in the discussion for a possible playoff spot, but it was still premature as the meat of the schedule awaited, including the all-important showdown with rival Brownwood.

As it turned out, the Yellow Jackets fell to Mineral Wells 26–14 the week before the Brownwood game, definitely deflating the excitement that was beginning to rise in the town. The loss only paused the brewing buzz, though, as fans in Stephenville were so hungry for success. They wanted a reason to believe. They wanted to know if this turnaround was for real.

And there was only one way to find out.

11. Tie = Win

"The past is last."

NOT LONG AFTER Art accepted the position of head coach/athletics director at Stephenville, he was invited to a community luncheon at the nearby country club. This was typical for a small town that loves its football.

Mayors, city councilmen, pastors, and football coaches are all revered by the locals, although not exactly in that order.

So one day in the early spring of 1987, Art accepted the lunch invitation and casually drove his pickup truck to the informal meeting, arriving to find 10 or 12 business leaders sitting at a corner table in the fancy dining room. There were handshakes all around, then a little small talk before the conversation shifted into questions about philosophy and personnel. Still, nothing too major. About an hour went by, and Art was thinking this was pretty painless and he'd probably be on his way. And that's when Stephenville-based lawyer Bob Glasgow, who later became a state senator, made a comment that would stick with Art forever.

"Coach, we haven't had a lot of success here lately, so if you go 1–9 and want to keep your job…that win better be against Brownwood."

The tongue-in-cheek comment received a few laughs around the table. None of the chuckles came from Art.

"I know I didn't take it as a joke at all," he recalled. "I know if someone is talking about my job, it's never funny. So I didn't take it as funny. I knew right then and there we had to figure out a way to compete with Brownwood on a yearly basis."

Easier said than done. Brownwood was as close to a Class 4A powerhouse as you had in the state of Texas during that time. Legendary head coach Gordon Wood had retired from Brownwood in 1985 after 26 years at the school, capturing seven state titles and winning more than 82 percent of his games with a 257–52–7 record. As the story goes, Paul "Bear" Bryant was once quoted after departing Texas A&M for Alabama that he had to leave Texas because "as long as Gordon Wood was there, I could never be the best coach in the state."

Wood might have stopped coaching the Lions, but their success continued on, especially against Stephenville.

★ ★ ★

In recent years, Yellow Jackets fans had grown accustomed to two rules when traveling to Brownwood:

1. Make sure and arrive early to eat at Underwood's.
2. Be prepared to drive home disappointed.

The family-owned restaurant that still stands today is a favorite among both locals and out-of-towners. For the Stephenville contingent that regularly traveled to district games, going to Underwood's Bar-B-Q for their famous ribs, chicken fried steak, or peach cobbler was a must. And considering Stephenville's lack of success in Brownwood, that proved to be the highlight of the road trip for nearly a quarter of a century.

Dr. Steve Steed, currently an accounting, finance, and economics professor at Tarleton State University, was one of the Stephenville locals who regularly supported the team, even in the heartache years. And he did so long before his kids were old enough to participate.

On this particular Friday afternoon in 1988, the plan in the Steed household was to do the Brownwood double-dip—Underwood's and the game. Steve told his family to get up and get moving so they could make the 60-mile trek and beat the expected long lines at the restaurant.

So as his seventh-grade son got up from the table, he put the lid on the can of peanuts he was snacking on, held it in the air, and shook it, making a racket as he yelled, "Go Jackets!"

Suddenly, the light bulb flashed profusely in Steve's head. "Wait just a minute," he said as he hurried into the garage. That's where he grabbed as many old coffee cans and metal containers as he could find. He scrounged around looking for nails, pens, marbles, and anything else that could help make a deafening sound. He put together a handful of cans for the entire family, and they hurried down to Brownwood, where they scarfed down some old-fashioned fried chicken before heading over to the aptly named Gordon Wood Stadium.

Naturally, like most things that are new, the fans surrounding Steve and his family weren't too thrilled with their creation. Then again, most of them probably weren't expecting a lot of reasons to make much noise at the ballgame.

As it turned out, there would be plenty to cheer about that night, and hundreds of more nights to come. What happened in that battle against Brownwood only cracked the surface of how Coach Briles was trying to build his program.

The same could be said for Steed, the original "can fan," who would go on to start a cultural innovation that would help change the attitude and image of his hometown forever.

★ ★ ★

Good football teams in high school typically have top-notch skill players. The great ones have dominating big men in the trenches.

And those that become dynasties have a consistent combination of both.

In Art Briles' first year as head coach, he had some talented guys on both sides of the ball, but he lacked the big horses on either line. There was one sitting in the stable, though, who was ready to be turned loose.

Brad Smith, a move-in from Nacogdoches, didn't grow up loving football. His family were dairy farmers and moved to Stephenville during the summer of 1988. Just before school started, he admittedly wasn't feeling the Stephenville vibe and moved back with his father in Nacogdoches. That didn't prove to be the right answer, either, so after one week of school, Smith came back to town to live with his mother and stepfather.

His family asked around about the possibility of his joining the team after the season had started. As it turned out, Smith was forced to sit out the first seven games on varsity, but he played junior varsity and dominated opposing offenses.

Oddly enough, he was finally eligible the week of the Brownwood game. Here was a guy who barely knew the system. He was a 16-year-old sophomore, and the Yellow Jackets were about to face the biggest, strongest, toughest team on their schedule.

So naturally, Smith stepped right in and started at defensive end. He proved to be one of the best players, if not the meanest, who ever suited up for Coach Briles.

★ ★ ★

Just 12 months earlier, Brownwood had handed the Yellow Jackets a 62–0 thrashing in Stephenville. But Art Briles wasn't at that game, and he told his players to leave that memory where it belonged—in the past.

At that point in the season, with the Yellow Jackets at 3–4 and still fighting for a playoff spot, he had them focused on 1988 and the task at hand. The goal was to beat Brownwood, something that seemed laughable considering the drought of wins versus the Lions over the past 25 years.

But on the field that Friday night in Brownwood, the Yellow Jackets didn't play like a team that hadn't won this rivalry in more than two decades. They didn't play like a team that was even aware of such a daunting streak.

Defensively, Stephenville played its best game of the season by far. One of many new faces on the coaching staff was defensive coordinator Steve Freeman, who ironically enough would later become head coach at Brownwood. He had his players on point from start to finish. They were tackling as a unit, swarming like their namesake Yellow Jackets would do, attacking the ball.

"We really did get after them that night," said Keith Graham, a sophomore linebacker who later went on to become one of Briles' more accomplished players. "We hadn't played great all year, but that particular night we were clicking on defense, and we had them frustrated."

Not only was Stephenville's defense stopping the Lions' offense, but it was providing some, as well. Mike Giles scored the only touchdown of the game for the Jackets, returning an interception for a score.

The fans on the visiting sideline didn't know what to think. Not only were they somewhat perplexed by Steve Steed shaking his unusually loud coffee can, but was their football team really hanging with Brownwood? Was this for real?

With the game tied 7–7 in the final minutes, it appeared the Lions were in a prime position to burst Stephenville's bubble. With a third-and-long at the Jackets' 12, Brownwood's quarterback rolled to his right and threw into the end zone, where the ball was broken up on a close play between the receiver and defender.

The quarterback was so upset on the non-call by the officials, he lost his cool and got in the face of the side judge, screaming for a flag.

"You've got to call that, ref! That's B.S.!" the quarterback barked.

Standing right next to Coach Briles, the official, Bob Burden, responded to the agitated player.

"Son, if you don't like that call, you're really going to hate this one." And he pulled out his flag and tossed it to the ground, calling an unsportsman-like penalty on the quarterback, which now pushed the ball back to the 27. Instead of a 29-yard field goal to win the game, the attempt had become a 44-yarder, which promptly sailed wide left, keeping the score knotted at 7–7 in the final minutes.

From there, Coach Briles decided to play it safe. He likely could've passed the ball around and attempted to get into scoring range, but considering the offense hadn't put up a point all game, and they were backed up in their own territory—not too mention what even a tie would mean to this team and the community—Stephenville ran the ball and stayed conservative.

There had been 24 years of heartache; it wasn't going to continue on this night.

★ ★ ★

There's a popular phrase often muttered after sporting events, especially in games where a team finds a way to collect a hard-fought victory: "A win's a win." After all, getting the W is what matters. They don't give out points for style.

Well, sometimes a tie can be a win. And that's what happened on that October night in 1988 in Brownwood, Texas. The Stephenville Yellow Jackets did not beat the Lions. But for the first time since 1963, they weren't beaten.

Stephenville 7, Brownwood 7. It had been a long time since the Yellow Jackets had been on the left side of a score line with the Lions. And with that, a tie became a win.

"It just depends on where you are with your program and what you need," Art said. "That's not always the case. But for us, right then, not losing to them was a big deal. I'm not sure how [Brownwood] felt; they were probably upset. I know to us it was a win."

And the town celebrated as such.

With a police escort leading the way, the team busses rolled back into Stephenville at about 1:00 AM, and to the surprise of the players and coaches, the welcoming group included a lot more than just the normal parents who were around to pick up their kids.

"You would've thought we won the state championship," said then–sophomore linebacker Joseph Gillespie, who later was an assistant on Briles' staff and eventually became a head coach at Stephenville, winning a state title in 2012. "There were thousands of people outside the school going nuts. It was crazy. We really had no business being on the field with them. They were really a better football team than we were. Fate was on our side. And, it was another example of how Coach Briles got us to play better than we were. That's something he has always been really good at. I think that night was the beginning of it all."

The Yellow Jackets won the next week, beating Joshua 10–0, and needed a win in the season finale against Cleburne to secure a playoff spot. While hanging tough through two quarters, Stephenville faltered in the second half, falling 21–6. Thus, the losing ways continued for the Yellow Jackets, who finished the year 4–5–1 for the school's fifth season below .500 in the last six years.

But for the first time in a while, hope was restored to the town of Stephenville. All because of a game they didn't lose in Brownwood. The game officially resulted in a tie. But try telling that to the Stephenville community that nearly burned the town down with overwhelming joy.

12. Making Some Noise

"Forget better late than never...better never late."

NOT LONG AFTER the 1988 schedule ended, a curious group of town supporters in the Stephenville Booster Club listened anxiously to their new football coach. He had one year under his belt, and now Art Briles was about to give the community his thoughts on the upcoming season.

A question from the audience was asked in reference to what his team needed the most.

What could it be? Bigger linemen up front? More speed on the edge? Depth at a certain position? Whatever it was, these Yellow Jackets die-hards were waiting for the scoop.

Coach Briles surprised the audience with his answer, which referred to the people in that exact room.

"I've got a problem here. I've got a lot of spectators, but I don't have many real fans," he said, raising a few eyebrows. That's certainly not what they were expecting to hear.

That had been Coach Briles' mantra since the day he arrived in Stephenville. He actually first made that statement to Steve Steed, who was part of the booster club in town and the originator of the Can Fans, which ironically debuted at Stephenville's epic 7–7 tie in Brownwood.

Steed was on board, making plenty of racket up in the stands with his family, but Art needed more help. So he went to the booster club and basically challenged the community to get completely behind the Yellow Jackets.

Local banker Monty Bedwell, considered somewhat of a town spokesman and community leader, also got involved early on with Coach Briles' unofficial campaign. Bedwell recalled the coach going to the booster club and requesting a combo deal where fans could purchase a Stephenville T-shirt and cap for about $15.

"He wanted color in the stands. He wanted support," Bedwell said. "He knew how to get support. It was something people could afford to do. It wasn't about big money. It was about getting people to support the team. And it didn't take long before he got that. But he also gave us something to cheer about, too."

Soon thereafter, Steed and Bedwell organized a small group who would take the normal tailgating experience to a new level. Instead of a parking-lot party with coolers, grills, and snacks, they would grab a bucket of chicken or a few large pizzas or possibly a takeout order from Peacocks, owned by Steve Peacock, also one of the original Can Fans. Others in the group included John Moore, Larry Branch, David Tomlinson, and Dan Dedivo, along with several members of their respective families. They became the foundation for a tradition that really took off in the 1990s when winning became not only cherished, but also expected.

Each game, home or away, this group that started out with 15 to 20 people would meet around the 40-yard line, about 20 rows up in the stands. And the big question every week would revolve around the type of can you had.

Was it an old Folgers Coffee container with nails inside? How about a smaller hand-sized can that used to be filled with vegetables but now has ball bearings? Or what about a bigger version that even had a duct-taped handle?

The cans came in all sizes. When things really started to take off, Steed and Bedwell would spend countless hours in the former's garage making noisy cans of all kinds to pass out at games. When the Can Fan sensation was at its peak, 75 percent of the crowd would all be shaking these cans—some as big as empty propane tanks and others as small as old Tylenol bottles filled with pennies for the kids.

If it made noise, it was accepted…at least by the members on the Stephenville side.

There were a few occasions when the opposing team would try to block them from bringing in the cans. It happened once in a playoff game at Bedford's Pennington Field, but Bedwell got resourceful and went to the one person who had a little pull.

"I just told Coach Briles they weren't going to let our cans in," Bedwell recalled. "He just laughed and said, 'I got it.' Then he told us to go to the side where the band was and we just snuck in our cans in the equipment. That happened once or twice. But after it got pretty big, it was something the other teams just expected."

On the field, Briles' team was making plenty of noise with its play.

★ ★ ★

On paper, the 1989 Stephenville Yellow Jackets didn't look much different than many other teams from previous seasons.

They weren't coming off a playoff run, failing to even finish with a winning record. But for the first time in 25 years, they could say they didn't lose to Brownwood the previous season. And that was enough to be optimistic about 1989.

More than that, Art Briles and his young staff of coaches were making headway. There was a sense of excitement brewing that year, evident by the larger number of fans and parents showing up for practice.

And the tickets were getting gobbled up fast for that first game of the season against Graham, an opponent that had edged the Jackets 9–7 to spoil Coach Briles' Blue & Gold debut the year before.

But 1989 was a new team. It was the start of something fresh. The Jackets whipped up on the Steers from Graham that day, 31–0, and if that wasn't enough, how about a 21–12 win over Springtown the next week? For the first time in seven years, the Jackets were 2–0, and the buzz around town was getting lively.

Even a loss to Sweetwater, where Coach Briles spent four seasons (1980–1983), couldn't slow down the Yellow Jackets. They rattled off four straight wins over Crowley, Breckenridge, Granbury, and Mineral Wells, which set up another showdown with their rivals in Brownwood. Because of district realignment, the rotating schedules were off, meaning Stephenville had to travel back to Brownwood one year after the 7–7 tie, a game that some would argue changed the football culture in Stephenville forever.

Unfortunately, the 1989 affair was more like the others, as Brownwood avenged that previous year's outcome with a 63–21 blowout, extending the streak to 26 years since the Yellow Jackets' last win over the Lions.

That setback didn't derail the team, though, which thumped Joshua and Cleburne to end the season at 8–2. More importantly, the finish put the town of Stephenville in a place where it hadn't been in 37 years: the playoffs.

"That was just a magical time for us," Bedwell recalled. "The season was over. We had played our 10 games. So you're telling us we get to drive over to Waco and play another game in the playoffs? I mean, you can't imagine how that was for our town back then. It was so exciting."

While it might have been easy to forgive the playoff-starved citizens for being satisfied with just getting there, the actual team decided they weren't quite done and were ready to do some postseason damage.

When you've been out of the playoffs for that long, the opponent doesn't matter much. And so the fact their first opponent was Belton, the No. 5 ranked team in the state, was irrelevant to the Yellow Jackets. And they played that way.

Thanks to huge efforts by wide receiver Jason Poston and dual threat Todd Bramlett, Stephenville controlled the game from start to finish, whipping Belton at Floyd Casey Stadium in Waco, 32–6.

"At that point, Briles had us believing we would win," said Graham, a junior linebacker on that team. "It was a miracle he did it as fast as he did. He always told us he would never 'line us up beat.' He would never put us in a position we couldn't win. I think we saw that against [Belton] that night. We were in position to win. He recognized personnel so well that he knew what it took to win."

Colin Shillinglaw served as Stephenville's head athletics trainer for 12 years and has now been with Art for more than 22, currently as the assistant athletics director for football operations at Baylor. So he's seen it all and then some. But when it comes to favorites, and the moments that really turn around programs, Shillinglaw says the Belton win was an all-timer.

"Back then, I didn't know much about high school football in Texas," said Shillinglaw, who grew up in Iowa and was fortunate to graduate from Texas Tech at the same time Art was calling around Lubbock looking for a new trainer. In fact, Art remembers Shillinglaw's car lost 50 percent of its power on the way to the interview, which made a big impression on his desire for the job. "But when we beat Belton the way we did, I knew we were getting there. No one gave us credit going into that game. They were ranked. It was our first playoff game. But I just remember we dominated both sides of the ball. That's when it clicked…we've got something here."

The fun ride of 1989 came to an end the next week. The Yellow Jackets were ousted by Fort Worth Brewer, 31–15. While Stephenville's arrow was certainly pointing upward as the 1980s came to a close, it wasn't exactly a decade of dominance, with just one playoff appearance and still no wins over Brownwood.

But the 1990s were right around the corner.

★   ★   ★

Most head coaches will tell you they're only as good as the players they have. A lot of them will also say the same about their assistant coaches.

Art Briles is no exception to either rule. He surrounded himself with a great coaching staff at Stephenville, something that was easier to do back then than today, as many coaches are under contracts with the school and/or district, so it's not as easy to let nearly an entire staff go like Briles did when he first got the job with the Yellow Jackets.

But he took advantage of the opportunity and used his resources and prior contacts to land some great assistants. One of those who joined his staff before the 1990 season was actually a complete stranger to Art, who needed some help coaching his offensive line. Nothing in particular stood out on Randy Clements' résumé until Briles scanned down toward the references. That's where he saw a familiar name in Bubba McGallion, a former teammate of Art's at Houston. McGallion was the head coach at Alto High School, where Clements had spent a year student teaching.

After a quick call to his former college buddy, Art liked enough of what he heard to hire Clements as the varsity offensive line coach. At the time, neither of them could've known they would be together for more than 20 years.

A few of the things that likely made Clements such an attractive hire was his age, his size, and his dedication to conditioning. Coach Briles didn't just want a good football coach; he also wanted assistants who weren't afraid to get their hands dirty in the weight room.

Clements was just two years removed from playing offensive line for a Division I-AA playoff team at Stephen F. Austin. Big and burly in stature, he eventually became Stephenville's head power-lifting coach as well.

But while lifting weights was no problem for a guy like Clements, all of the coaches were pushed by the man running the show.

"If you didn't like to lift weights, you weren't at the right spot," Clements said. "We had a few coaches who didn't like to work out. [Briles] took issue with that, and they didn't stay the whole time. But we were hands on. I was young and could get in there and do it. But he pushed you because you'd be lifting or something, and you'd look over and this old man is in here kicking our ass."

Thanks to countless pull-ups and extensive work on the monkey bars since he was a kid, Art was freakishly strong in his upper body. When it came to the bench press, he was hard to beat, even by a young lineman like Clements.

"Yeah, he'd always bench more than me," Clements recalled. "But every time he'd be cockin' off about the bench, I'd say, 'Let's go look at that squat rack over there.' He'd say something like, 'Hold on, I gotta make me a couple of phone calls. Be right back.'"

★ ★ ★

One mid-morning in early March, the phone rang in defensive coordinator Mike Copeland's office. He picked it up and started chatting with a man who said he was from the Discovery Channel. While the coach didn't exactly know where this was headed, he finally realized the cable TV network was doing a documentary on small-town football in the state of Texas, and Stephenville had been chosen for its centerpiece.

Basically, all they wanted to know was when would be the best time to send their trucks, camera crew, and equipment down during the 1990 season?

Now, Copeland had a good idea what game might work the best, and again, this was national TV, so you certainly didn't want to be embarrassed by anyone. He mentioned a few options to the gentleman on the other end of the call, but all the while he was telling himself that this needed conformation from Coach Briles.

"Let me run this by him and get back to you," Copeland told the caller from Discovery.

So later that afternoon, Copeland walked up to Coach Briles on the practice field, knowing Art wasn't opposed to media coverage, especially with the program beginning to turn the corner.

After a few funny looks, followed by the typical response of, "The Discovery Channel?…Football?" they both agreed it would be a good idea to have them out. The question then became which game. As soon as Copeland started spouting off a few of the non-district opponents that might make sense, Art cut him off abruptly:

"Brownwood. Tell them to come to the Brownwood game."

Don't forget how long Coach Copeland had been around the Stephenville program. At this point, it had been 21 seasons, and none of them had included a win over their neighbors to the south.

"Hmm, I don't know coach. You sure about that? Brownwood?" Copeland asked. "Let's rethink that a little. It's going on the Discovery Channel."

So Art did rethink it. For about three seconds. He looked up and with a deadpan glare said, "Yeah, Brownwood. Let's bring 'em here for Brownwood."

★   ★   ★

A few weeks later, a relatively unknown and undersized seventh-grader was wrapping up another track practice. Jason Bragg was dead tired after about two hours of pole vaulting. It was around 5:00 PM, and he had just called his mother to come pick him up. But in the meantime, something to drink would be nice.

Bragg was thirsty for a soda but only had a dollar bill. As he searched for anyone who might have four quarters to exchange, he came across an older man with a Stephenville shirt, who seemed like a coach. He asked him for change, and the man told him to follow him over to the office. As the coach was looking through his drawer to find the necessary coins, he made some small talk.

"You coming from track practice?" the coach asked, knowing the answer already.

"Umm, yeah," said Bragg.

"That's sir."

"Oh, sorry. Yes, sir."

And that's when Bragg realized whom he was talking to. Even without seeing a nameplate on the desk or hearing an introduction, he knew that this wasn't just a coach, but *the* coach. And more importantly, it was about to be *his* coach.

Bragg went into the field house that day looking for some change. In a matter of minutes, he realized just how much *change* he had coming.

13. "I Feel Like a Winner"

"No is not the answer."

IF THE EXCITEMENT around town before the 1989 season could be described as a buzz, it was only magnified the next year. In 1990 Art Briles had the Stephenville program swarming like mad Yellow Jackets, ready to attack. That's exactly what they did to kick-start a decade they would eventually dominate across the state of Texas.

While the defense seemed to be further along than the offense in the first two seasons of Briles' tenure, Stephenville became a complete team in his third year. The Jackets' only regular season loss occurred to Sweetwater, who held Stephenville to 27 points, their lowest offensive output of the regular season.

With the Can Fans shaking each week, the wins just piled up for the Jackets, who started off district with a 28–0 victory over Granbury. Three more wins had already clinched a share of the district title for the Yellow Jackets going into the final regular season game. But, despite their 8–1 record, nothing had been settled for Stephenville. Not until they got that monkey, which looked more like a (Brownwood) lion, off their backs.

With the Discovery Channel crew in town all week, interviewing Art, members of the faculty, media, and some of the fans, it was time to take the field and see if Stephenville could finally get that elusive W against Brownwood.

For so many years, the Yellow Jackets had been pushed around by the Lions, but it was going to change on this night. In fact, Art made sure of that long before kickoff. Because of district realignment the year before, Stephenville had to play two straight road games at Brownwood in 1988 and 1989. So, since Art had taken over, he had never hosted his neighbors from the south.

By word of mouth, a tradition Brownwood players liked to do before road games was brought to Coach Briles' attention. As the players warmed up and made a lap around the field, each player would spit on the goal post, typically right on the colored mat that protected the players from the post. In this case, the padding was navy with a Stephenville logo.

Well, Art wasn't about to let that happen, so a few hours before the game, he made some calls, reaching out to a few of his former players who had recently graduated but were in town for this epic showdown. Once he shared his concern, it didn't take much convincing for these guys to defend their school, protect their property, and more than anything, support their coach.

So Briles instructed them to get into two groups and stand shoulder-to-shoulder in a circle surrounding both goal posts. He specifically told them not to start a fight or even say anything.

"But I did tell them this: 'If someone spits on you, then it's up to you to do what you think is right.' I can't tell a grown man how to react if he gets spit on," Art recalled.

Sure enough, about 6:00 PM in Stephenville, some 90 minutes before kickoff with most of the fans still making their way to Memorial Stadium on the campus of Tarleton State, the Brownwood players came out, lapped the fields, and were met by some rowdy individuals with folded arms and blank stares.

As it turned out, the Stephenville alums stayed dry. No spitting incidents occurred, although there were a few verbal exchanges. In fact, Brownwood's coach at the time, Randy Allen, had a few words with Art, even threatening to turn him into the UIL for what he deemed "inciting a riot." Art just shrugged it off with a laugh and said he was "protecting school property from being vandalized."

But he knew there was more to it. He knew he was sending a message to both teams: things were about to be different.

★   ★   ★

To this day, the crowd was one of the largest ever to watch a Stephenville game. Bleachers were brought in from area junior highs and placed in the end zone for additional seating. Fans lined up on the sidelines and in the end zone corners, while others simply sat in the aisles of Memorial Stadium, which holds just 7,000 in the stands.

All around town, people were saying this would finally be the year Stephenville beat Brownwood, and so it appeared the good folks actually had to see it for themselves.

But right away, it didn't look much different than previous SHS-BHS games. The Yellow Jackets fumbled away the opening kickoff and eventually trailed 14–0, but closed the score to 17–14 at the half. But again, they fell behind 24–14 early in the third quarter.

But that's when everything shifted, from the momentum of the game to the actual score to perhaps even the balance of power in Class 4A football.

After the Yellow Jackets rallied back to take the lead early in the fourth, Stephenville's offense really began to fire on all cylinders as wide receiver Jason Poston took a slant over the middle and coasted for a 60-yard touchdown. The defense then turned up the heat and hauled in an interception for another touchdown late in the game, adding one more exclamation point.

That last score sent the entire sideline into a frenzy, including Coach Briles, who is typically the calmest voice on the headsets. But this was different. This was Brownwood. And it was time to celebrate.

"Yes, yeeeesss, yeeeeeeeesss!" Coach Briles shouted with arms raised in a way that more resembled a preacher at Stephenville's First Baptist Church.

As the final seconds ticked off in Stephenville's come-from-behind 42–24 victory over Brownwood, Art roamed the sideline with a five-word message that he continued to repeat, making sure all of his players, coaches, trainers, and anyone else within earshot could hear: "I feel like a winner. I feel like a winner."

Art said it numerous times. He did feel like a winner. He wanted his team to feel it, too. When something finally gets accomplished for the first time in 27 years, it's more than enough reason to feel that way.

After the game, Art did one last video for the Discovery Channel, saying, "This is what high school football is all about." Picking the Brownwood game for that documentary turned out to be the right choice. Stephenville football wasn't just back, it was on the map.

★ ★ ★

Beating Brownwood in 1990 will be a game remembered in Stephenville forever. In fact, thanks to YouTube, the seven-minute video the Discovery Channel aired can and has been reviewed often. That is, of course, for all the people who don't already have a VHS copy, which many Stephenville residents transferred to DVD long ago. Sure, there were bigger and more meaningful victories throughout the 1990s, but that first win over Brown-wood paved the way.

Stephenville is a town full of pride. They don't forget where they came from. And they certainly don't forget that game.

But the Yellow Jackets couldn't relish in the victory for too long. It was time for the playoffs once again, and this year, Stephenville had plans to stick around for longer than just two weeks. The postseason started with a shootout win over Wichita Falls Hirschi, a team loaded with speed. The Jackets were clicking too well on offense, though, and outlasted the Huskies 49–40. The next week saw another nail-biter, this time against Fort Worth Brewer, but the Yellow Jackets prevailed once more, 28–21.

Next up was Snyder, a program that passed on hiring Coach Briles to be its head coach just three years earlier. In the 1990 regional round, the Tigers were no match for Stephenville, which cruised to a 34–13 win, setting up a quarterfinal showdown with Burkburnett and its star running back Skip Hicks, who would later play for UCLA and spend four years in the NFL.

While Stephenville wasn't always loaded with skill players, they made up for it with big men in the trenches. Brad Smith, a move-in from Nacogdoches two years before, anchored the offensive line in 1990. He had a mean streak that often couldn't be corralled—by himself or even by his coach.

Against Burkburnett, the Yellow Jackets had a commanding two-score lead late in the fourth quarter. With a timeout on the field, Coach Briles called the entire offense over to the sideline and specifically told Smith to keep his cool and not to retaliate to anything that might warrant a flag. That was usually easier said than done for Smith, who admits he was worth about "45 yards a game" in personal foul penalties.

And, despite a direct order from Coach Briles, Smith couldn't help himself on the very next play. "All I remember is that I'm punching one of their players right in the face," Smith said. "I get a flag. I get ejected. Coach specifically told me to tell the other guys not to start something, and I'm the one doing it."

The Yellow Jackets won 32–16 over Burkburnett but dropped a hard-fought game the next week to Wilmer-Hutchins in the state semifinals, 35–18 at Texas Stadium, a site Wilmer-Hutchins had played the previous three games. Art learned a lesson that day on the importance of having experience—not just in the actual scheme or game plan, but with the surroundings. Stephenville players were imitating Troy Aikman and Emmitt Smith while playing on the very turf as the young superstars. Meanwhile, the Hutchins players were used to the surroundings, and the Jackets paid for it.

After just three years with his program, Art Briles had taken Stephenville five games deep into the playoffs. They weren't satisfied, but they had the entire town in a football frenzy and hungry for more.

★ ★ ★

The start of the 1991 season did nothing to quell the excitement from the previous year's 13–2 squad. The Yellow Jackets were 3–1 after four games, their last victory coming thanks to a 28–0 thrashing of Burkburnett and Hicks, now a senior. The Yellow Jackets steamrolled through district play, which included one three-game stretch over Granbury, Crowley, and Joshua when they won by a combined score of 90–3.

To no one's surprise, the biggest victory came against Brownwood in the regular season finale. It seemed like Stephenville kept checking things off the list. In 1988 it was ending a 25-year losing streak with a tie. In 1990 they were able to win for the first time in 27 years. And then in 1991 they won at Brownwood for the first time in 30 seasons. A late touchdown pass to receiver Chris Harkey gave the Yellow Jackets a dramatic come-from-behind win over the Lions, 13–9. That game gave Stephenville a second straight district title and led them into the bi-district round against Burkburnett again, marking the fourth time in two seasons facing the Bulldogs.

While it was much closer than the four-touchdown whipping they gave Burkburnett earlier in the schedule, Stephenville held on for a 10–7 win, setting up a match with Fort Worth Boswell in the area round at Pennington Field in Bedford.

On a cold, windy day that kept both teams from passing the ball with effectiveness, the Yellow Jackets were behind 15–13 in the final minutes but were on the move despite a stiff crosswind. The Jackets moved the ball to the Boswell 27 and faced third-and-four. But a three-yard loss proved to be costly. On fourth down from the 30, Coach Briles had no choice but to attempt the game-winning field goal by Jody Bennett, who had made clutch kicks all season long. Bennett's kick was solid and definitely long enough, but as the ball traveled up into the air and wasn't protected by the surrounding walls at the stadium known as HEB, it got caught into the teeth of the breeze and hit the upright. The ball immediately dropped down just short of the crossbar.

Just like that the season ended for Stephenville, losing a heartbreaker to Boswell and Mother Nature, 15–13.

★ ★ ★

The first game of the 1992 season provided a lot of excitement for Stephenville fans. And that's not easy to do when you lose by three touchdowns. Despite being defeated 42–21 by Abilene, the Yellow Jackets were able to look past that 0–1 start and foresee good times ahead, mainly because of the two legs and right arm of junior quarterback Branndon Stewart.

While there are many factors that lead to great high school players and teams—coaching, the weight room program, financial support that leads to better facilities, etc.—sometimes success comes down to things that can't be controlled, such as human growth and development.

Even as a junior, Stewart was the prototype of a quarterback. He was 6'2", 190 pounds, with an already chiseled upper body. As great as he could throw, he was oftentimes an even better runner, showing flashes of both in that loss to Abilene.

The 1992 team not only had a first-year starter behind center in Stewart, but a plethora of talented sophomores, including Mitch Copeland, the son of defensive coordinator Mike Copeland, along with Jeffery Thompson, and eventually Jason Bragg, who was on the eighth and ninth grade B teams before starting on varsity by the end of his sophomore year—just another example of how some players physically mature differently than others.

After beating Brownwood two straight years, the tide turned back to the Maroon & White in 1992. The Lions raced out to a 21–0 lead in the first quarter, and midway through the second were driving again at the 10-yard line.

Mike Copeland was Art's defensive coordinator for all 12 seasons in Stephenville and said there was only one occasion during those dozen years in which Coach Briles made a sideline comment referring to his defensive strategy. Down by three touchdowns, Art raced toward Copeland and yelled with a fiery look in his eyes, "Mike, I don't want them scoring another point the rest of the game!"

Puzzled by the statement, which was out-of-character for Art, Copeland looked back to the field and saw where the Lions had the ball. He shouted back "What do you want to do?"

"I don't care. You figure it out. I just don't want them scoring another point."

Brownwood missed the field goal two plays later, and as it turned out, added nothing more to its score that day. Problem was, neither did Stephenville and the game ended with a disappointing 21–0 defeat.

It was an inexperienced team that made inexperienced mistakes. Consistency is hard to sustain with players that young, evidenced by Stephenville failing to win three straight games until the end of the regular season, when they wrapped up the schedule with a 7–3 record, which was good enough to get into the playoffs.

But that's when this team of youngsters came to life, growing up in a matter of just a month. Fingernails were gone in Stephenville thanks to a series of close playoff wins, starting with a 10–6 triumph over Azle. A key fumble recovery by Shane Freels with four minutes to play, followed by hard-nosed running from Mark Blackburn, sent the Yellow Jackets to the area round in Weatherford. That's where Stephenville would face Fort Worth Arlington Heights in a contest filled with turnovers, mostly by the Jackets.

Despite coughing the ball up five times, Stephenville got back possession thanks to an interception by Thompson. The Jackets trailed by only four points, 17–13, with 55 seconds left but were 70 yards from the end zone. Stewart and the offense marched the ball quickly and got into Arlington Heights territory. And that's when Thompson, one of the fastest players the Stephenville program has ever seen, got past the defense again, hauling in a perfectly lobbed pass from Stewart with just 15 seconds on the clock.

Pandemonium, both in the stands with the Can Fans rocking the entire west sideline, and on the field. So much so that they drew a 15-yard penalty from the officials. But it was a comeback win for Stephenville and a play that put Stewart and the Jackets in the spotlight.

A 9–6 win over Plainview in Wichita Falls, thanks to a game-winning field goal by Brad Couch, advanced the Jackets to the state quarterfinals against Lubbock Estacado in San Angelo. Estacado featured a quarterback named Zebbie Lethridge, who later went on to star at Texas Tech before appearing in two games as a defensive back with the Miami Dolphins.

Temperatures hovered around freezing and a 25–30 mph wind made it feel even colder. Late in the first quarter, with Stephenville up 7–0, Coach Briles called a timeout before the last few seconds ticked off the clock. With the wind at his back, he wanted the Yellow Jackets' punting unit to possibly create some better field position. What it did was give Lethridge more room to operate as he weaved through Stephenville's coverage for 78 yards, down to the 3, which set up a game-tying touchdown on the next play.

After a turnover later in the quarter, Lethridge threw a touchdown pass that gave the Matadors a 13–7 lead. No team would score again. Another great season for the Jackets had ended in heartache.

Minutes after the final gun sounded, reporters stopped Briles for a quote about the game, but the coach took a broader approach.

"I'm very proud of our players; they're good people, No. 1," he said without hiding his disappointment. "They were relentless in their effort to win. They're champions in our eyes."

While that defeat ended the 1992 season, Stephenville's next loss wouldn't occur until 1995. They would soon be champions in everyone's eyes.

14. A High You Can't Buy

"You be the one everyone wants to be."

BY THE FOURTH game of the 1993 season, the culture change Art Briles was looking for in Stephenville had been completed. The town believed in this team that was now one of the top powerhouses in Class 4A.

Beating Brownwood had been crossed off the checklist, and making the playoffs was becoming routine, something the Yellow Jackets had done for four straight years.

But if there was any school that probably hadn't noticed a big difference, it was one of Art's former employers. Excuse Sweetwater if they weren't convinced. For all the success Stephenville enjoyed in Briles' first five seasons, they had yet to defeat the Mustangs from Sweetwater, a place where Briles served as an assistant from 1980 to 1983. In fact, after a loss to Sweetwater in 1991, Art told his coaches in the locker room to get familiar with the Mustangs. "We're not going to stop playing them until we beat them."

Briles felt like his 1993 team was better. The players were bigger and stronger. And even their new uniforms, featuring all white jerseys and pants, gave the Yellow Jackets a sleeker look.

But on this late-September night in Sweetwater, Briles was about to make another change.

Sweetwater held a sizable home-field advantage in its Mustang Bowl, a unique high school stadium where the seats didn't go more than 25 rows up, but circled the entire field in a setting that was rather intimidating for opposing players.

Even more so, the visitors' entrance to the field was also daunting. Not only was there a 25-foot inclined ramp the players walked down, but it funneled right through the concession-stand area, which was oftentimes packed by heckling fans from Sweetwater, who wouldn't just yell and scream, but also had been known to toss a drink or two or possibly even spit on the opposition.

Art knew all about this, and decided that on this night his players would take the field another way. However, what was the real reason?

"We did it because they didn't want us to," Art said. "They didn't want us to do it because it had never been done. This was our way of saying, 'Things have changed, pardner. We're not waiting for you to throw the first punch.'"

The move wasn't without some controversy, of course. Right as the Yellow Jackets came out of the locker room, an elderly lady working as an usher pointed toward the ramp to guide them. But she was horrified when the team started veering in another direction, so much so that she ordered a nearby sheriff from Sweetwater to stop Briles and his squad.

Briefly, out of confusion, the players came to a halt. In football, the referees are usually the only authority that counts, but now officers were getting involved. Stephenville's sheriff stepped in. Words were exchanged between the two policemen. That's when Art yelled to his team, "We're going!"

Instead they went to the side, underneath the grandstands, and while the Stephenville fans with can-shakers in hand were anticipating the team emerging from the end zone, here the Yellow Jackets came charging down through the stands, decked in white.

Things were about to be different. Not just this game, but this season.

"You could've heard the boos from El Paso," then–junior defensive back/receiver Jeffrey Thompson recalled.

But it didn't matter. Stephenville blasted the Mustangs 42–14, a lopsided win that probably would've occurred whether the Jackets had entered the field through the ramp, the stands, or by helicopter. The Yellow Jackets were dominating on defense, keeping the Mustangs out of the end zone. Sweetwater's two scores came on special teams and defense. Senior quarterback Brandon Stewart accounted for five touchdowns, running for three and tossing two to junior receiver Jason Bragg.

But to this day, people remember that game for the entrance.

"Coach just had a knack for being spot on in the decisions he made," defensive tackle Mitch Copeland said. "We were ready to play. We were the better team. But when he did that, we got even more fired up. We had never beaten them, so it was a huge confidence boost to us."

The message was clear: there was a new sheriff in town…in more ways than one.

★ ★ ★

The 1993 team is remembered mostly for players like Stewart and Bragg, who both went on to play major college football and were eventually teammates at Texas A&M. But what made that team so dominant was the defense. In fact, if there is one misconception about Coach Briles, it's probably the importance he places on defense. That's something he did right away with Mike Copeland, Stephenville's defensive coordinator.

"Every year when we discussed personnel, he'd take the quarterback and the running back and he would say, 'You can take anyone else you want for defense,'" Copeland said. "I tested him right off the bat and said I wanted the center, who was all-district at the time. He said 'You got him,' and that's the way he was. He knew defense was extremely important."

As the 1993 season rolled along, the Yellow Jackets won five non-district games by a combined score of 220–23, yielding just one offensive touchdown. In fact, that would be the only score allowed by Stephenville's defense during the entire regular season, as they did not allow a single offensive touchdown in district play. They completely shut out Mineral Wells, Granbury, and Joshua to the tune of 168–0 combined.

Of course, the Brownwood game is always a big one, regardless of records, but Stephenville rolled over the Lions 30–7, with Brownwood's only score coming off an interception return.

The Yellow Jackets entered the playoffs with a perfect 10–0 record and were ranked No. 2 in the state behind defending 4A champion Waxahachie. First up was familiar foe Azle in the bi-district round, a rematch from Week 2 that saw Stephenville pummel the Hornets 38–6.

But the playoffs are a different animal, and Art worried about this game more than he was letting on. The bi-district round can often be tough on teams that have visions of going to state. Sometimes you're looking at a possible matchup five or six weeks later and forget about the first one, especially if it's an opponent that was beaten badly earlier in the year.

Art also knew that defeating a team twice in one season could be challenging. In fact, this would be Stephenville's fourth meeting in two years with Azle, a team that was young and rebuilding a program using a pass-happy offense.

The Jackets found out early this game would be a different story. Azle took a quick 14–0 lead, only to see Stewart score three rushing touchdowns in the second quarter for a 21–14 halftime advantage.

Stephenville went up later in the fourth, 24–21, but Azle was driving in the final minutes. In 1993 overtime had yet to be implemented in high school football. Games in the regular season ended with a tie, and in the playoffs, the winner was determined by having the most penetrations (advancing the ball inside the opponent's 20-yard line). If that was also equal, the tiebreaker went to first downs.

At the point in the game, the Jackets led by three, but were tied on penetrations. Azle had a fourth-and-five from the 25-yard line. All they had to do was convert the first, which would extend the drive and also put them ahead on penetrations. If they then made the field goal to tie the score, that would give them the win. But Stephenville's defense, having been so dominant throughout the season, came up big once again with a stop, the Yellow Jackets holding on for a huge first-round victory.

Around town, it was a head-scratcher for the fans that remembered a 32-point blowout over Azle a few months back. But to Art Briles, a scare was exactly what the team needed.

"When you get in the playoffs, style points go out the window," he said. "For that team, we really hadn't been tested at all. We needed a game like that. We survived a tough game and moved on."

Bill Hart, longtime columnist of the *Abilene Reporter-News*, wrote that week: "The Jackets needed a close shave without getting cut."

He was right about that because it gave Stephenville more incentive to stay focused for the next game against Fort Worth Arlington Heights, the same school the Jackets beat in the final seconds of the area round last year.

But the rematch…was no match. Stewart threw four touchdowns and ran for another as the starters got to rest in the second half in preparation for Sweetwater. Stephenville won in a blowout, 45–0.

About two months after trekking his players down through the stands at the Mustang Bowl, the rematch had much less pregame drama. Sweetwater appeared ready for the fight and had the Jackets pinned back late in the first quarter with the score tied 7–7. But that's when Stewart showed why he wasn't just a good quarterback, but a player who had many of the top colleges interested in his services. From his own 8-yard line, he took the snap, darted right up the middle on a draw, and never looked back, scoring on a 92-yard touchdown and breaking Sweetwater's back. The Jackets would score 26 points in the second quarter and take a commanding 40–7 halftime lead. They put it on cruise control in the second half and won 46–21.

One week after beating the school where he spent four years as an assistant, Art would now face the former head coach of those Sweetwater squads, W.T. Stapler, who had moved on to Andrews High School. Stapler had referred Briles for his last three head coaching jobs in Hamlin, Georgetown, and Stephenville, the latter a position he actually turned down himself.

Stapler knew facing Stephenville was going to be tough. It would've been even tougher, though, had they played in Sweetwater, where he figured many of the locals were still upset with him for leaving back in 1987, two years after the Mustangs won the state championship.

Art and his wife Jan actually met W.T. in Sweetwater the week before the game to exchange film and set up the location for the upcoming matchup. Sometimes the host stadium is decided by a coin flip, but in this case, Stapler didn't care so much where it was played, as long as it wasn't in Sweetwater.

Eventually the decision was made that the game would be played in San Angelo. Of course, the always-superstitious Coach Briles didn't exactly love that idea because his team had lost there to Estacado the year before. But the 1993 team was different, and so he agreed.

Just the meeting itself was an emotional time for Stapler because of what Art meant to him. He wanted to win for his team and his kids and his program, but he certainly didn't want to be the reason Art Briles' season came to an end.

Before the game, Stapler joked with Art, handing him a $100 bill if he would go easy on his team. Briles declined the C-note—he was pretty nervous himself about winning the game and knocking out the coach he thought of as his mentor.

In the end, Stephenville prevailed because of better athletes. The Jackets didn't execute well on offense, and Stapler's group was well coached and fought hard, but Andrews came up short, losing 17–7.

For the second time in the school's history, Stephenville was headed to the state semifinals. They were undefeated and flying high at 14–0. The problem was, their next opponent was not only unscathed, but sitting on a 30-game winning streak, having not lost a game in the last two years.

★   ★   ★

In the spring of 1993, a few assistant coaches at Stephenville were sitting in the stands at the state track meet in Austin. Randy Clements, the offensive line coach at the time and one of Coach Briles' top assistants, ran into some coaches from Waxahachie. Regardless of the fact that it was April, Texas is Texas. Before too long, football was brought up.

Waxahachie went 16–0 the year before and dominated Class 4A. Just one week after Estacado edged Stephenville 13–7 in the quarterfinals, the Indians completely annihilated the Lubbock school, 70–6, in the semis.

In fact, Boots Elliott, longtime voice of the Yellow Jackets, said Stephenville's loss in 1992 to Estacado might have been the best thing to happen to the program. Had they won that game, it's doubtful they would've been very competitive against Waxahachie, and who knows what that does to the psyche the next year? As it turned out, the close defeat to Estacado made them hungrier heading into 1993, and they were much more prepared for Waxahachie this time around.

Still, coaches have egos, too, so in the stands at Texas Memorial Stadium, now known as Darrell K. Royal–Texas Memorial Stadium, Clements made small talk with his opposing colleagues and said, "We sure wish we would've been able to get by Estacado and play you guys…would've been fun."

One Waxahachie coach responded quickly. "No, you don't. Would've been ugly."

With that, it was on. Clements didn't say much. He barely even turned around. He just nodded to himself and stored that in the memory bank.

Maybe it was true. Maybe Stephenville would've been no match for Waxahachie in 1992, but it didn't matter now. This was 1993, and the stage was different. This Stephenville team was different. It was more talented. It was tougher. And it was battle-tested.

The Yellow Jackets needed to be all that and more come kickoff in Waco.

★   ★   ★

The ironic part of Art Briles becoming the head coach at Baylor and turning the program around so dramatically is that despite some of the great moments he experienced in his first five years with the Bears, he'd already enjoyed plenty of unforgettable memories at Floyd Casey Stadium. Not only was this the site of his first playoff victory with Stephenville, it was about to be the site of arguably the biggest win of his high school coaching career.

Before the game, the school busses for both teams were driving to the stadium at the same time. Already in game mode, Art leaned over to the bus driver and told him to "step on it…we're going to beat these guys in something tonight."

Make no mistake. Art was confident about winning more than just a bus race.

It was quite a showdown between Stephenville and Waxahachie, which had an intimidating pregame ritual that included Indian war chants done in unison, resembling a scene from *Remember the Titans*, a movie that didn't come out until 2000.

The Yellow Jackets' walk back into the locker room was a rather quiet and stoic one. They were too busy gawking at the confident Waxahachie bunch that hadn't lost a game in two full seasons. As much as Stephenville had done this year, the Indians had more than doubled it.

Coach Briles entered a locker room full of wide-eyed players who seemingly had met their match this time around.

"Men, it looks like we've just lost our 10th pregame in a row," Art told his team. "But it doesn't matter. We're about to start this game, and if we do what we're supposed to do and take care of us…we'll win. We are good enough to win, I promise you that."

That's all they needed to hear. Now, it was war on the field. Back and forth all game long with huge momentum swings for each team. One of the biggest plays of the night, though, came from the most unexpected source.

Not a player. Not a coach. But…a band director?

That's right, Jim Alexander was the longtime leader of the Stephenville marching band and was one of the most enthusiastic, football-loving directors of his time. He had a knack for playing a song appropriate for the occasion, as he also understood the game. He knew about momentum and when the defense needed to get a key stop.

So, just before halftime, with the band already filling up the sideline in preparation for their performance during the break, Alexander watched as Waxahachie drove for a potential late score in the final seconds. With his band ready, he prompted them to fire up the school's fight song right in the middle of the action. This wasn't just a routine tune from the stands; there were trumpets, tubas, and clarinets literally standing behind the chain gang holding the first-down markers. As a result, Waxahachie fumbled two snaps and was flagged for a false-start penalty. Backed up, they missed a field goal to keep the score tied at halftime, 7–7.

In the third quarter, Stewart gave the Jackets a 14–7 lead on a 62-yard touchdown run, only to see the Indians quickly respond, the game tied again heading into the final 12 minutes of play.

Driving for the go-ahead score, Stephenville coughed up the ball, straight into the hands of Waxahachie's defensive star Montae Reagor, a future Texas Tech Raider and NFL player with the Broncos, Colts, and Eagles, who raced 71 yards to the end zone, giving the Indians a 21–14 lead. It was a wild play that the Yellow Jackets' estimated crowd of about 13,000 fans feared would be a crushing blow.

Instead, Stewart and Co. came right back down the field. With a little under six minutes remaining, the quarterback barked out the first of two plays that many people believe changed Stephenville football forever.

"Gun Gold Right, 500 Fly."

It sounds a lot more technical than it is. Basically the play calls for Bragg to run by his defender and Stewart to throw it as far as he can with the hope that they hook up in the end zone. Bragg's only concern was getting off the line. Playing just about every snap on both sides of the ball, he was worn out at that point. But he managed to get free from the cornerback, and when he looked up for the ball, all he saw was a perfectly thrown pass already in midair. Bragg caught up to the heave, snatched the prize with his mitts, and leaned over the goal line for the touchdown.

The sideline completely erupted. It was a chaotic scene with coaches, players, and anyone else nearby jumping for joy. The problem was, the Yellow Jackets were still trailing 21–20. Their work wasn't done.

Fortunately, Coach Briles asked for clarification with the officials regarding the tiebreakers, penetrations, and first downs. Up in the booth, the staff basically knew they were equal in both categories, but with five minutes on the clock, Waxahachie would've been able to pick up a few first downs and advance to the finals, even with a tie on the scoreboard.

So going for a two-point conversion was the only option. Art admitted the extra time for the officials to sort out the numbers helped calm down his team a bit, but it didn't help him decide on what play to run. That was a call designed specifically for this moment and at this spot on the field. And more importantly, it was practiced more than a 1,000 times during the season.

"Special Blue Tackle Over 18 Sprint-Out Pass."

Again, nothing fancy. Bragg lines up in the slot and Stewart rolls to his right. It's a run-pass option depending on the coverages of the defense. Bragg simply runs a sharp out route to the front-corner pylon. In this case, Stewart fired it into Bragg who snuck across the goal line for the additional two points.

Of course, with more than five minutes on the clock, there was plenty of time for Waxahachie to score, although they weren't the best passing team around. They liked to grind it out; this was out of their comfort zone.

The Indians did get the ball around midfield, but junior linebacker Jody Brown, a two-time all-state performer, made what he calls the most memorable play of his career.

"I remember the running back catching the ball in the flat, and it was just me and him," Brown said. "He made an inside cut, and I just grabbed his jersey and held on. He wasn't getting free. I made the tackle short of the first down."

Moments later, a fourth-down pass failed. The upset was complete. Stephenville 22, Waxahachie 21.

"That is one of the most epic wins of my career," said Briles. "And it's probably the win, other than maybe the Brownwood game in '90, that really put Stephenville on the map. Beating Brownwood was really big for us and our community. Beating Waxahachie in the state semifinals showed all of Texas who we are and that we're here to stay. It was a humbling experience for our football team."

★ ★ ★

As the final seconds ticked off the clock against Waxahachie, Briles saw a couple of his coaches who had been scouting teams from the other semifinal game, La Marque and Corpus Christi Calallen. He asked one of them not only who won, but how it was looking in terms of matchups.

"Coach, I'll be honest," the young assistant said to Art. "The state championship was won here tonight. They can't beat you."

That sounded good to Briles, but he didn't celebrate early. He knew La Marque, their next opponent, had talent, speed, and history. And he'd been there before as a player. While the stage was bigger now, Art was a senior star quarterback for Rule in 1973 and lost the Class B state championship to Big Sandy. Nothing is a sure thing.

And for a while, this game was far from that. Played at Texas Memorial Stadium, it took awhile for Stephenville to get going. Down 13–6 just before the half, Coach Briles called a "swinging gate" play that freed Bragg for 40 yards to the 7-yard line, setting up a touchdown run by Shane Freels.

At halftime the score was tied at 13–13, but just as it had all year, the defense tightened up and shut down the Cougars the rest of the way. Stephenville did its part on offense, as well, with two more touchdowns, including a nifty 32-yard run by Stewart, who had been named the Associated Press' Texas Class 4A Player of the Year a few days earlier.

"Great players have great games in championship games," said La Marque head coach Alan Weddell, who later joined Briles' staff in college. "Stewart was unbelievable in that game."

Bill Hart has seen his share of football games while working for the Abilene paper. To this day, he ranks Stewart's side-armed pass to receiver Travis Lewis over the middle while falling to the ground as one of his all-time favorites. That play led to Stewart's go-ahead score. Later in the game, defensive back Jobe Lewis picked off a La Marque pass, which resulted in a touchdown by running back Heath Haynes.

Just like that, the Stephenville Yellow Jackets were state champions. The final score, 26–13.

"What an accomplishment for our team, our program, and our community," Art said. "There's no better feeling. To see the looks on the kids' faces… it's truly the best feeling in the world. It's a high you can't buy."

★ ★ ★

Before the bus ride home from Austin, the players were starving. With the school's first state championship secured, they had dreams of big things. Steak? Shrimp? What about both?

Coach Briles stood up and told the players how proud he was of them, but he also reminded them to act right before they got to Luby's.

"Luby's?!" could be heard from Jeffrey Thompson in the back of the bus.

"What's wrong, Tommy, you don't like Luby's?" coach quipped back. "Come on, Luby's is good."

Nothing against the cafeteria, which was probably the best setting at that time of night to host more than 150 people. And it's likely those hungry boys grubbed three or four plates each.

As the bus rolled into Stephenville around 2:30 AM, Thompson was the last one to get off. He saw Briles standing outside and was anticipating what he was about to hear from his coach. He was part of a team that delivered Art Briles his first state championship. Surely, the words were about to be epic.

Thompson stepped off with his gym bag over his shoulder and walked right past Coach Briles, who uttered one message before he turned around and went into the field house.

"Weight room will be open Monday at 8:00 AM."

Granted, the state title game finished up late Saturday. It was now Sunday morning. Officially the off-season had begun. Time to get geared up for next year.

And it should go without saying, the weight room was full.

15. Something to Bragg About

"No excuses, no complaints, no comparisons."

CHAMPIONSHIPS bring credibility. Any way you slice it, Stephenville football wasn't just on the map, it was shining for all of Texas to see.

As a community and football program, people were taking notice. Individuals were getting their credit, too.

Branndon Stewart wasn't exactly a highly rated recruit heading into his senior year, but after leading the Yellow Jackets to the school's first state title, and doing so in a fashion that showed off both his arm and running ability, he was suddenly a hot commodity. For a quarterback like Stewart to have to wait until after his final season to start entertaining offers, though, is very rare. Usually, colleges have their incoming classes all but filled by then.

But teams were opening up spots for him, including the University of Tennessee. Volunteers head coach Phillip Fulmer spent a few days in Briles' kitchen and living room where they held Stewart's in-home visit.

This also gave Art a chance to reconnect with another blast from his past. A Tennessee assistant coach at the time was Lovie Smith, who played against Art in the 1973 state championship game between Rule and Big Sandy. Smith was a defensive backs coach, but as a native Texan, he paid attention to players from the Lone Star State, especially ones where he knew their head coach.

While Tennessee badly wanted Stewart, they also had their eyes on another top prospect—Peyton Manning, whose father, Archie, had gone to Ole Miss. It was expected Manning would play for the Rebels, as well, but right before signing day, he surprised everyone and chose Tennessee. Fulmer and the Vols were telling Stewart he would be their guy, but once Manning became available, they couldn't turn him down.

Coach Briles isn't a sugar-coater, so when he talked to Stewart for the first time after the situation went down, he was up-front with his now former quarterback.

"It's pretty simple, Stew," said Briles. "Peyton's dad is named Archie. Your dad is named Reg. His dad played for the Saints. Your dad builds houses. He may not be any better than you, but they're going to go with him. That's reality. We're not dealing in fictions. It's a fact."

But Stewart was also more of a go-with-the-flow guy. While many of his high school teammates were big ol' country boys who bled Navy & Gold with a passion, Stewart was more down to earth. Some people around town or even in the locker room could mistake that easiness for not loving the game. Others might say football just wasn't his only interest.

Either way, Stewart wasn't devastated upon hearing the news that Manning received a scholarship. Instead, both went to Tennessee as two of the best quarterback recruits in the country. And in their freshman year, they each saw action in the 1994 season opener against UCLA, a 25–23 loss. Stewart played rather well, but Manning led the team down for a touchdown. Obviously, the rest is history.

It wasn't long before Stewart's time at Tennessee was, as well. But during that freshman year, Smith would take him into his office to call Coach Briles back in Stephenville. Not only was the phone conversation a way for the former Yellow Jacket to hear a familiar voice, but it gave Smith and Art the chance to stay connected, too.

Stewart played in 11 games as a freshman, but watched Manning start the final eight. He transferred after one year in Knoxville and headed to Texas A&M, where he played three seasons, starting 34 games. He led the Aggies to their only Big 12 championship with a win over Kansas State in 1998, which sent A&M to the Sugar Bowl.

As it turned out, Stewart wasn't the only Yellow Jacket on that Aggies squad.

★ ★ ★

One player whose mailbox was already getting stuffed with recruitment letters even before the start of the 1994 season was Jason Bragg. That wasn't a surprise to Coach Briles, who actually had an eye-opening conversation with his versatile do-it-all back a year earlier.

After a track practice in April 1993, Bragg saw Art outside as he was walking into the Green Room, Stephenville's indoor workout facility. The coach stopped him to make small talk about next season, which would be his junior campaign. Bragg was considered a late-bloomer, having played three years on the B team before starting at the end of his sophomore season on varsity, a feat that's typically rare.

But on this particular day, reality was about to set in.

Some might say Bragg never really knew how good he was, even after his senior year, so as a sophomore and junior-to-be, he was still oblivious to his potential.

"Jason, if you take care of your school, come to work every day, do what you're supposed to do," said Briles, "you can pick any college in the country to play Division I football."

Bragg thought Coach had lost his mind. Division I football? Like the guys on TV? No, that wasn't him. His parents didn't even go to college. That's just something he never imagined. But standing outside after his pole-vault practice, that pipe dream suddenly looked more realistic.

As it turns out, Coach Briles was more than right. By his senior season, Bragg was fielding letter after letter from just about every school in the nation. Notre Dame, USC, Miami, Texas, Arkansas, Oklahoma, Texas Tech, Baylor, Texas A&M, and Houston, just to name a few. There were hundreds more and multiple letters from each on a weekly basis.

College was now in Bragg's future, but it wasn't his top priority heading into his final year at Stephenville. Getting his team back to the championship was the ultimate goal, although it was one that nearly ended before it even started.

★ ★ ★

Just a few weeks prior to the opening of the 1994 season, it was apparent how important Bragg would be to the Jackets' returning to state.

With Glenn Odell taking over for Stewart at quarterback, there were obvious question marks about the offense, but as long as Bragg was back there in a wide receiver/running back role, along with his safety duties on defense, Stephenville seemed to be in good hands.

The offensive line had some studs in Curtis Lowery, whom Art referred to as "Big City," and Shaylor Pryor, and Briles was quoted in that year's *Dave*

Campbell's Texas Football—a popular preseason magazine (bible) for everything football in Texas—saying that Jody Brown was the best linebacker in the state.

Jeffrey Thompson was one of the more intriguing players on the team. Not only was he the fastest player, he was also the smartest, his GPA hovering right at a 4.0. Other than Bragg, he was arguably the second-most durable athlete on the squad, starring at both receiver and defensive back. Thompson also led the Yellow Jackets in trash-talking, end zone dancing, and Coach Briles imitating, something he would put on display in the 16th game of the season, also known as the state championship.

So the pieces were in place. There was a strong supporting cast around Bragg. However, it was clear he was the centerpiece.

On a steamy hot day in early August, Bragg was standing still, waiting to start a drill when a punt returner sideswiped him to the ground, crashing into his knee. After trying to walk off the pain and regain his strength, he eventually had to go to the locker room and get an MRI to check for ligament damage.

The defending state champs, prepping for the start of the season, were now holding their breaths as their star player limped off the field.

But when it came time to kick off the 1994 campaign against Saginaw Boswell, Bragg didn't just suit up and play, he was the star of the night with three touchdowns, including a 53-yarder to open the scoring that set the tone for a 44–6 win.

Actually, that victory set the tone for the entire season because the Yellow Jackets were rarely contested all year. The defense was dominant, holding every opponent, both in the regular season and playoffs, to less than 20 points. Considering Stephenville's offense never put up fewer than 24 in a single game, and the average score for each contest was around 42–11, there was really only one goal for the Yellow Jackets: repeat.

Mitch Copeland was a defensive tackle in 1994 and is said to be Stephenville's all-time leader in varsity starts with 46, edging out Thompson by one because he didn't start the opener in his sophomore year. Copeland says his biggest regret was not enjoying that season more.

"We were just so loaded with talent in '94," Copeland said. "If we finished with anything less than a state championship, it would've been a failure. That was just our mentality going into it."

So much so that, when flyers were passed around to order senior class rings, the majority of the football players declined.

"We said no thanks," Copeland said. "We expected to get a different kind of ring that year."

After ripping Boswell and destroying Abilene 59–14, the stage was set for a showdown in Stephenville with Roosevelt, an inner-city high school from Dallas.

Being a master motivator, Art liked to use whatever he could to provoke his team, so he rattled off a few names of the opposing players, constantly mentioning them in practice during the week. He'd go up to Lowery and tell him about some defensive end who was the best player in Texas and how he's got to be focused. Or he'd tell Thompson about a wide receiver who won state last year in track and how he'll run by him all day if he's not prepared.

But the Jackets were ready for this one. After a 7–7 tie through the first quarter, Stephenville poured it on from all angles, dominating Roosevelt 56–13. The signature play came from Bragg, who took a direct snap and darted straight up the middle 70 yards for a touchdown, going untouched against a secondary that featured most of the members of their state-advancing track team.

The next week, Stephenville's country boys were again facing a different demographic, this time Dallas Jesuit, a talented private school that won its state class the year before. As the Yellow Jackets ran onto the field in warm-ups, the opposing student section sang "Old McDonald Had a Farm," continuing the nursery rhyme into the first quarter. Of course, once the score was 19–0 Jackets after the first and 33–8 by halftime, the music and singing stopped. Stephenville went to 4–0 with a 47–15 thrashing of Jesuit.

That was one of many games in which the Yellow Jackets employed an offensive formation called "Hammer Time," lining up some of the biggest, strongest players on the team to simply maul the opponent in goal-line and short-yardage situations. But it was more than a powerful running scheme. "Hammer Time" was the epitome of Stephenville football during that era. The hard-nosed linebacker Brown, inserted as a fullback, would often point toward a defender and yell, "We're coming right at you. Get ready!" Sure enough, the play would go right where he said it would, yet no one could stop it.

By the time district began, Stephenville was a well-oiled machine. The margins of victory were 38, 47, 52, and 36 before Stephenville beat Mineral Wells 25–0 in the regular season finale. Imagine what it would've been without the second half being called because of lightning. In fact, once the playoffs began, some teams even called the Mineral Wells staff to see how they were able to hold the Jackets to such a low score.

The closest game of that group wasn't even close at all. The Yellow Jackets destroyed rival Brownwood 42–6, outrushing the Lions 503 yards to six yards in the process. As Stephenville was starting to pour it on, Copeland had some words with the Brownwood quarterback, who fired back with: "We're going to kick your ass in baseball this year."

What? In the middle of such a heated rivalry, the quarterback tries to get back with a jab about baseball? Nice try, but in Stephenville the main sport during the months of March and April is spring football. That's followed closely by power lifting, which helps maintain the strength for football; track, which helps endurance and staying fit for football; and baseball, which maybe helps them stay competitive and coordinated. In Stephenville, it's always about football.

★ ★ ★

Throughout the season, Bragg had his moments of pure dominance. Against Brownwood, he only carried the ball 10 times, but that was enough for him to rush for 232 yards, including touchdowns of 60 and 67 yards that came from the "Hammer Time" formation. He also caught three passes for 57 more, totaling 289 yards from scrimmage.

One of the more memorable moments of his prep career occurred in a laugher game at Cleburne, where it had rained most of the night, muddying the field to a point where injuries were always a concern. While he ran the ball, caught the ball, played safety, returned kicks, and sometimes lined up at quarterback, Bragg was also the punter. Of course, with him doing all of those other things, Stephenville didn't need to kick the ball away too often, anyway.

But late in the game, with the Yellow Jackets leading Cleburne 45–0, a punt was necessary. By this time, Bragg had long been pulled, so Coach Briles told him: "Just don't get tackled and get yourself hurt. If they get close to blocking it, don't have your leg extended out there. So just run around with the ball."

It seems Bragg just heard the "don't get tackled" part. He took the snap and was off, weaving through a few defenders. Before you knew it, he had gone on a 47-yard touchdown run. Unfortunately, to the folks on the Cleburne side, the play looked like the defending state champions were trying to rub it in their face with a fake punt, despite owning a commanding lead.

Briles knew how the situation appeared from the other side of the field. In this case, though, perception wasn't reality. He knew Bragg wasn't in the wrong, but as a coach, sometimes you have to take care of perception and hide the reality.

Coach grabbed Bragg by the jersey, got right in his face, and starting yelling, putting on quite a show. "I'm not sure what I'm supposed to say to you right now!" Coach shouted. "That made me look like the biggest ass in high school football. So you just act like I'm yelling at you. But…that was one hell of a run."

The boos from the opposite bleachers were deafening. And since the game was well out of hand, the coaches normally in the press box had already departed for the sidelines. That left play-by-play announcer Boots Elliott as the only Stephenville-attired person on that side of the field. Needless to say, he was hearing it from fans shouting up toward him and anyone else who happened to be in the press box.

Getting called "low-class" and "cheap" for the rest of the game and into the postgame show, Elliott let most of it go as he continued to call the game. But as the regular cohost of *Coffee with Coach* with Art during his Friday morning radio show, Elliott finally fired back as he was packing up his equipment.

"I just call the games on the radio," he said. "Go yell at the other balding guy over there."

They certainly did. Art got plenty of hate mail from the Cleburne faithful over that play, but he knew the truth. He knew his intentions. And, he learned a valuable lesson: always have a backup punter.

16. Defending Their Honor

"Tough Guys Finish First"

WHEN THE YELLOW Jackets won their first state championship in 1993, they virtually flew under the radar statewide. Sure, they were ranked because of their undefeated record, but there weren't many in Texas who thought Stephenville had a shot to unseat Waxahachie, the champions from 1992.

But as the Yellow Jackets prepared for the 1994 playoffs and looked to repeat in Class 4A, being under the radar was a thing of the past. Everything they did was getting noticed. In fact, some things they weren't doing were garnering attention, as well.

When a team comes out of nowhere and becomes this good, this fast, accusations are going to arise. And they did, mostly in surrounding areas where Stephenville was handing out weekly whippings.

Steroid accusations were beginning to surface. What started out as loose talk picked up steam and became rumors Stephenville simply couldn't control.

Art Briles laughed it off. He did back then. He does today. Actually, it was more of a compliment. He knew how much his team busted their butts in the weight room. He knew how coaches from across the state would make the trip to Stephenville. That's a common occurrence even today, to check out how another team practices and prepares. But these schools were coming to see the off-season workout program.

Players such as Jody Brown, Jason Bragg, and Mitch Copeland have various opinions about the allegations. They knew the truth and pinned the rumors on misinformed jealousy.

"I always said this, 'Come test us and come watch us work,'" Copeland said.

The sad part of it all was that many believe the accusations started from within. A former Stephenville basketball coach whose son didn't win the starting quarterback job over Branndon Stewart, allegedly went to the University Interscholastic League (UIL), the governing body over the state's high school sports, and the Stephenville school board, hinting that Yellow Jackets football players were on steroids. He also blew the whistle on violations of improper use of the weight room, which was a UIL rule at the time.

Of the 10 allegations sent to the UIL, eight were cleared, with only two private reprimands doled out that were viewed as nothing more than a slap on the wrist. Stephenville had been using a sign-in sheet in the weight room to keep track of the players attending. That suggested they were required to participate in what was supposed to be voluntary workouts. Stephenville decided to open up the weight room to the entire community, which sidestepped a rule that has since been abolished.

But the steroid accusations didn't go away. They became more prominent as the Yellow Jackets rolled through their 1994 schedule. It was a storm that brewed all season and was about to boil to a head.

★   ★   ★

Unlike the 1993 campaign that saw the Yellow Jackets survive a nail-biter in bi-district play, this 1994 squad was much more dominant and could out-muscle weaker teams. Stephenville turned a 14–14 tie game with Lubbock Estacado into a 34–14 win, before a pair of one-sided contests against Denison and Borger in the next two rounds.

That set up a quarterfinal match with Sherman, an 11–1 team ranked No. 6 in the state. The Bearcats had won 10 straight, outscoring their opponents 354–46. Since a Week 2 loss to 5A Garland High School, Sherman hadn't allowed more than 13 points in a game. Meanwhile, the Yellow Jackets hadn't been held under 31 points in any four-quarter contest all season, so something had to give.

But the Sherman-Stephenville matchup proved to be just as nasty off the field as anything that could've happened on it.

It started a week earlier in Wichita Falls, where Sherman thrashed Canyon Randall 45–6. The Yellow Jackets had defeated Borger on Friday night, allowing Art to get up to Wichita Falls the next day to not only check out his next opponent, but also meet with the winning coach and hash out the details for the next week.

Art talked with Sherman's head coach John Outlaw afterward to discuss how many game tapes would be exchanged. Coaches can be quirky about this practice, not wanting to show their hand too much, but at the same time wanting to evaluate the opponent. But what Outlaw didn't realize is that because he had apparently rubbed some opponents the wrong way throughout the year, those teams had already given their game tapes to Briles and the Stephenville staff.

He knew they would already have 12 games of Sherman, so when it came time to discuss the exchange, Art said, "Well, coach, I know I don't want to trade much."

"Well, that's fine then. How about we don't trade any at all," Outlaw said, trying to call Art's bluff…only to have it backfire.

"Okay, then. That's what we'll do. We won't trade any."

Outlaw quickly tried to come back and offer up three or four tapes, thinking he would do Briles a favor. But Art stuck to his guns.

"Nah, you said none. Let's do none," as he tried to walk out the door.

"Art, you're going to be like that?"

"Yes, sir!"

That's when Outlaw informed him that the Sherman booster club had a private jet that would take him around to every town and every team Stephenville had played and he would gather as much tape on them as he could.

Coach Briles looked him square in the eyes and didn't blink with his two-word response: "Safe travels."

And with that, it was on.

★　★　★

A few days prior to the Sherman game, Art Briles had several messages waiting for him on his office phone. Most of them were from a lady who identified herself as "Penny."

Her calls, of which many were getting intercepted by other coaches, were insinuating an improper relationship with Art. The calls kept coming and even a fax was sent with a picture of an attractive lady. She also made threats that she would take their relationship to the newspaper.

Not exactly sure of her intentions, Art shrugged it off as he had the steroids accusations. He told his wife Jan about it and wasn't too worried, knowing he had done nothing wrong. Finally, it got to the point, though, where he had to screen all of his calls and even stop taking them as the game got closer.

By the time Saturday rolled around, Coach Briles hadn't thought much about it, but once he stepped onto Pennington Field in Bedford, he now realized from where it all stemmed. Chants of "Pen-ny! Pen-ny!" came from the student section. He knew this was a setup from Sherman, possibly even from the top down.

Once again, all he could do was chuckle. However, the actual game with Sherman was no laughing matter as Briles and his No. 1 ranked Yellow Jackets were about to find out.

Surprisingly, the noise from the stands was hardly the worst thing that occurred on the Sherman sideline. By the time most of the Stephenville fans had crammed into their side of the field, they had noticed several homemade signs from the Sherman faithful, taking the steroids accusations to a new, nastier level.

The signs read, "Body by Art," and, "Shoot 'Em Up, Art!" and featured syringes and needles. Stephenville officials were heated. They confronted members of the Sherman school district, and before too long, they were all removed. The signs didn't even last until kickoff.

But the damage was done. Every player involved in that game remembers the signs more than anything. Same for the coaches, radio announcers, and even a 12-year-old ball boy named Kendal Briles, who, despite his age, understood what was being accused of his dad's team.

It was ugly. It was dirty. And not a single play had been run.

★ ★ ★

Usually, it's hard for any football game with so much surrounding hype to live up to the billing. This one surpassed it.

There wasn't a single seat to be had on this day, the fans even overflowing onto the playing field. Coach Briles recalled that he knew there was no way he could be flagged for being outside of the coaching box because it was simply filled with spectators.

From the 25-yard line to each goal line on both sides of the field, the fans were lined up 10-deep, from the field to the back wall. The crowd was estimated at 14,500, but many witnesses suggest it had to be closer to 20,000.

As for the game itself, Sherman came out like a team possessed. Bearcats running back Jerwayne Parker was a load to handle, ripping off a pair of 50-plus yard runs in the first half. He scored the first touchdown of the game, only to be answered by the Yellow Jackets on a Glenn Odell strike to Howard

Art Briles (above right) in a family portrait—older brother Eddie (above left), father Dennis, and mother Wanda. Art (below left) before his first birthday and with Tottie (below right), his "foster grandmother," during an annual camping trip in Colorado.

(Clockwise from top left) Art's senior class picture; Art holding plaque after Rule won Class B state track title in Austin in 1974; Art in the middle of a joyous locker room in 1973; Coach Dennis Briles with his son Art, during Rule's loss to Big Sandy in the state championship game; Art's high school track team. (Opposite page) Art at the University of Houston.

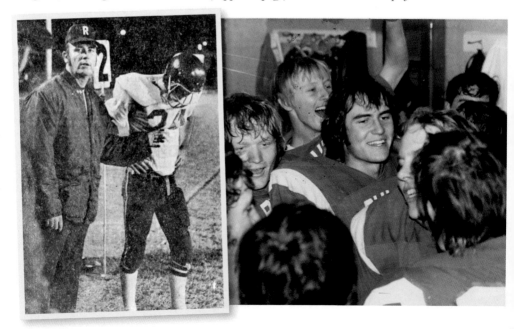

Dennis and Wanda Briles' headstone, located at the cemetery in Rule, Texas. Brothers Eddie and Art picked out that headstone the Sunday following the accident. Elsie Kittley, or "Tottie," was buried at the same grave site, near other family members.

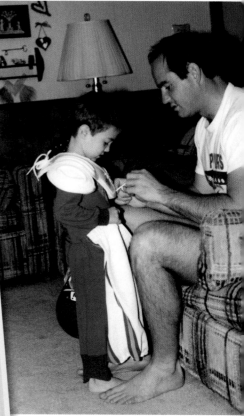

Art and Jan (above left) in college; Art helps Kendal (above) with his first football uniform; and Art holds Jancy (left) at their Sweetwater, Texas, home.

(Clockwise from top left) Art impressed his players by working out alongside them; Art on the Stephenville sideline before the 1993 state title game vs. La Marque in Austin; Jan and Staley with their own noise-making can; Art took his Yellow Jackets team through the stands in a memorable 1993 game vs. Sweetwater.

Kendal (above left) as a ball boy for Stephenville; in an epic game vs. Sherman in 1994, Jackets QB Glenn Odell (21, above right) gets ready to throw; Art gives Jason Bragg a kiss (below) after Stephenville once again won state in 1994 vs. La Marque.

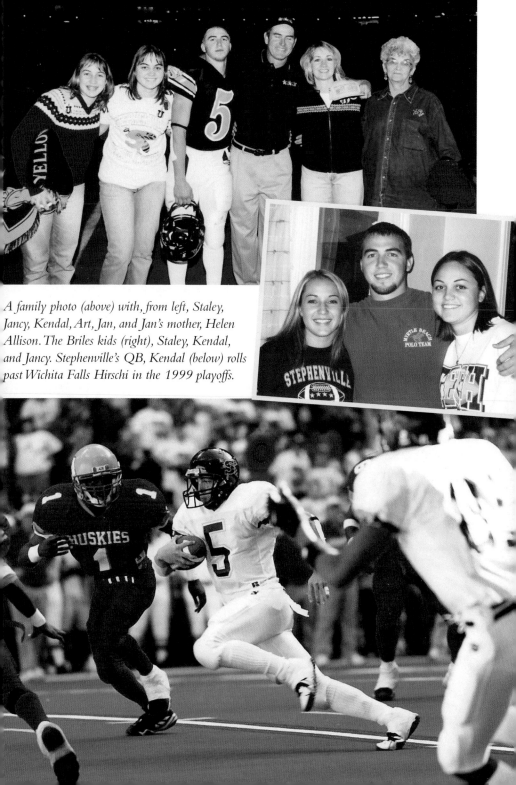

A family photo (above) with, from left, Staley, Jancy, Kendal, Art, Jan, and Jan's mother, Helen Allison. The Briles kids (right), Staley, Kendal, and Jancy. Stephenville's QB, Kendal (below) rolls past Wichita Falls Hirschi in the 1999 playoffs.

Kendal and Art Briles (right) walk onto the Astrodome field prior to the 1999 state title game vs. Port-Neches Grove. It proved to be Art's last game as Stephenville's head coach. (Below right) Against PNG, Stephenville was outnumbered in fans, but not in noise, thanks to the most extreme Can Fans. (Bottom) With Kendal Briles (not pictured) leading the charge, Stephenville won its fourth state title of the 1990s with a 28–18 win over PNG in the Class 4A Division II championship. As a team, the players dyed their hair blond together, they won state together, and they celebrated the championship together.

Phillips. Another long run by Parker led to a field goal for a 10–7 lead before Sherman then capitalized on Jason Bragg's second fumble of the game, turning it into a late second-quarter touchdown. Stephenville went into halftime trailing for the first time all season, 17–7.

Stunned to see his team making uncanny mistakes and not overpowering the Bearcats like they had done against teams all year long, Art shook his head as he walked in between Jeffery Thompson and Bragg.

"Man, this is gonna be tough, guys," Coach Briles told the players as he shook his head.

Like the rest of his teammates, Thompson didn't make a habit out of talking back to this coach. But this moment called for an exception.

"Nah, coach, we've got this. We'll come back. We're better."

What Thompson said made the coach feel a little more confident. What Bragg would do minutes later proved to be a defining moment of the season.

As the coaches huddled in a small room to orchestrate a second-half game plan, they heard a resounding knock on the door. That was uncommon during halftime, but the rap was loud enough to get their attention. It was Bragg, the team's best player who had already coughed up the ball twice in the first half. He didn't have a long message.

"Give me the football in the second half, and we're going to win."

Bragg turned around and walked out. Coach Briles looked at the other coaches and smiled. "It looks like we've got our game plan."

And that's exactly what happened. Bragg was fed the football and did what he'd done all year—dominate with his running prowess. He rushed for 101 yards in the second half alone and finished with 148, scoring the go-ahead, 26-yard touchdown with 2:43 to play. If that wasn't enough, he also picked off two passes on defense, including one in the final two minutes. Thompson would later haul in an interception, as well, in the remaining seconds to preserve the 24–17 win.

The two guys who assured Coach Briles things would be all right in the second half were the two making it happen when the team needed them most.

For all the talk, the signs, the chants of "Pen-ny!" and "Ster-roids!" that Stephenville endured all week and all game, they had the last laugh...or flex.

Some of the Jackets flexed their muscles toward the Sherman crowd, but the most telling moment occurred right at the final gun. That's when two basketballs came rolling onto the field from the Stephenville side.

Sherman had been sending messages all week. The Yellow Jackets just fired one back: Your football season is over. Your basketball season has just begun.

★ ★ ★

If you think you've truly seen it all on the football field, you had better be able to say that you were at the Sherman-Stephenville game in 1994. That's when you would've seen a referee bite a player on the leg.

That's right, a full-fledged bite.

Thompson was the unlucky recipient of the official chomp, which occurred right on the Stephenville sideline at the end of a play. Thompson recalls getting "ear-holed" by a Sherman lineman and going to the ground, where he fell right into the side judge. Unaware of who he ran into, but hearing an awful groaning sound right behind him, Thompson started to feel pain on his thigh. He looked down to see the official was biting his leg as he writhed in agony after suffering a broken ankle. Thompson was laying on him, and that was the referee's way of dealing with the sudden trauma.

Thompson threw three straight punches at the official and "was rearing back for a fourth" when defensive coordinator Mike Copeland stopped him, not knowing exactly what was transpiring.

Thompson got up and told every single person within earshot what happened. He told all of the players on the sideline, "The ref bit me!" He went into the Sherman huddle, the Stephenville offensive huddle. Anyone who would listen, he wanted to make sure they heard of the strangest thing he had ever seen (or felt) on a football field.

The official had to be carried to the locker room. Thompson remained in the game, but later had a nasty bruise with teeth marks that he didn't mind showing off to anyone who cared to see.

★ ★ ★

A few days after the Sherman game ended, Coach Briles got another call in his office from an anonymous woman. He had put the "Penny" fiasco behind him but was afraid the harassment was about to start again.

As it turned out, though, the lady on the other end was calling to apologize. She told Art that she was the wife of a Sherman assistant coach, and the idea behind the prank was to get Briles rattled and perhaps divert his concentration ahead of what proved to be the hardest game Stephenville played all year.

The Yellow Jackets had a difficult time winning that battle mainly because the Bearcats were that good. But all the distractions likely didn't help the matter.

"That was just a weird deal. I wasn't sure if someone was going to come up to me," Art recalled. "It just shows how crazy stuff gets."

Over the years, Outlaw developed a good friendship with Art before the former Sherman coach passed away in 2011.

★ ★ ★

And to think, getting by Sherman was just the quarterfinal round. But Stephenville was rolling now, and they wiped out Corsicana the next week in Waco, the site of the epic win over Waxahachie in the semifinals a year earlier. This 28–6 victory came thanks to a dominating defense, which shut down Tigers' running back Ketric Sanford, who set a state record that season with 475 attempts, which now ranks second all-time, while rushing for 2,761 yards. Against Stephenville, though, he had a season-low 82 yards.

The Yellow Jackets also enjoyed strong offensive performances from Odell and Bragg in leading the team into another championship showdown with La Marque. For the second straight year, the undefeated sides would square off with the Class 4A title at stake. This time, it would be a trip to the Astrodome in Houston.

Coach Briles once received some advice from former Lewisville High School coach Ronnie Gage, who told him to let the players cherish their trip to the state championship game. That's why Briles always arranged to stay in a hotel the night before, which allowed the kids to get the experience of a big-game atmosphere.

At halftime, La Marque, who was much closer to home this time around, led Stephenville 14–0. As the players jogged to the dressing room, the sideline reporter from HSE (Home Sports Entertainment) stopped Coach Briles and asked him to share his thoughts about the two-score deficit.

"We're fine. We're in good shape. We're going to come back and win."

Art believed in these players. He knew his team was better than how they were playing. And he knew he had Jason Bragg and Jeffrey Thompson. They were the two who led the comeback against Sherman, and once again, they sparked a comeback in Houston.

With a field goal and a quick touchdown pass to Thompson, the Jackets got it back to a manageable 14–11 score. Bragg went to work on the ground, and the defense stiffened in the second half like it had done all year. After Thompson's second touchdown catch—a 67-yard bomb down the sideline, the Jackets went on top 25–17. In Deion Sanders fashion, he high-stepped most of the way into the end zone and then did a dance that mimicked Briles' sideline antics. (The coach was known for throwing his cap down when a player would get hit on the sideline, saying, "Oooh-weee, that's late.") Thompson scored, threw down his imaginary cap and yelled, but it's likely even his teammates didn't hear or catch on to his latest creation.

The last score of the game—by Bragg, fittingly—involved a touchdown celebration of another sort. For weeks, the all-everything back had told Briles of his intention to dunk the ball over the goal post. Every time, Coach would firmly shake his head and tell him don't do it, don't be disrespectful toward the other team and don't get a penalty. Bragg often thought about celebrating in such a way, but he never did.

So after he broke free for a 32-yard run to ice the game against La Marque, the thoughts of slamming the ball over the crossbar—the way Cowboys receiver Alvin Harper had been doing so frequently in the NFL—entered his mind briefly. He still didn't know if it was a good idea, but just as he was contemplating the slam, the ball was ripped from his hands in the back of the end zone. Young Kendal Briles, the coach's kid who was probably a better athlete at 12 years old than some of the players on the team, took the ball away from Bragg as he was always instructed to do by his dad, returning it to the official.

But Bragg didn't care. He knew his team had just won another state title. Mission accomplished. He returned to the sideline expecting a big hug from his coach, who instead was wearing a perplexed look on his face.

"Why didn't you dunk it?"

In a classic case of foreshadowing, that ball-boy strip turned out to be the first interception of Kendal Briles' career. Who knew five years later he would be doing the same on a much bigger stage?

★ ★ ★

The championship game ended with jubilation once again. Getting to the mountain was hard enough, but staying there for another season proved to be an even greater challenge. Art was overwhelmed with joy. The second time around seemed to be more satisfactory because of the target placed on his team's chest all season long.

From the allegations sent to the UIL earlier in the year to keeping his team motivated despite facing lesser competition to the continued steroid accusations to the soap opera drama against Sherman to then playing and beating La Marque once again...the season proved to be a wild ride for the Jackets, but will go down as one of the best in Texas high school football history.

Coach Briles walked off the field arm in arm with Bragg, the horse his team rode all season long. Winning state titles can bring a person out of character, evident by the big kiss Art planted on Bragg's right cheek.

In the locker room, the players doused their coach with Gatorade, although they dropped the bucket in the process, leaving him with quite a bruise. But Coach Art Briles, the guy who took what was considered a dead-end job in Stephenville just six years ago, was now a two-time state champion. Nothing could deter that excitement—not even a small bump on the head.

17. Family Man

"If you're going to miss...miss big."

IF YOU WANTED to locate Art Briles in Stephenville, there were two solid bets on where to find him each week. Friday nights on the Yellow Jackets sideline was the safest choice. Sunday mornings at First Baptist Church was a close second.

Art, Jan, and the kids were fixtures there, rain or shine—which in Stephenville equated to a loss or a win that previous Friday. The Yellow Jackets even had a few Saturday playoff games over the years, but that didn't stop Briles from bringing the family to church the next day.

"I remember when we played in Austin for the state championship in 1993," said Monty Bedwell. "They didn't get the busses back in town until about two or three in the morning. You'd think if you just won your first state title, you'd get a pass from church. But that Sunday morning, there he was with his family like it was any other day."

Now, you wouldn't catch them on the front row of the service. In fact, they usually found a pew close to the back, or sometimes went up to the balcony seating. But that was Art's style. He wasn't going to be seen. He was going because that's how he was raised. And that's how he and Jan wanted to raise their family.

To the Briles family, church wasn't a big social event, a place to sit and chitchat afterward. In fact, if there was a third bet on where you might find Art and his family on a regular basis, it would be at Mazzio's, a chain restaurant known for its pizza. In what became a weekly tradition, they would get out of church, get to the car, and hurry over to Mazzio's, where they could grab this one particular booth that gave their family of five plenty of space.

And, perhaps more importantly, the spot was in perfect view of two big screens that were showing both NFL games being aired locally. And they weren't just going to watch the Cowboys, the clear-cut hometown team in

Stephenville and really all of Texas. Art just liked to watch whatever game was on. He didn't mind the pizza, either, nor did the kids, who were usually taking turns dropping quarters in the Street Fighter video game while their dad enjoyed a little down time.

Watching football, eating pizza, and playing video games might not have been the ideal gathering for some families, but it was for this family in the mid-1990s.

* * *

When it came to playing sports, the three children usually made their own choices.

Neither of the girls ever played little league soccer, and Kendal only did for one year. He was always more interested in football.

Jancy played softball in high school, but her focus was on basketball, where she started three years on the Honey Bees varsity squad in Stephenville.

Staley played basketball and volleyball for parts of her prep career, but was more interested in softball. During her freshman year at Frenship High School near Lubbock, she was playing third base when she applied a tag on a runner, severely injuring her left thumb. Immediately thinking it was broken, she fought through the pain for the next out and went to the dugout where she took her glove off and figured she was done for this game, and probably a few more. While Art didn't make all of her events because of his busy schedule, he was in attendance for this one and quickly got down from the bleachers and went to the dugout where he talked to Staley through the fence. Surely, he wanted to know how bad her injury was and ask her how she was feeling.

"Hey, open up that Gatorade cooler and go stick your hand in there.... You're on deck. Get up and get ready to bat."

So Staley shoved her thumb into the ice-cold water before going up to the plate. While she recalls somehow getting a base hit despite a loose grip on the bat, she eventually was taken out of the game for what was officially diagnosed as a fractured left thumb on her glove hand.

While his kids had a variety of tastes in sports and could decide on their own what to play, where track and field was concerned, Art made the call for them—they would run.

He might have been a better football player and knew that was his primary ticket to college, but he had a true passion for track and field, and still does today. Track is the one sport he believes teaches lessons along the way, a sport he views like he does life—rather bluntly at times. It's either good or bad. Yes or no. Black or white. Track is no different.

"The thing I loved about track is you can't hide," he said. "The guy who is the fastest wins. That's just the way it is. It's that way in football or basketball, too, but not as prominent. I really enjoyed track for that reason because when I get on the track, I do my thing and no one can question how things turned out the way they did. Results don't lie."

Art always signed them up for summer track in Stephenville until they were old enough to compete for the middle school.

"He wanted us to do it because it makes you tough," Staley said. "It shows you, 'Can you handle it? Do you have the guts?' Track is all about you versus yourself. It does make you tough. You get that sick feeling in your stomach before you go. It's now or never. I don't think I appreciated it then because I hated it, but I think track makes you mentally and physically tough. I'm glad he made us do it."

Jancy ran track until her sophomore year, and Kendal was part of a 1600-meter relay team as a sophomore that qualified for state. He also went to regionals in the pole vault, jumping 13′6″ as a sophomore. However, injuries to his shoulder prevented him from participating in track as a junior and senior.

Whether they went to state every year as he had done didn't matter to Art. Just the will to compete was good enough for this dad.

★　★　★

Whether it was their parenting skills or simply lucking out, Art and Jan were fortunate that their first child gave them little to no problems. Jancy was independent way beyond her years. In the sixth grade, she started working for a local flower shop, Flowerland Florist, where she would prepare bouquets and mums and help with whatever was needed.

She also started to drive at the age of 11, learning on the farm with her grandfather, Wallace Allison, whom the kids simply called "Pop." She was driving on the streets and highways around Rule at age 13, and because the flower shop needed her to start making deliveries, she applied and received a hardship license so she could drive anywhere when she was 15.

There were no major—or even minor—incidents that led to Jancy being disciplined. To this day, she can't recall a spanking by her parents, although that wasn't the case for Kendal and Staley, who both got in trouble once for going across the street to swim in the neighbor's pool despite being told not to. When they got called back to their house and were told to await a spanking, the brother and sister—around the ages of 12 and nine, respectively—hurried into the house to load up numerous amounts of clothes and underwear to help pad themselves for the licks.

But Jancy never gave them much trouble. She certainly wasn't a party girl, but after her graduation in 1998, having already been accepted to Texas Tech in Lubbock, one particular celebration got the best of her. Her experience with alcohol left her extremely sick the next morning—to the point that Jan stayed home with her while Art and the rest of the family went to church.

This was not the Jancy her parents were used to, by any means. She felt horrible, both physically and emotionally. She knew she had disappointed them, especially her father, whom she still looks up to with the utmost respect.

Later in the afternoon, Art hadn't said a word about the incident to Jancy when he asked her to go up to the school with him to run an errand. She knew right then what was coming. She knew he was going to express his disappointment in her, and even at the age of 18, Jancy dreaded the thought that she had let him down.

When they got in the car, he spoke what was on his mind.

"Jancy, I just want you to know how proud I am of you for the person you've become. You've been such a great role model to your brother and sister. And me and your mom appreciate you helping us out with them the way you do. I'm proud to have you as my daughter."

And that was it. Nothing more. No hidden meanings. Art knew exactly what had happened the night before. He knew how she was feeling at the time. But parenting and coaching can have some parallels. At times, you have to know when to press certain buttons.

His daughter was hurting. And while he had no immediate cure for her hangover, Dad knew exactly how to lift her spirits.

★ ★ ★

Being a coach's kid isn't easy. Coaches work long hours and are usually out of town on a regular basis. When they are home, the stress level is always high and their thoughts are typically on the upcoming game that week.

Throw in the possibility of picking up and moving at a moment's notice, and the situation can be difficult on the kids.

But you won't hear any of Art Briles' three children utter phrases such as, "He never told me he loved me." No, Jancy, Kendal, and Staley heard those words from their parents quite often and still do today.

He might be busy, but Art has never lost sight of parenthood's importance.

"As a father, he has always been incredibly supportive, understanding, and easy to talk to," Staley said. "He expected us to act right and be respectful. He never pushed us too hard but encouraged us to be our best. He has always been very busy with coaching, but never too busy to be a great dad and role model."

That love has now extended out to daughter-in-law Sarah, who married Kendal in April 2009, and his son-in-law, Jeff, who joined the family in March 2011. Jeff is currently on the Baylor football staff as a running backs coach. As the son of Art's good friend, Mike Lebby, a fellow assistant coach at Sweetwater, Jeff grew up with the Briles family, playing sports with and against Kendal. He also maintained a good relationship with Staley over the years, and when he joined the Bears' staff as a graduate assistant in 2008, he began dating her while she was still finishing up school in Houston.

Obviously they weren't sure how to break the news to Art, but Jeff realized one day he didn't have to.

"She was coming into town for the weekend, and we had been spending a lot of time together," Jeff said. "One day, coach says, 'Lebb, you think I'm going to get to see my daughter this weekend?' From there, I guess he just knew and never really said anything about it. He just has a way of making things comfortable."

They dated for two years before he proposed. Jeff was admittedly nervous when he went to visit Art and Jan, although he wasn't sure why. Jeff had known them his entire life. He worked with the coach daily, and it's likely they knew this was coming. Still, Jeff was nervous when he met with Art to ask for his blessing.

"Well Lebb, you've pretty much been family for 27 years. Why not make it official?"

While the family didn't know Sarah quite as well, they liked her from the start because she was able to do something they hadn't seen too often— beat Kendal athletically. His parents' first introduction to his new girlfriend occurred at Barnaby's Café in Houston. Sarah, who lettered in tennis at the University of Houston, had just finished whipping Kendal in a friendly match.

"From the first time I met them—even though I desperately needed a shower—they've welcomed me with loving arms," Sarah said. "They surround the entire family with great love and support."

Sarah and Kendal gave Art and Jan their first two grandchildren. Jaytn was born in October 2009, just days before Baylor played Oklahoma State at home. Kinley arrived in May 2012. Art, who goes by "Roro," loves them both dearly, but treats them differently, of course.

"Jaytn fits right in with this competitive family, and Art loves to see him grow and strive to be the little athlete he is," Sarah said. "He's always asking if he's the fastest boy in class and is all eyes to watch Jaytn do something amazing.

"But you can see his extra-soft side with Kinley. He's not as eager to see her meet little milestones like he was with Jaytn. He would stay on Jaytn's progress more about him crawling, walking, and throwing a ball, just wanting him to be a stud. With Kinley, he'll talk about how pretty and tuned-in she is, and that nothing's getting passed her. That she's on her time and she'll walk when she wants to walk, and he's okay with that."

Even his own kids love the "Roro" side of their dad.

"As a grandfather, he is just so goofy and playful," Staley said. "His grandkids bring out a different side of him. They love being around him and wrestling with him. They bring him such joy. I can't wait to eventually see him with my child."

★ ★ ★

A day hasn't gone by in Art Briles' life when he doesn't think about his parents' tragic death. But those recurring thoughts are rarely shared, even within the close-knit family. Jancy, Kendal, and Staley have never had a full discussion with their father about him losing his parents back in 1976. Yet they know the pain is still there, and every so often something will trigger his emotions.

Once, when the family was living in Lubbock, they all went to a local theater in late November 2002. Art enjoys going to the movies, as long as the terms are right. When the family shows up to the ticket booth, whatever is playing right then will typically win out as the film of choice. On this day, and probably because of the convenient show time, they picked *Eight Crazy Nights*, an animated film written by Adam Sandler, who also voiced the lead character. The movie was listed as one for the holidays, but certainly was meant for adults, with language and other innuendos.

This certainly wasn't Art's type of movie, and at one point, his daughters looked over to see just how badly their dad was hating it. He was, but for reasons they didn't realize.

In the movie, Sandler's character, Davey Stone, is a troubled adult who has no respect for others. His life has gone down a dark path that includes a battle with alcoholism and a long criminal record. When a mentor tries to help him, he realizes Davey seems like a lost cause. The film then has a flashback to 20 years earlier, showing the events that likely led to his troublesome behavior.

Davey was playing a basketball game at the local recreation center when his parents were driving to the game. Their car skidded on a patch of ice and collided with an oncoming truck, killing them instantly. After the game, the police informed Davey of the accident.

The majority of the movie included slapstick comedy with crass jokes, but while the rest of the theater, including his family members, chuckled along at the bathroom humor, Art Briles wiped away tears. The irony was too much.

Even though 26 years had passed since that fateful day when he lost his parents, the emotions were overwhelming. He missed them more than ever.

18. Hunters to Hunted

"A happy man is a beat man."

WITH CLASS 4A considered one of the elite levels of Texas high school football, getting a player who's experienced that kind of competition to ink a college letter of intent is indeed a big score. Having that player make an announcement at his high school on signing day, with members of the media in attendance, is an exciting deal for all involved, creating quite the spectacle.

So imagine the scene when nine Yellow Jackets are on one stage signing letters of intent, including seven to Division I schools.

Jason Bragg's signature was the most monitored, but he ended speculation by agreeing to go to Texas A&M, edging out Nebraska, Texas, and Florida in the end. Named the Texas Player of the Year by *USA Today*, he actually signed as an athlete and began his career as a defensive back, before moving around to running back and fullback and even backing up at punter, although current Pro Bowler Shane Lechler didn't need much help.

But if winning two state titles didn't have Stephenville's place on the football landscape firmly established, having nine players sign college scholarships certainly did the trick. Three of those were starting offensive linemen: Shaylor Pryor (Iowa), Curtis Lowery (Texas Tech), and Travis McKinney (New Mexico State). McKinney was joined by Jeffrey Thompson and Jobe Lewis, while Glenn Odell followed his head coach's footsteps and signed with Houston. Mitch Copeland and Jody Brown went to nearby Abilene Christian, which had signed three Jackets from the previous season.

While that attention was big for the school, it didn't exactly sit well around the town. Sure, they were happy for their own, the boys who took advantage of the opportunity to advance their lives through football and go on to college, a road many people in Stephenville had never traveled. At the same time, however, having nine players sign college scholarships meant nearly two handfuls of high school superstars had to be replaced.

And before too long, word started to spread that the Yellow Jackets might be losing their biggest puzzle piece of all.

★ ★ ★

By 1995, if you needed a blueprint on how to turn around a high school football program, Art Briles seemed to have the master copy. Not only did he do so in Hamlin about 10 years earlier, but he also oversaw a complete rebuilding in Stephenville, with two state titles in the trophy case.

And other schools were definitely taking notice. Some wanted to come visit and check out how they practiced and prepared, and perhaps steal a few pointers.

Some wanted to simply steal the mastermind himself.

Just north of Dallas lay the budding community of Allen, which was growing by the day. They had plans for a multimillion dollar stadium and were headed toward the Class 5A level. The superintendent at the time, Barbara Irwin, made no bones about her attempts to hire Art to become the new head coach and athletics director at the local high school.

After interviews both on the phone and later in person, Art and Jan finally decided it was time to go. Their work in Stephenville was done: seven years, six playoff appearances, two state titles, and a 4–2–1 record vs. Brownwood. To Coach Briles, he had done enough; it was time for a greater challenge.

Jancy Briles was a freshman in the middle of basketball practice one early morning when she was told to meet her dad out in the hallway. He explained to her that they were leaving for Allen, and the next thing she knew, she was in the car with the entire family, headed north.

To Art, this seemed like a good decision. It was going to be more money, more opportunity to grow, and another challenge to build a winner. At least that was the mindset just out of Stephenville. But as the car approached Fort Worth, his thoughts started to change.

Maybe this isn't such a great move. Why would I want to leave the comfort of Stephenville? Is this really the best place for our family?

With those concerns dominating his mind, Art finally stopped the car to talk it over with Jan a little more. They decided to keep going, but that lasted only a minute or two before Art had convinced himself and the family to turn around. They weren't moving to Allen. They weren't going to leave Stephenville behind after all.

The car went about 25 miles down the road, when thoughts crept back into Art's mind.

But what if Allen is really as special as this lady says it is? What if we can't grow any more at Stephenville?

So guess what? The car turned around. Allen was back on. The family was moving yet again. But as soon as the Briles clan traveled north for a few more miles, it became painfully clear that Art's heart wasn't in it. He couldn't do it. He didn't want to make that move just yet.

They stopped in Tolar, Texas, a small town outside of Fort Worth. From a gas station pay phone, the coach called Irwin and told her he couldn't go. While she all but begged him to change his mind, he didn't have the heart to tell her that he had already changed it—back and forth—several times.

And despite her efforts to bring a busload of student athletes down to Stephenville to recruit him and hopefully pick up and return him to Allen, the flattered, yet humbled coach turned her down yet again.

For Art, it wasn't time to leave Stephenville. He didn't rule it out from ever happening, but at the moment, he just wasn't ready.

Coach Briles already had a great job, although he knew he was the reason for it being so. The Stephenville head coaching position wasn't exactly viewed that way in 1987 when he accepted the gig. He turned it into a destination job. He worked hard to put a great product on the field and to get the support of the community. And it was rewarding when Stephenville started to win.

The position was also a great one financially, which again was something Coach Briles had to work for. At one point while with Stephenville, Art wasn't just the highest-salaried football coach in the state, but his earnings—in the ballpark of $105,000, which included an annual stipend for his radio show—made him the highest-paid prep football coach in the nation.

As with any top salary, there is always negative feedback and jealousy. Other faculty members at Stephenville were initially unhappy with the discrepancy of pay between Coach Briles and the teachers. But, they quickly learned that he was also one of them. He attended the evening faculty meetings, often a rarity for head coaches. He even participated in discussions and debate. While there will always be sour grapes for some, Coach Briles earned respect around town and at the school.

Stephenville's principal in 1998, Curtis Rhodes, commented at the time about Art's salary in an article featured in the *Dallas Morning News,* saying,

"Coach Briles has put Stephenville football on the map. And it helps the businesses in the community. It does a lot for this community. He earns everything he makes."

★   ★   ★

Heading into the 1995 season, there was one number mentioned more often than any other when it came to the team's recent success: 32.

As in 32–0, the unblemished record of the Jackets the past two seasons. The national record for consecutive wins was 44. To make it, Stephenville would need to stay perfect through the first two rounds of the playoffs.

Art Briles said he tried to downplay the achievement with his players, but inevitably, the 32 straight wins was hard for a proud town like Stephenville to ignore.

The streak never even made it to 33. In the first game of the 1995 season, Boswell, a team that lost 44–6 to the Jackets in the 1994 opener, turned the tables with a 17–10 victory that stunned the two-time defending champs.

Coach Briles didn't get many Gatorade baths when his team won, but he got doused during the postgame handshake at midfield. "That didn't bother me at all," Art recalled. "That was a big win for them. We had won two straight titles. But I thought it was good for us. We needed to taste that defeat. I remember thinking it was a good thing."

His oldest daughter didn't see it that way. Jancy, now a sophomore at the age of 15, was standing outside the fence where the players and coaches exited the field. This wasn't just a disappointed, teary-eyed daughter waiting to comfort her dad. Jancy was crying her eyes out and needed consoling herself. Remember, this was the first time as a teenager she had seen her father's team lose.

No longer Art or Coach Briles, he became Daddy. He hugged Jancy as tight as he could and told her the truth. "Jancy, it's okay," he said. "We're going to be all right. Trust me, if this is the worst thing that ever happens to me, we're going to be okay."

He assured her things would be fine, not only that night but for the rest of the season. Coach Briles was correct, as the Yellow Jackets went to a more run-oriented offense and churned out 12 straight victories, including a 50–9 win over Brownwood and his mentor W.T. Stapler, who had taken over the Lions program that season. Stephenville got another huge win over Sherman in the area round, 28–3, although the game didn't have the drama or emotions from the previous year. In the quarterfinal round, the Jackets then fell to Denison 38–13, ending their quest for a third straight title.

★ ★ ★

One of Art Briles' qualities that nearly all of his former players will mention is his knack for making every kid on the team feel important. From the superstar to the guy with the least ability who rarely saw the field, he found a way to get them involved, either with a personalized nickname or giving them a special job or task. Regardless, they all felt like the big boss was in their corner.

And it was no different with the coaches. While the varsity assistants were the ones interacting with Art the most, he made sure to keep in contact with the junior high coaches, as well. Not only were they required to use the same schemes in correlation with the overall philosophy of the program, but they also helped out with advanced scouting, going on the road to help the varsity get ready for upcoming games.

Before the 1996 season, one particular junior high coach, Phillip Montgomery, had returned to Stephenville after a quick coaching stint in East Texas. He coached Kendal Briles in the sixth grade two years earlier and now, serving as a student teacher while earning his degree at Tarleton State, he had him again in the eighth.

But Montgomery, quickly known as "Monty," was one of those tireless workers who never quit. He loved being a part of Stephenville's football scene as much as possible, so he stayed late during the weekends when it wasn't required. He sat in the back of the coaches' room and soaked up as much knowledge as possible.

One of his first assignments was to go on the road with another assistant coach and scout a team the Yellow Jackets would play early in the season. So Monty headed out to a scrimmage, primed to come back with a detailed description of this future opponent. He had charts and diagrams and a good read on what this team liked to do defensively. Monty was sure he would be more than prepared to give Coach Briles and the staff a detailed scouting report.

When it came time to watch the film, Art's first question caught the young coach off guard.

"Who's the best player on defense?"

Now Monty knew how much they liked to play a 3-4 scheme versus the 4-3 front. He knew how they were disguising coverages in the secondary. He knew where the blitz was coming from and knew how often the corners would be in press coverage. But the best player? A specific number? He wasn't ready for that. But to appease the coach, Monty rattled off a linebacker, No. 32.

Right when the film started, Briles directed the red laser pointer at the screen and focused on No. 32, who proceeds to get dominated on about four straight snaps. The small light is fixated on this player, who can't get off his block, misses a tackle, and is nowhere near making a play on the ball. Coach Briles stopped the film momentarily and made eye contact with Monty in the back of the room.

"Nice pick."

And they moved on. Coach Briles likely forgot about that soon afterward. Phillip Montgomery never did. Going forward, that was the first thing he looked for when advance scouting. And he also got familiar with the types of questions Art might ask him in the meeting, just to see if he was on his toes.

"That sounds like something small, but it really made me a better coach," Montgomery said. "It was just about paying attention to detail. It's not all about scheme, but making sure you understand personnel and how everything fits into that picture. I always look back at that one story and how that small detail changed the way I approached what I did."

Montgomery eventually stayed on the Stephenville staff even past Coach Briles, and then rejoined him in Houston. He is now at Baylor, serving as the offensive coordinator and quarterbacks coach who assists with the play-calling duties. These days, locating a team's best player is more than a habit, but rather his primary responsibility.

★   ★   ★

In 1996 Stephenville had six games in which they either lost or tied. Yet it might have been one of Coach Briles' better coaching seasons. After a 42–39 overtime loss to Coach Stapler and Brownwood, the first overtime result for either program, the Yellow Jackets were 3–4–1 with one of those victories obtained by forfeit. Even reaching the playoffs looked bleak, much less making another postseason run.

But Stephenville once again got hot at the right time and won the last two regular season games to sneak in as the third team from the district. The 1996 campaign was the first to have three teams advance to the playoffs from each district. That late surge and a timely rule change saved the Jackets' playoff streak, extending it to eight straight years.

Throughout the season, Coach Briles had been grooming young sophomore quarterback Kelan Luker, a strong-armed passer with natural mechanics. Luker would get reps sparingly, splitting time with Kyle Dempsey, who was nursing an injured shoulder.

"I was just a puppy sophomore back then, but I think coach saw potential in me," Luker said. "He would put me in passing situations, and that's all I would really do. But we had some success early on."

Despite sneaking into the playoffs, Stephenville transformed into its usual postseason self. They outlasted Forth Worth Arlington Heights 23–14 and then met up with 11–0 Boswell again in the area round in Waco. With the score tied 20–20, a nervous Luker even thought to himself: *Man, I hope I don't go in*. Sure enough, seconds later...

"Luke, you're in."

Luker took the field and made the first of what would be many big-time plays during his high school career. Running "Shift Right 19 Fade," he actually didn't throw it to the right receiver. Initially, the design was to toss it to Dempsey, who would shift over from quarterback at times when the coaches wanted to capitalize on his 6'4" height. Instead, Luker improvised on his rollout and went back toward the middle of the field where he hit a wide-open Brad Brammlett for a 60-yard touchdown with about three minutes left to play. That proved to be the game-winner as Stephenville advanced with a 27–20 victory. They then beat Sweetwater 7–0 in the next round before the season again came to an end with a 27–16 loss to Denison in the state quarterfinals.

The following season, 1997, which now featured Luker as the full-time junior starter, saw the Jackets turn a shaky 2–3 beginning into another winning regular season, at 7–3, only to lose to Denison for a third straight year, 43–18, this time in the area round.

Meanwhile, head coach Alan Weddell's La Marque team went on to win their third straight championship, having defeated Denison in all three title clashes.

That's just another example of how football is a game of matchups. For three years, Stephenville simply couldn't beat Denison, who had no answers for La Marque, who had twice been overmatched by Stephenville.

And that last point was soon to be revisited.

19. Luker to Cardwell

"They don't ask how, they ask how many."

AS THE MAN running the show, Art Briles had enough to worry about each year with his own varsity players. He made sure to learn the names of everyone in his program, but there were underclassmen with whom he wasn't too familiar.

But not among the quarterbacks. From junior high on, Art knew the kids who could throw the ball and who couldn't. And back in 1995, one particular freshman stood out more than the rest.

Kelan Luker wasn't a finished product by any means—it's hard to find a freshman who is—but he had qualities about him that are just difficult to coach. One day in practice, Briles walked over to the young quarterback and said, "Luke, did you know you have a really quick release?"

"I don't know, umm…is that good?"

Coach Briles then threw out a comparison to Dan Marino, and Luker quickly realized that having a quick release is without a doubt a good thing.

So by his senior year, Luker was about do something that was rare for Coach Briles and Stephenville—start consecutive seasons at the position. Branndon Stewart led the team in 1992, then returned in 1993 as a senior and promptly won a state title.

Obviously, that was the primary goal for the Yellow Jackets heading into the 1998 campaign, but Coach Briles and Luker also sat down before the season and wrote out some more specific goals.

"He told me I was the best pure passer in the country," Luker recalled. "And he made me believe that. He told me that every day. He always believed in me, and that made me believe in myself."

But a great quarterback typically has great weapons around him, and there was no exception to that rule in 1998 with Cody Cardwell in the mix. A dynamic wide receiver who also returned kicks and occasionally ran the ball, Cardwell wasn't the biggest player on the team. In fact, at 5′9″ and 165 pounds, he was one of the smallest.

Cardwell wasn't the player other teams were worried about as they gazed across the field during pregame warm-ups. Cardwell was the guy they worried about when he ran past them for a touchdown—and let's just say that happened quite a bit during the 1998 season.

With Luker, Cardwell, and a junior tailback named Zac Hunter, a jitterbug who earned the nickname "Zac Rabbit" for his elusiveness, the Jackets expected to have a formidable offensive attack.

"We knew we had a chance to be pretty good," Art said. "We had guys coming back. We had Kelan for a second year. Cody was a dynamic, do-it-all player who, when he's on the field, you have a chance to win. We just had the feeling we were going to be good."

Even Coach Briles didn't know it would turn out to be "record-setting" good.

If there were any legitimate concerns about the 1998 team before the season started, they were on defense, where the experience was limited. Only two starters returned from the previous year, and just four seniors cracked the starting lineup.

Defensive coordinator Mike Copeland typically didn't have to beg Coach Briles for too many players. The system they used was simple. Art took the quarterback and running back each season and would let Copeland pick the next 11 guys to round out his unit. But this year, there was one particular kid Copeland didn't get right away. And it's not because Art wanted him on offense; he was just unsure if the player was ready for varsity.

Actually, Art knew his son Kendal was good enough physically as a sophomore, but always guarding against the perception of favoritism, he balked at first. Finally, Copeland told him, "Coach, he's one the top two or three players we've got right now. I need him."

Art finally agreed to the request, and as it would eventually turn out, the decision not only proved to be the right call, but also a needed one.

In the season opener, however, any doubt surrounding the defensive unit was put to rest with a 45–0 blowout of Richland High School from the Fort Worth suburb of North Richland Hills. The Jackets saw everything they needed to see. Luker was stellar, completing 14 of 20 attempts for 394 passing yards and four touchdowns. Cardwell and receiver Chris Evatt both posted more than 100 receiving yards, and the defense pitched a shutout, the first of four that season. Talk about a tone-setter.

The Jackets' dominant win set up a showdown with Round Rock, a Class 5A school outside of Austin. No matter how prestigious a football program already is, if a 4A team can defeat a 5A squad, it's a big deal. So the 31–12 victory over the Dragons was important in its own right, although getting to 2–0 was perhaps a more important feat for the Yellow Jackets, who hadn't started a season with two straight wins since 1994, the last time they won the state title.

Figuring out Stephenville's recipe for success didn't take a football guru: get the ball in Cardwell's hands and let him create. Typically, Briles tried to free his young star out in space in order to utilize his speed, but Cardwell would occasionally take an inside handoff and use his great vision and cat-like quickness to find his own opening.

In the third game against Weatherford, Stephenville led 21–7 at the half and kicked off to start the third quarter. After a three-and-out forced by the defense, the ensuing punt was fielded by Cardwell, who weaved through the entire return team before being ruled out of bounds at the 17-yard line, setting up a touchdown by Hunter on the very next snap.

Plays like that are why Coach Briles always referred to the 1998 squad as being "explosive." One minute the lead is two touchdowns, but before the bands can settle back in the stands after their halftime performances, and the fans can even reach for their noisemaking cans, the score is 28–7 thanks to Cardwell and Hunter.

After the 49–21 win over Weatherford, Coach Briles, completely out of character, jumped into the showers, fully clothed, while yelling with excitement. Those were the little things that always kept the players on their toes— they just never knew what he might do.

District play opened the next week against Everman, a team that hadn't played Stephenville since beating the Yellow Jackets 13–0 in 1991. All week long, Briles and Copeland stressed to their players the importance of gang-tackling and wrapping up, but on the first play from scrimmage, Bulldogs tailback Dondy Kennedy took a screen pass in the flat, juked and jived about six defenders, and rumbled for a 52-yard touchdown that ignited the home crowd. Everman then missed the extra point. They wouldn't score again.

Stephenville spotted the early six points, only to fire off 50 straight, thanks again to the prowess of Cardwell, who scored on pass receptions of 48 and 63 yards that were sandwiched around a 58-yard touchdown run. He racked up 211 total yards for the game, most of which came in the first half, as Stephenville rolled to 4–0 with a 50–6 victory.

Minutes before taking the field against Crowley the next week at home, Coach Briles had a simple message to his squad:

"We can turn this 48-minute game into a 12-minute one if we take care of business in the first quarter."

And that they did, scoring 28 points in those first 12 minutes of play. Cardwell was limited to just two catches, although he managed 125 yards and scored on both receptions, including a 93-yard backbreaker to make it 21–0. The Jackets' second touchdown came from sophomore Kendal Briles on a 46-yard punt return. Meanwhile, Luker again put up impressive stats despite attempting just seven passes. Five of those were completed with three reaching paydirt, as he threw for more than 200 yards in limited action.

The town was buzzing. That feeling the Stephenville community enjoyed a few years back was surfacing once again. The offense was explosive. The defense was dominating, and more importantly, the Jackets had superstar players who now knew how to take over a game.

At 5–0, Stephenville was cruising. But they were headed for a large speed bump, one with a familiar, yet undesirable shade of maroon.

★ ★ ★

Coach Briles walked into the Stephenville job 10 years ago and was quickly informed of the mutual dislike between his new school's football program and Brownwood's. But he didn't run from the challenge. In fact, he embraced it, and after that initial 7–7 tie in 1988, followed by a huge win over the Lions in 1990, the rivalry was back and better than ever.

But like some coaches who downplayed the animosity, Art seemed to provoke it, at least within his own team. While he was rather complimentary of his opponents on his weekly radio show, *Coffee with Coach*, especially to the usually successful Lions, he fueled the fire during practices.

Not long after he took over as head coach of the Jackets, Art shocked his players during the week leading up to the Brownwood game when he passed out different jerseys for his players to wear over the next few days. The players didn't mind so much; they were old and raggedy, some with a few tears. The problem was, they were…maroon?

In a way to motivate his troops, keep them focused on their opponent, but do so with an element of surprise, Art told the offense to wear the maroon jerseys during the Brownwood week, in which the festivities around town included a bonfire. As the story goes, those maroon jerseys made their way to the Wednesday night rally at Stephenville City Park as the community members gathered in excitement for the big game. And when the maroon jerseys got tossed in the bonfire, it became the highlight of the night.

Stephenville-Brownwood is always big, no matter the records, but when both teams are undefeated and ranked among the top 10 in the state, the game goes to another level—and good luck finding a seat. This one was truly standing room only as more than 8,000 fans jammed their way into Stephenville's Memorial Stadium.

As if this rivalry needed any more ammunition, Brownwood's coach, Steve Freeman, who replaced W.T. Stapler in 1997, was once an assistant under Briles in Stephenville. While respect always remains, the familiarity of two head coaches unequivocally raises the stakes. Art remembered the feeling he had in facing Stapler at Andrews back in 1993, so he knew Freeman likely shared the same sentiments.

In terms of classics, this one was true to form. With four touchdowns in the first quarter—two by each team—the game looked more like a track meet that would go down to the very end. Brownwood actually took a 34–21 advantage late in the third quarter, but Luker and Cardwell played pitch-and-catch on a pair of possessions that were both capped off by short touchdown runs from Jimmy Ferrazas to give the Jackets a 35–34 lead.

Not yet finished, the Lions, quarterbacked by the coach's son, Colby Freeman, engineered a go-ahead drive that put Brownwood on top 40–35 with 4:17 left to play. That was more than enough time for Luker, but in the final minute, facing a fourth-and-two at the Lions' 40, Cardwell was tripped up for no gain on a quick lateral run. And although Stephenville managed to get the ball back in the final seconds, Luker's desperation heave was intercepted.

The perfect season was over. The chance to win district was likely out of the question now, too. But not all was lost for the Yellow Jackets despite the defeat. Coach Briles knew that, and he wanted to make sure his team was aware, too.

Standing at the doorway to the locker room after the game, he watched all of his players, distraught, exit the field. The coach spotted Luker passing by with his head down, trying not to make eye contact with anyone, particularly his coach.

"Luke, get your head...up!" the coach said with force.

That was all Briles had to say. He didn't need to explain how three district teams make the playoffs. He didn't have to tell them they played a great game but came up short. He knew he had a good football team, one that simply "ran out of time" as he told a reporter after the game.

He couldn't feel sorry for himself or allow his players to feel that way. The Jackets had to go to Cleburne the next week and face another undefeated team determined to join the district party that typically included only Stephenville and Brownwood. Cleburne was back in their district for the first time in three years, and the Jackets had whipped them 52–0 and 45–18 in the previous two meetings between the schools.

But Cleburne, also nicknamed the Yellow Jackets, had improved dramatically, and Stephenville soon knew it, trailing 14–6 heading into the fourth quarter. Luker and Cardwell then connected to narrow the deficit, which was later followed by Luker's quarterback sneak to give Stephenville a 20–14 lead. After a field goal made it a two-score game with 3:08 left, Kendal Briles picked off a late Cleburne pass to secure the win.

"That was a turning point in that season," Luker said. "Against Cleburne, it really brought us back up. It's not something you think about at the time, especially because it was Brownwood, but losing to them may have been the best thing that happened to that team."

Just moments after the conclusion of the Cleburne victory, defensive coordinator Copeland entered a raucous locker room and shouted, "I love football!" sending the already-jubilant players into a frenzy.

Little did any of them know that they hadn't seen anything yet.

★ ★ ★

Following the bounce-back win over Cleburne, Stephenville rolled into the playoffs by annihilating Joshua 63–0, Burleson 58–0, and then Granbury 65–14. The offense was turning heads, but where the Jackets were really coming together was on defense. Against Joshua, the nine touchdowns garnered most of the attention, but defensive performers were quietly making plays, as well. Safety B.J. Mercer had a game to remember with 14 tackles, a blocked field goal, an interception, and a fumble recovery.

Vocal leader Jack Hodges was one of the toughest on defense. He played with an attitude that seemed to spread throughout, not only on his side of the ball but across the entire squad.

And while the Jackets always felt they could outscore opponents with their explosive offense, the playoffs are different. You survive behind a stingy defense.

Stephenville entered the postseason at 9–1 and ranked No. 9 in the state. Even though that one loss to Brownwood didn't prevent them from making the playoffs, it did set up arguably the greatest bi-district matchup in the history of Texas high school football. Because the Jackets finished second in the district, they were paired against undefeated Andrews, the No. 1–ranked team in Texas.

For Coach Briles, this wasn't just a game between two of the top schools in the state. The head coach on the other side was none other than Mike Lebby, a dear friend who coached with Art in Sweetwater and even lived in the Briles household, sharing a room with Kendal for a few weeks when Lebby was head coach at Dublin, a small 2A school near Stephenville.

Lebby was a colleague, former staff member, and a lifelong family friend, which made the game one of the hardest he ever coached.

"It wasn't very fun," Lebby said. "We knew if we were going to be successful in the playoffs, we'd have to eventually play Stephenville and Art. It was a great game, but I didn't enjoy it, against a good friend like that. It was just hard to do."

And it was difficult on Coach Briles, too. Throughout the year, the two would call each other and discuss everything from strategy and philosophies to each other's family. But on this beautiful afternoon at the Mustang Bowl in Sweetwater, Lebby was another opponent standing in the way of Stephenville's ultimate goal.

What worried Briles more than the head coach, though, was Andrews' running back. Shaud Williams was the best tailback Stephenville would face all year, and it took only one series and a 79-yard touchdown run for him to send a quick message about what type of game this would be. Stephenville returned the favor on a 69-yard run by Cardwell; Williams came back with a two-yard score; and Cardwell tied it up again on a 24-yard touchdown catch from receiver Chris Evatt. The two most explosive players on the field, Williams and Cardwell, had each scored twice in the first quarter. This was indeed a shootout.

Andrews and Stephenville continued to trade blows, with the Mustangs leading 21–17, thanks in large part to four first-half turnovers by the Jackets, and then later 28–24 in the third quarter after a 48-yard score by Williams. But Stephenville prided itself on being a strong second-half team. The reason Coach Briles worked them tirelessly in the off-season was to be tougher in the end—the end of a game and the end of a season.

Both were under consideration in this battle against Andrews. The Yellow Jackets came back to lead 31–28 before Hunter broke it open with a 56-yard touchdown run early in the fourth quarter. That's when the defense came up big yet again, with Kendal Briles picking off a pass and returning it inside the Mustangs' 30-yard line to set up a final field goal.

Williams, who rushed for 253 yards and earned all five of Andrews' touchdowns, reached the end zone on the last play of the game to make the score appear a tad closer. But that was only fitting because it was a classic, Stephenville winning 41–35.

While Kendal Briles called it the "most exciting football game" he had ever been a part of, his father and head coach had a strange feeling afterward.

"It's always hard when you face one of your friends," Art recalled of playing Lebby, whose son Kyle was a senior. "But they were the No. 1 team in the state. When we won that game out there, we felt like we had played the state championship game. We just felt like it was hard for someone to be that much better than Andrews."

Sure enough, someone would be.

★ ★ ★

Riding the high of their huge win over Andrews, Stephenville poured it on against Denton, 48–28, in the area round. Next up was Pampa, who faced the Yellow Jackets at Texas Stadium, although Coach Briles wasn't too keen on going back to the Cowboys' home field, especially when Dallas' senior vice president Bruce Hardy, an advisor for Texas Stadium, told him there wasn't enough space to put the team in a locker room.

"I told him we could put him up in the Stadium Club [a large ballroom that often hosted parties and functions but had open windows that looked out onto the playing field] where his team would have a lot of room," Hardy said. "Oh, man, Art didn't want that at all."

Hardy finally convinced Briles that it would work out, and they set up the large area with makeshift lockers and training tables. It was bigger than any locker room the Yellow Jackets had ever seen, but more than serviceable.

As it turned out, despite the improvised facilities, Stephenville smashed Pampa 42–0. Maybe that Stadium Club wasn't so bad after all. In fact, when the Yellow Jackets won the coin toss to play at home again the next week against Wichita Falls Hirschi, Art got on the phone with Hardy.

"He wanted that Stadium Club again," he said. "I told Art we didn't have to do that this time. We had open locker rooms. Plus, we had a big event up there that night that we couldn't move. But Art just had to have that ballroom. He was superstitious like that. So I pulled some strings. Every game they played that season, they were up there."

More important than where they dressed was actually what they did on the field. Stephenville met up with an intriguing Hirschi team in the quarter-finals that went just 5–5 in the regular season but got hot with three straight wins, including a shocking 23–21 victory over Brownwood.

"We were upset with that because we wanted them again," the safety Mercer said of Brownwood. "But at that point, you just want to survive and advance."

Hirschi had plenty of team speed, and early on in the game, hung in there with the Yellow Jackets. Nick Gholson, a longtime sports editor of the Wichita Falls *Times Record News* said there was a big difference between the teams.

"Hirschi had more talent. Hirschi had more speed. Stephenville had more Briles," Gholson said.

The Jackets pulled away in the second half, 42–21, to advance in a win Art said on the postgame show was more of a blowout than the score indicated.

Style points didn't matter now, though. What mattered was facing South-lake Carroll, a suburban Dallas school that had already won two 3A championships in the early 1990s, but had moved up in class without suffering a major drop-off.

Much like the 1993 semifinal clash with Waxahachie, Art had a feeling this matchup with Carroll would once again be the *real* state title game. Just a few weeks back he might have thought Andrews was the toughest challenge in his way, but the Dragons from Southlake proved him wrong.

"I remember watching them on tape, and what stuck out to me was how easy they made everything look," Briles said of his next opponent. "They never got into a panic. Their athletes looked like they weren't overextending their abilities. That's what worried me as a coach. When you make it look easy, it means you're just really good at what you're doing. They were destroying people in the Metroplex area."

With Texas Stadium only about 20 minutes away from Southlake, this semifinal matchup was considered a home game for the Dragons. They packed their half of the field, just as the Stephenville faithful did on the opposite side. The crowd was estimated at around 18,000, but you would've never thought it was that low, considering the noise being generated from both sections.

Fans rocking, cans shaking, TV camera crews surrounding the field...this is what high school football is all about. The only thing that topped the pageantry leading up to this game was the actual game itself.

This was one of the all-timers for both teams. A true back-and-forth affair, Carroll and Stephenville traded blows for four quarters with no team ever grabbing a two-score advantage.

Carroll led 7–3 early in the game and looked to capitalize when the Yellow Jackets fumbled in their own territory. But Kendal Briles picked off a pass at the Stephenville 12, and two plays later, that deadly duo of Luker-to-Cardwell struck big with a 77-yard touchdown to give the Jackets the lead.

"We knew we could score fast; we had done it all year long," Coach Briles said. "But Southlake was just a really, really good team on both sides of the ball. We felt like we could score, but we also felt like we had to just to keep up."

In the third quarter, Stephenville went ahead 24–21 on Luker's 43-yard touchdown to Cardwell, but the advantage didn't last long. Carroll responded with a 10-play drive that ended with an 18-yard touchdown pass from quarterback Nathan Chandler, who would go on to play at Texas Tech and eventually transfer to Iowa.

With Southlake still clinging to a 28–24 lead, the Dragons made a huge fourth-down stop when they sacked Luker at the Jackets' 26-yard line with 2:34 remaining in the fourth quarter. All Carroll had to do was get one first down, and the game was over. Ten yards and they would advance to the state final.

They got nine and a half. Facing a fourth-and-two at the Stephenville 18, the Dragons elected to go for the first down and win it. But the swarming Yellow Jackets defense, led first by end Cal Jillson, and followed up by Keith McCormick, stopped running back Clay McNutt just inches from the first-down marker.

Fort Worth Star-Telegram reporter Rick Herrin, who covered Southlake all season long in 1998 and is considered a historian for the football program, points out an ironic twist of fate for the Dragons.

"Southlake has always had great kickers," Herrin said of a program that has produced future NFLers like Garrett Hartley and Kris Brown, as well as elite collegiate kickers in Cade Foster and Mac McGuire. "But that year, they didn't have one they trusted. They might not have even wanted to kick a field goal and go up seven, but it wasn't even an option right then because they had struggled in the previous few games."

Stephenville had new life, albeit just 1:33 was left on the clock, and they had no timeouts. But all year long the Jackets had been an explosive, quick-scoring offense, and that's what they needed now more than ever, some 83 yards from the end zone.

Coach Briles knew what had worked for Southlake on the series before, watching them blitz Luker up the middle two straight plays. So on first down, his hunch was the Dragons were coming again.

He was right, and he was ready.

A middle screen right over the blitz to Cardwell was wide open and nearly went for a touchdown, but a desperate Southlake defender tripped up Cardwell after a 22-yard gain. A nine-yard pass to K.C. Steed on the sideline then set up a play for the ages. Like they had done all game, and all season, Luker hit Cardwell on a 52-yard strike down the left sideline for a touchdown that sent the Stephenville fans into raucous euphoria with 1:04 remaining in the game.

Stephenville play-by-play voice Boots Elliott never lacks for excitement, but prides himself on staying composed and always respectful of the opposition. But even he lost himself in the moment, uttering a call that he still regrets to this day.

Elliott's booth location was next to the Southlake coaches in the press box. With just a clear glass window separating them, this allowed Elliott to often glance over for a reaction. After Cardwell's touchdown, he took what he saw to the air.

"Stephenville is on top 30–28 with the extra point coming…and look at the gloom and doom on the faces of the Southlake Carroll coaching staff sitting next to us."

Down by three, Carroll was by no means done. They moved the ball inside the Stephenville 40-yard line with about 30 seconds to play.

Mercer, who initially wasn't sold on the idea of Kendal Briles taking his free safety spot and forcing him over to strong safety, said the noise at Texas Stadium was so deafening at one point that he missed a call and played the wrong defense, leaving his receiver running free down the seam. But Kendal ran over in time to swat the ball away, saving Mercer.

"At that point, I remember thinking how much I loved that kid," Mercer said. "I guess that was the right move after all."

The Yellow Jackets held on for the 31–28 victory in a game Coach Briles said will always go down as one of his all-time favorites.

★　★　★

Like the 1993 win over Waxahachie in the semifinals, beating Southlake Carroll was also considered the virtual state championship, although that's odd to say considering their next opponent, the La Marque Cougars, were the three-time defending state champions, looking for an unprecedented "fourpeat." In fact, had La Marque not lost two straight title games to Stephenville in 1993 and 1994, they might have reeled off five consecutive 4A titles heading into this matchup, which marked the fourth straight game the Jackets would play at Texas Stadium.

La Marque had a new coach after Alan Weddell left for an assistant job at Texas A&M, a move that opened Coach Briles' eyes a bit, considering the success Weddell had enjoyed at the high school level. But Weddell was apparently ready for a new challenge.

All Briles could focus on now, though, was the current La Marque squad, coached by Larry Walker. The Cougars owned an impressive 13–0 record, but they weren't exactly winning in impressive fashion. La Marque's five playoff wins had produced a total of 92 points, just an 18.4 average, and included some close shaves against Crosby and Dayton.

Meanwhile, the Yellow Jackets had posted 204 points in their five games leading up to this state final, an average of 40.8 points per game. Another stat that suggested something had to give centered on La Marque having scored more than 27 points only three times all season, while the Jackets were held to under 27 points just once the entire year. And they still managed to beat Cleburne in that game.

Sure enough, all of the signs proved to be accurate predictions of the eventual outcome.

As they had in their previous two showdowns against La Marque, the Jackets spotted the Cougars an early touchdown. But that would be all they would allow as the defense then stepped up to stifle La Marque. Stephenville's offense did the rest, scoring 34 unanswered points to cruise past the Cougars for their third championship of the decade, and the third in a six-year span.

Beating La Marque wasn't even the most surprising feat of the day for Stephenville, which put an impressive capper on the season by breaking a few prolific offensive records during the state title game. The biggest was the Yellow Jackets setting the national high school mark with 8,641 total yards, although Luker also posted some Texas records, as well, including 4,700 passing yards for the season and 8,297 career passing yards, bettering Koy Detmer. In addition, Cardwell set a new state best with 112 receptions, which has since been broken but remains a Stephenville single-season record.

By the early fourth quarter, with Luker's day over, he glanced up to the video board at Texas Stadium as they flashed the national record. The players were all congratulating each other on that accomplishment, along with the ultimate goal of taking Stephenville football to the top once again.

Standing on the sideline as the final minutes rolled off the clock, Luker started to face reality. While victory had never tasted sweeter, the ride had now come to an end. Tears of joy turned into sobs that he didn't bother holding in.

Coach Briles was also thinking about the big picture as he was nearing his third state title. While the jubilation was gaining steam in the final seconds, Art started thinking about his seniors. And there were plenty of great ones, including none better than Luker and Cardwell.

But he also realized right then just how many key players were juniors and sophomores. He hadn't officially hoisted his third title just yet, but he was already thinking about their chances of winning a fourth.

20. Roger & Charlie

"Normal don't fly."

DURING A LATE-SEASON practice one day during the 1994 campaign, Stephenville was gearing up for another critical playoff game. With excitement in the town building, there could be anywhere from 50 to oftentimes 300 spectators watching the Yellow Jackets work out.

During one particular drill, a pass sailed over a receiver's head and out of bounds some 30 yards down the field. It rolled off the sideline, sending the equipment managers scrambling to get a new ball in the huddle for the next play.

Out of nowhere, the same ball that was incomplete 15 seconds earlier, came sailing in with the tightest of spirals and landed right in the middle of the group, tossed about 40 yards in the air, on a rope.

"Who threw that ball?" one of the assistants wondered, figuring it was a backup quarterback or possibly one from the JV or freshman teams.

Turns out it was Kendal Briles, the coach's son who was only in the fifth grade. The athletic 11-year-old was always around the practice fields and served as a ball boy for the Stephenville games during the 1993 and 1994 seasons.

The players and coaches always knew Kendal was going to eventually be a star for the Yellow Jackets. Even then, his passes were as good as some of the varsity quarterbacks. From age six to about 10, Kendal spent his Friday nights at the same stadium where the Jackets would be playing. But he had his own games going on, usually two-hand touch, or maybe even tackle football if the administrators weren't looking. Knowing the importance of the "big game" taking place out on the field, Kendal would always keep a close eye on the score. He knew what was happening, but back then, his competitive nature didn't allow for much sitting around.

Even on Sundays before church, while his mom and two sisters were still getting ready, Kendal would ask Art to toss him a few passes in the yard, dress shirt, slacks, and all. The opportunity to impress Dad was always worth being the sweaty kid in Sunday School.

Other days, Art would find himself as the all-time quarterback, throwing the ball to Kendal and his other neighborhood buddies for mean games of street ball. If there was a chance to compete, Kendal was out there doing so, especially if he got the opportunity to beat his dad.

As he grew older, the basketball wars grew more intense. Kendal saw himself inching closer and closer to bettering Art but was never actually able to do so until his freshman year, a day he still remembers.

As both head football coach and athletics director, Art had seemingly endless responsibilities at the high school, and thus never coached any of the kids' recreational teams. Still, he tried to attend as many of Kendal's soccer or baseball games as he could, along with any sporting event in which Jancy and Staley were involved. He may have never pitched as a volunteer coach, but make no mistake, Art did plenty of coaching to Kendal in the pickup truck on the ride home.

When Kendal was about eight years old, he was one of the star players for his youth baseball team. This was his second year playing in a kid-pitch league, a step up from machine-pitch. Near the end of the second-to-last game of the season, Kendal struck out for the first time all year, on a called third strike no less.

With his dad watching, Kendal knew he was going to hear about it. Of course, immediately afterward there wasn't a peep from his father, who was standing along the fence.

"On the way home, I understood that from now on I would never look at another pitch," Kendal said. "I cried during the entire 10-minute ride because of the way he was telling me about it. I was disappointed because I disappointed him."

But Art was far from done. Bright and early at 8:00 AM the next morning, he rounded up not only Kendal, but the entire family and took them to nearby Jaycee Park. Jancy, Staley, and Jan scattered around the field, and with a bucket of balls, Art stood on the mound and fired pitch after pitch.

Many of them were over the plate. Some were way out of the strike zone. Others even ended up hitting Kendal, who fought back tears as he diligently swung at every pitch. The family stayed out there for a few hours, and although the message was meant for Kendal, Jancy and Staley were paying close attention, as well. From that day on, there weren't many pitches the Briles children let go by.

★ ★ ★

Just like his dad, Kendal grew up as one of the fastest on the block. A natural, he was a kid who excelled at just about everything. Give him a few tries on water skis, and he'd be skimming all over the lake in a matter of minutes. His great hand-eye coordination helped him become a good jump-shooter, an accurate passer, and a decent pitcher.

Of course, add those qualities in with his speed, and he was just an all-around athlete who was used to coming out on top. But it almost didn't work out that way for Kendal, who escaped what could've been a horrific accident at the age of six. The Briles family was relocating across town from a rental home to a four-bedroom house just three blocks from the school. Hiring movers or even renting a truck was not in the cards. A whole group of football players were willing to run through a wall for their head coach; they'd definitely pitch in to help move some furniture.

But at one point during the day, Art was backing his truck and trailer into the driveway, with Jancy sitting in the bed and Kendal at the edge of the trailer with his legs dangling off. As the trailer started inching upward into the driveway, Kendal's feet got caught on the pavement while the truck continued to move backward. With Kendal yelling and screaming, it took Jancy banging on the back of the window to get Art to notice in time to stop the truck.

By then, Kendal was laying in the driveway with blood everywhere. The trailer had ripped his left calf muscle with a deep gash that sent a large stream of blood running down into the street.

"That's the only time I've ever seen him really scared," said Keith Graham, a standout linebacker from 1988 to 1990. "Coach wasn't scared of anything or anyone when we were on that field. He was scared that day."

Neighbor Steve Keenum, a college coach with Tarleton State at the time whose son Case would eventually star for Art at Houston, heard the frantic screams. He scooped up Kendal in a blanket, and since it would've taken too long to unhook the trailer, he and Art rushed the boy to the hospital in Steve's car.

Laying in his father's lap, Kendal was in shock and felt little pain. He kept asking Art to let him see the wound. His frightened father refused every time. At the hospital, Kendal would need 22 staples to close the gash. He lost all feeling on the inside of his ankle for a while but eventually returned to full strength, although he still has scars from the accident.

That might have been the scariest incident Kendal had involving a truck, but unfortunately it wasn't the only one. At the age of 15, he and some high school buddies were planning to camp out in the woods behind his family's new home. That's where Kendal had carved out a trail on which he would often go hunt for raccoons or rabbits. With no intentions of hurting anyone, just to be mischievous and adventurous, they built a bomb, filling balloons with acetylene. One of his friends drove it in from the country to the Briles house, and they then hid it under blankets in the bed of Art's Chevy pickup.

With backpacks, coolers, and all of their other necessities already loaded, Kendal and Jan were trying to get their dog, Tate, in the back, as well. The bomb had endured being driven nearly 40 miles, as well as sitting outside in the sun for hours. But when the black lab jumped into the bed, the jolt, though small, proved to be the final straw. It exploded, creating an enormous flame that flashed right in their faces.

Thankfully, no one was seriously hurt, although Kendal had to get all of his eyelashes plucked after they were singed, and the emergency room doctors also removed the contacts that had been burnt into his eyes, scratching his corneas. Kendal's friend, Sterling Doty, had his shorts melt to his skin.

And Jan, she might have received the worst of it. Her eyebrows were burnt, her hair frizzed straight up in the air, and she had a smoke-black face, reminiscent of an electrocuted cartoon character. The poor dog? He ran away for two weeks and hid in the neighbor's garage before finally returning home. As for the truck, it wasn't totaled but did suffer major damage to the back end as the bomb put a four-inch dent in the bed.

Art was at the high school watching a basketball game, while Jancy was cheering, when he was notified. He immediately left for the hospital to check on his wife and son. To this day, Kendal doesn't even recall getting into trouble over the incident. Perhaps the scare itself, or having to walk around the hallways as a high school freshman without any eyebrows, was punishment enough.

★ ★ ★

On the football field, player-coach conversations are usually one-sided. Coaches do most of the talking, while players nod and listen. Occasionally, there is back-and-forth dialogue, but usually the talk ends with a "yes, sir" or "yes, sir, coach."

"Yes, sir, Dad" just doesn't really work. Or at least it didn't feel right to Art and Kendal. Art never gave any special treatment to Kendal. In fact, he was oftentimes tougher on him. He didn't get the same high-fives the other players did. Art gave Kendal his share of praise, but he never went overboard. He expected great things from all of his players, especially his son.

On the flip side, Kendal didn't want special treatment. He wanted to play on varsity as a sophomore because he was good enough. He wanted to be the starting quarterback because he simply was the best player for the job.

Neither one of them wanted to be viewed as father and son, so one day Kendal started referring to his dad as Roger. Kendal had a friend whose own father had that name, and he called him "Rog." Kendal said it enough that he eventually dubbed Art the same.

Somehow Art became Roger, and soon thereafter coach then started replying to his son with an off-name, as well, going with "Charlie." Neither Art nor Kendal specifically recall how or why the nicknames "Roger" and "Charlie" came about, but over time they eventually made it to the field during practices and even in games. (The names wore off as they both got older, although Kendal's son, Jaytn, Art's first grandchild, refers to his grand-father as "Roro."

Whatever the name used, Kendal learned during his elementary and junior high days that being the coach's kid meant he was going to be held to a higher standard. Just because his dad was Art Briles, Kendal had to be exceptional. Fortunately, he was.

Those expectations didn't just come on the field, either, but also in the classroom, the lunchroom, the hallways at school, really anywhere in the town. To his close buddies and certainly around the house, he was Kendal. To every-one else, he was the coach's kid.

"It was pressure," Kendal admitted. "When you grow up in Stephenville, where it's one high school and your dad is the head football coach, and the success of the town is centered on football, I was always taught that all eyes are on me. He always told me that everyone is looking for me to screw up. With him, coming to baseball practice, it wasn't like, 'Hey, there's Dad.' It was more like, 'Hey, I better do really, really well because the coach is watching me.' And that made me a lot better."

Typically, the best athlete on any football team is the running back. And the smartest kid with the greatest understanding of the game is oftentimes the quarterback. Well, Kendal was both, which made him quite the dual threat, starting as far back as the seventh grade.

For three straight years, Kendal's teams were downright dominant. They were 6–2–1 as seventh graders before going 9–0 in the eighth grade. That was followed by a perfect 10–0 season as freshmen at Stephenville High.

Entering his sophomore year, any talk about Kendal moving up to the varsity to play quarterback was quashed the moment Kelan Luker threw the ball. As they would each prove in 1998 and 1999, respectively, both Luker and Kendal could get the job done. But considering Art had often said that Luker had the best release of any quarterback he'd ever seen, there was no way he would bench him as a senior for his sophomore son.

In fact, Art's plan was for Kendal to play quarterback on JV in 1998 before coordinator Mike Copeland convinced him that Kendal would be one of the best defensive players on the varsity. But that doesn't mean Copeland didn't notice his quarterbacking skills, as well.

During the '98 playoffs, the Yellow Jackets were riding in separate busses through Dallas traffic following a practice. Usually, the offensive and defensive players were split up, and on this day, the offense's bus was in front when the wheels got turned sideways, causing it to slide across two lanes of the highway and nearly get hit by an 18-wheeler.

All the passengers could do in the defense's bus was watch. Copeland, who was sitting in the front, had the best view of the near-accident. Even after the first bus straightened out and eventually got back on track, those in the second were a bit rattled.

Copeland broke the tension. "Oh, we would've been fine. We've got Kendal on this bus. He could've played quarterback." Laughter erupted after the joke, but in a matter of months, that very scenario would be the centerpiece of yet another run for a championship.

★ ★ ★

By March 1999 the excitement of winning a state title just a few months earlier still hadn't worn off. Also, the fact that Stephenville did so with such offensive prowess—setting numerous records, including a national high school mark of 8,641 total yards in a single-season—grew the fever pitch to an all-time high around the town.

But the two key components of that offense, Luker and wide receiver Cody Cardwell, were graduating seniors, and both were headed for SMU in Dallas.

As for Kendal, he was headed for Stephenville's starting quarterback duties. He knew he would be judged against Luker in the fall, but when spring ball got underway, that was the least of his worries.

"When I started taking quarterback reps that spring…it was one of the worst times of my life," he said. "[Art] expected so much of me, and he had just had Kelan Luker, and they set the national record in offense that year. I wasn't exactly what he wanted, but I was a different style."

Kendal had quick feet and was more of a playmaker. Luker had a cannon of an arm and was the prototypical high school quarterback. Luker was a pass-first, pass-second quarterback and would run if and only if there wasn't an open receiver he could find. Quite the opposite, Kendal was run first, pass second.

Stephenville assistant coach Phillip Montgomery, who worked with the quarterbacks during that time and has been the offensive coordinator at both Houston and Baylor with Art, was an important go-between. He admits that there were some difficulties on the practice field.

"Coaches are always going to be harder on their own kids," Montgomery said. "And knowing them both now, they're both very headstrong. So it was sticky. That spring was really rough."

Around the dinner table at home, Jan and the two girls could always tell what kind of day it had been at practice. Not only would there be nights when Kendal and Art didn't speak to each other, they wouldn't talk to anyone at all, creating an awkward tension that spread throughout the entire household.

One day during workouts, Kendal found himself struggling. The ball was coming out slower than Art wanted, the passes weren't crisp, and his attempts often fell off target. After another incomplete pass, Art had seen enough.

"Get him out of here…. Get him out! I don't want to see his face."

Kendal walked to the sideline, making sure he kept his helmet on. He didn't want any of his teammates to see the tears rolling down his cheeks. Sure, he called the man "Roger" or "coach," but at this very moment, hearing those specific words...that was his dad.

Now, he only sat out for a play or two before Art yelled over, "Get your butt back in there!" But the damage was done for that day. Letting down his dad was the ultimate failure. At that point in his life, Kendal would take 10 straight losses to Brownwood before disappointing his father on an isolated practice field in March.

By the end of the spring, however, Kendal had started to figure it out. The plays were run more smoothly and with more efficiency. With each passing day, the tension came less and the compliments more. Kendal was winning over his father's respect—whether he knew it or not—and was primed and ready to lead the Yellow Jackets into the 1999 season.

Defending a state title is never an easy task, but Kendal knew he was more than ready, especially after what he had just endured.

21. Decade of Dominance

"Happy teams don't win...determined teams do."

EVERYBODY WANTS TO be part of a winner.

Heading into the 1999 season, Stephenville football was more than just a powerhouse around the state. Because of Art Briles' unique schemes and play-calling, he was being dubbed an offensive genius. High school teams weren't using the motion, shifting, and consistent shotgun snaps that Stephenville had already mastered.

The Jackets won three state titles in a six-year span using three different starting quarterbacks. If you had a passer who needed a fresh start, the perfect place for him to be was with Briles.

About 100 miles north of Stephenville is the town of Decatur, Texas. And in the previous two years, a middle schooler named Kevin Kolb had been lighting up the competition in just about every sport. He was the biggest kid, with the strongest arm, the best curveball and the sweetest jump shot around. But with his father, Roy, as his junior high coach, Kevin wasn't always well received. Many in the community thought Kevin was benefitting from special favoritism, and as a result, Roy was called to the school board on two occasions and had to fight for his job.

At that point, frustration had set in throughout the entire family, mostly with Kevin. He couldn't believe how his father was being disrespected. In fact, he told his parents he wanted to move, and so the search went out. That's when the Kolbs caught wind about what was happening down in Stephenville.

During the 1998 playoffs, Roy and Kevin actually made it to Texas Stadium for the epic clash with Southlake Carroll, and with the help of a janitor, they made it down to the sideline where both Kelan Luker and Art Briles walked right by Kevin, who had Christmas-morning eyes as he watched in awe. He knew right then and there that he wanted to play for Stephenville.

After the season, Roy and Kevin approached Art about a possible transfer, and the Stephenville district happened to have a coaching spot open at one of the junior highs. But with the Kolb family deciding to let Kevin finish out his eighth-grade year, things seemed to have settled down around Decatur—or so they thought.

By the end of the spring semester, the family had decided not to move to Stephenville after all. On the last day of school, however, as Kevin waited for his dad to give him his usual ride home, he soon found out that Roy had been called in front of the school board yet again.

That was it. Final straw. Kevin stormed into the house, the 14-year-old telling his family it was time to move. He asked Roy to call up Art and ask about the job, which was still open. And just like that, the Kolbs were on their way. The sleepy 3A city of Decatur had just run a future NFL starting quarterback out of its town.

In a classic case of the rich getting richer, Stephenville was waiting with open arms.

★ ★ ★

The Yellow Jackets knew a thing or two about defending a title. In 1994 the team was coming off its first state championship. They lost a quarterback in Branndon Stewart, but had nine returning seniors who would eventually sign college scholarships, including their do-it-all leader, Jason Bragg. So it wasn't a surprise when that team went 16–0 and repeated as state champs.

In 1999 the Jackets were again replacing a senior quarterback, one who was coming off a record-setting campaign. Luker was gone, but it was time for Kendal Briles to run the show. Here's a kid who grew up on the Stephenville practice fields. He had seen it all and heard it all, and now it was his chance to lead the Jackets back to the promised land. Pretty hefty expectations for any 17-year-old kid, especially the son of the head coach.

With Stephenville ranked No. 1 in the state to open the 1999 season, Kendal was suddenly seeing his picture in magazines and newspapers, including the *Dallas Morning News,* which at the time had one of the most-recognized sports sections in the country. The Yellow Jackets received fantastic coverage from local papers such as the *Stephenville Empire-Tribune* and certainly with the *Abilene Reporter News,* where longtime columnist Bill Hart was always kind to the Jackets, and in particular Art, who gave Hart the nickname "Legend."

While they had nothing but respect for those smaller papers, the players and coaches always knew they had made it big when the *Dallas Morning News* profiled one of their own or wrote an advance for an upcoming contest. Usually that didn't happen until the playoffs, but with Stephenville listed atop the preseason polls, the Dallas newspaper ran a feature on Art and Kendal and their chances of repeating.

Kendal told the paper there was much more pressure to replace Luker than suiting up for his dad: "But I still think we have a chance to win state again. That's the best part of playing for my dad—that I can be there with him when we win."

Not an *if* but a *when.* Just like the '94 team chose not to order senior class rings because they expected to earn another ring at state, this '99 squad had the same intentions. Nothing short of winning it all would be accepted.

Led by Kendal and Zac Hunter on offense and a host of defensive seniors, the Jackets were a close-knit group that played together on the field and hung together off it. They acted alike, talked alike, and when they took their helmets off, they all pretty much looked alike, the latter being more about the dyed-hair phase that Kendal and defensive back/receiver Brady Gunn started before the 1998 state final.

"Actually, that game my hair was pretty orange because we had no idea what we were doing," Kendal laughed.

They eventually not only got better at bleaching, but also recruiting other teammates to go blond, as well. By the end of the 1999 season, about 75 percent of the squad were rocking gold domes. And the players even made a bet with coaches Phillip Montgomery and Mike Copeland to dye their hair if the Jackets won state for the second straight year.

Regardless of the targets on their chests as defending champs, the Yellow Jackets overpowered nearly every regular season opponent. With Kendal getting more comfortable behind center each week, and the Jackets' defense—led by Cal Jillson, who had switched from defensive end to middle linebacker—holding its opponents to under 21 points for five straight games, Stephenville cruised to a 5–0 mark.

Next came the all-important Brownwood affair. The year before, the Lions were the only blemish for Stephenville's 15–1 title team. Not that the Yellow Jackets ever needed extra motivation to face this opponent, but avenging the only loss from the previous season was weighing on Kendal's mind. That's the Brownwood team on which Stephenville focused, and not the one that lost 39–34 seven days earlier to Everman, a team the Jackets shellacked 43–20 two weeks prior.

Of course, rivalry games are always unpredictable. The standing-room-only crowd in Brownwood saw an evenly played battle that had the Lions on top 14–7 in the third quarter. But that's when the Jackets went to work as Kendal scored on a 33-yard touchdown to tie things up with 7:02 to play in the third. After a fumble recovery, Stephenville then grabbed the lead in the fourth on a 19-yard run by Hunter, which was followed by a 68-yard pass from Kendal to Toby O'Neal down the right sideline to put the game away.

Kendal's night included three touchdowns and 148 rushing yards, but Montgomery, the Jackets' quarterbacks coach and constant intermediary between Kendal and Art, recalled some overall concern afterward.

"Kendal really won that Brownwood game for us with his legs," he said. "He didn't throw for many yards, though. We were worried about that a little bit. Kendal was playing great, but we hadn't really opened it up yet. So we went into the next game against Cleburne with the mindset to throw."

Five scoring tosses and 441 passing yards later, the young Briles showed he could be the kind of dual-threat player the coaching staff had been wanting. While it was merely a 54–31 shootout win to improve to 7–0, the combination of running past Brownwood and throwing over Cleburne in a seven-day span was viewed by many as the turning point in the season.

As the playoffs neared, the Jackets had improved their winning streak to 17 straight, and once again, dreams of taking home another state title were becoming closer to reality for the Stephenville community.

The stadium was filled beyond capacity for just about every home game, the crowd also including Art's oldest child. Sure, his son Kendal was the star of this show, but Art also cherished his Friday afternoon visits from Jancy, who was then a sophomore at Texas Tech. After her 8:00 AM English class, she would bolt Lubbock for Stephenville—even admitting to occasional triple-digit speeds so she could get to the field house in time to meet her dad, who always had some down time in the afternoons following the weekly coaches lunch at nearby Chi Hua Huas, just a few blocks from campus.

She was a college student now, but Jancy has always been a family-and-football-first type of girl. And especially in this glorious 1999 season in which her little brother "Kendy" was leading the way, she wasn't about to miss a snap.

Now firing on all cylinders, blowouts over Joshua (56–7) and Burleson (49–0), along with a 32–16 win over Granbury gave the Yellow Jackets their first undefeated regular season since 1994.

★ ★ ★

For the second straight year, Stephenville's first playoff opponent in the bi-district was Andrews, coached by Art's close friend, Mike Lebby, whose oldest son, Kyle, had graduated, but his younger son, Jeff, was a now sophomore offensive tackle. Jeff and Kendal had been good friends for as long as either could remember, stemming from the days Mike coached at Dublin, a small town about 15 minutes outside of Stephenville and the site of some mean wars of Sega Genesis between the two boys, not to mention any other form of competition they could find.

There will always be a debate around Stephenville about which Yellow Jackets team was better—1998 or 1999. That isn't the case for Andrews, which went 10–0 in 1998 only to lose to the eventual state champions. The Mustangs weren't as dominant the following season, although they were still good enough to finish 8–2 and reel off four consecutive wins, including a 28–27 victory over Sweetwater, where Mike and Art both coached in the early 1980s.

While not many expected a repeat of the 41–35 shootout from the year before in the bi-district round, this rematch had the makings of something special. Andrews' crowd countered Stephenville's Can Fans with a giant horn that blew the entire game. Stephenville quarterbacks coach Phillip Montgomery said, "It was like a train running through the stadium all day long."

Jeff Lebby was just a freshman and stood next to his dad on the sideline during the 1998 classic. This time, he wasn't just playing or starting, but was doing a lot of talking, too. His good friend growing up was the opponent's starting quarterback. His dad's best friend was their head coach. This was a huge deal to Jeff, and he made sure everyone else knew it.

"I can remember talking noise to their sideline, noise to their players, and nodding my head," said Jeff. "All their guys were doing it to us. There was no holding back. I was an arrogant ass who thought I was better than everyone, but really wasn't worth anything. But I was going to act like it. That's what made it fun. We were great friends who loved to compete against each other and still do to this day."

For a while, Jeff and his Andrews teammates had plenty of reason for the swagger. They led 14–10 before Stephenville scored two touchdowns late in the second quarter, including a backbreaking 80-yard run by Hunter. In the third, the Jackets then scored 19 unanswered points, eventually pulling away, 49–20. However, the gain didn't come without a little pain for Kendal, who took a vicious hit by an Andrews linebacker late in the fourth quarter. Not coincidentally, Kendal was soon pulled from the game and replaced by freshman Kevin Kolb to run out the clock.

Afterward, the two families were back to what they had always been. Jeff gave big hugs to Kendal and Art with similar messages for both: "Love ya… good luck moving forward. Go win it again."

Stephenville advanced to face Wichita Falls Hirschi for the second straight year, although for the second straight week, the Jackets again trailed early. Speed helped the Huskies jump out to a 12–0 lead, but by the half, Stephenville was back on top, 22–19, thanks to the nifty running of Hunter. The Jackets would eventually pull away for a 35–19 win, ready for the next week's matchup with Frenship High School out of Wolfforth, Texas, near Lubbock.

In the regional round game against the Tigers, Stephenville benefited from a big interception return by Gunn in the second quarter and later a clutch field goal by Eben Nelson to break a tie and lift the Jackets to a 31–28 win. Stephenville then handled Canyon 38–10 in the quarterfinal round, which led to a meeting with Ennis, a showdown between two of the state's top 4A teams. Once again, the semifinal round proved to be the setting for one of the best games of the season. The 1993 semifinal win over Waxahachie and the 1998 thriller against Southlake Carroll probably stand alone, but the 1999 clash with Ennis isn't far behind.

Ennis' head coach, Sam Harrell, played for Gordon Wood at Brownwood, a school that went without losing to Stephenville for an incredible 26-year period, 1964 to 1989. Maybe Harrell didn't consider the Jackets a big-time threat when he played for the Lions in the mid-1970s, but none of that mattered now. Stephenville was Goliath here in 1999, especially against an inexperienced Ennis team that was far from battle-tested.

Playing on a cold and rainy day at Texas Stadium, the two sides went back and forth for four quarters. Stephenville led 31–24 late in the game, but Ennis' stocky quarterback, O'Neil Peterson, scrambled to his left before breaking four tackles en route to a game-tying touchdown with 2:12 left on the clock.

That was more than enough time for Briles and Hunter to go to work. On the second play of Stephenville's next possession, Hunter rushed 23 yards to midfield, with a personal foul penalty for a late hit tacked on after the play. The Jackets stayed conservative and kept the ball on the ground, moving to the 2-yard line before Nelson, the savvy left-footed kicker, hit a 19-yard field goal to send the Jackets to the state final for the fourth time of the decade.

★ ★ ★

Before the team traveled down to the Astrodome to face Port Neches-Groves for the state championship, a few concerns had started to surface around Stephenville...and it had nothing to do with finding time for Christmas shopping or simply figuring out a way to make another out-of-town trip in late December.

The folks in Stephenville could always handle those dilemmas. But they were starting to worry about one lingering situation that could be damaging for the next game, as well as another possible rumor that could hinder the entire program.

Kendal had an injury to his right little finger that wasn't getting any better as the postseason march continued. For most players, extra tape or simply a padded glove would do the trick, but for a quarterback who has to field every snap, hold onto the ball and also throw, this wounded pinky was becoming quite the problem.

Now there was never a doubt Kendal would be able to play. He had recently been named the Texas 4A Player of the Year, an honor that rarely went to a junior. But that's the type of season Kendal had produced, and that was the type of respect Stephenville had earned.

So not even the most pessimistic of Yellow Jacket fans thought Kendal wouldn't be able to play because of this injury. Still, when you're that close to another title, it doesn't take much to dig up some concerns.

What the town was really worried about, however, was the fact that Texas Tech head coach Mike Leach had been spotted near the bench during the last game. Leach wasn't a well-known name at the time and had just been hired to take over the Red Raiders, but word was spreading that Briles was again entertaining the thought of moving on. By the time the Jackets rolled into Houston on Friday night, many of the traveling fans were already worried that this would be the last time they'd see their coach roam the sideline for Stephenville.

While this type of talk might have made good coffee-shop fodder around town, rarely did the gossip leak into the Yellow Jackets' locker room. Just like the steroid claims or the allegations from the former basketball coach a few years earlier, Coach Briles did a nice job of shielding his players from most of the rumors. And even if the players were aware, he made sure the focus always remained on the task at hand.

Of course, he didn't have to convince his guys to keep their attention on Port Neches-Groves. After all, Stephenville was 15–0, winners of 25 straight, and trying to defend their title. Staying focused was the easiest of things to do for the Jackets.

What wasn't easy to fathom, though, was the crowd PNG had in attendance at the Astrodome on December 18, 1999. Stephenville's fans had always been the largest in attendance and the loudest in noise, thanks to the Can Fans. But because the finale was being televised on HSE so close to Christmas, not to mention many had already been to five playoff games, Stephenville had only about 5,000 loyalists make the nearly five-hour trek to Houston. Meanwhile, it was just a 95-mile drive for the fans of Port Neches, which is located in the southeastern corner of the state.

One of the largest crowds in Texas high school football history, 39,102, was on hand for the championship, so running onto the field and seeing what appeared to be 35,000 fans decked in purple caught the Stephenville players and coaches by surprise.

"I still remember seeing that crowd for PNG," Jillson said. "It was the biggest crowd we had ever played in front of, and it was the first time someone else had more fans than us. We ran out on the field and heard boos. That was a different feeling, but a good feeling. They didn't like us, probably because we were good. I think that motivated us."

None more so than Kendal. The Jackets quarterback was simply amazing under the Astrodome lights. Banged-up pinky and all, he completely stole the show and silenced the PNG crowd early with a breathtaking touchdown run from the 15, although he actually covered more like 50 yards. The quarterback initially darted to the left before reversing course and running backward 15 yards, making two defenders miss before getting all the way to the right sideline, where he tiptoed the final steps into the end zone for an early score.

Back on the bench, Kendal was gasping for air—not only because he had just gone on a lengthy run to cap an 80-yard drive, but also because the air conditioner in the Astrodome was not turned on, creating a steamy, muggy atmosphere throughout the stadium.

Then again, Kendal was hot regardless, as he ran for two more touchdowns that kept the Yellow Jackets comfortably in front all game. Even when the Indians appeared to have some momentum early in the third, cutting the lead to 21–12, Kendal came right back with a 79-yard drive that ended with another 15-yard run to the end zone with only 14 seconds remaining in the quarter.

Leading by two scores for most of the second half, Stephenville kept PNG at bay with a stingy defense. Jillson's interception in the fourth quarter brought Coach Briles out of character and into a fist-pumping, pad-slapping frenzy.

"That is complete satisfaction, especially because coach was always more into the offense," Jillson said. "So getting him excited like that about a defensive play...that is probably the most satisfaction there is. We made a huge stop, and you can tell he's so satisfied. That's the best."

But it was two other interceptions that really grabbed the headlines. Along with rushing for 94 yards, passing for 130, and totaling three touchdowns, Kendal made the most of his 10 to 12 defensive snaps. The state's best offensive player also came up with two picks from his safety position—his first two of the season. They couldn't have come at a better time. The last occurred in the final seconds, allowing him and the offense to simply take a knee and run out the clock. Stephenville 28, Port Neches-Groves 18.

The descriptions of Kendal's performance varied, but they all had the same message. Former Jackets standout Mitch Copeland, who was the tight ends coach for that 1999 season, said it was "the single greatest individual performance" he had ever witnessed. Stephenville's longtime athletics trainer, Colin Shillinglaw, who also handled many of the day-to-day operations for the team, dubbed the game the "Kendal Briles Show." As for Art, he called it a "superb individual performance" and the best game his son ever played, considering the magnitude of the situation.

Walking off the Astrodome turf, Coach Briles was thinking about more than just the 10-point victory that had now made him a four-time champion and undoubtedly given Stephenville the title of "Team of the Decade." He also couldn't help but think back 26 years earlier when he was the quarter-back for his father's team in the state final. But after an undefeated season in 1973, the Rule Bobcats came up short to Big Sandy, 25–0, to lose the Class B championship.

This time, the father-son combination pulled it off.

Still, while all of those thoughts were rolling through his head, there was another that kept creeping in, as well. Amid the excitement of the players, the smiles, and joyful tears, Art was soaking it all in as best he could.

For he knew things would never be the same.

22. A New Challenge

"Don't wait for it to get bad to get good."

AT THE START of the 1990s, Art Briles was still a salesman. He was trying to convince not only his players and coaches, but also the entire community that Stephenville had what it took to be a winner. The tools were there. All he needed was hard work and dedication from within, as well as the outside support of the town.

He received both, and the Yellow Jackets won. They won big, dominating Class 4A with a pair of back-to-back championship seasons, including the last two of the decade. But as crazy as it seemed to Art, both then and even now, he sensed Stephenville's residents were starting to take for granted the excitement of winning state. Once desperate just to beat Brownwood, Yellow Jackets fans now expected to bring home titles. And anything less than that was considered a failure.

In Art's mind, the time had come to move on. And that belief alone was a surprising one, considering his son Kendal still had his senior season of high school ahead. All of the pieces were in place to lead Stephenville to a third straight trophy.

Instead, he was ready for a new challenge. Just as he did more than 25 years ago, Art Briles was going off to college. This time he was headed to his alma mater, Texas Tech, to be a part of Mike Leach's first coaching staff in Lubbock. Leach got the job in December 1999 and was relatively new to the state. In building his staff, both he and then–athletics director Gerald Myers thought hiring some assistants with Texas ties to help in recruiting was crucial.

What better man for the job than a guy who had won four titles in the last seven seasons—someone who also had climbed the ladder from his first job at Sundown High School 20 years earlier. Art had been on the bottom floor, doing the laundry and chalking the fields for a Class A school. To work his way through the ranks like he had, which included becoming the president of the Texas High School Coaches Association, meant building a solid rapport with hundreds of his peers across the state.

And that's what Texas Tech needed. Who knew that first staff Leach put together would eventually produce as many as nine college head coaches or coordinators, including current Division I head coaches Dana Holgorsen (West Virginia), Ruffin McNeill (East Carolina), and Sonny Dykes (UC-Berkeley). (His first quarterback in Lubbock, Kliff Kingsbury, was named the head coach for the Red Raiders in December 2012.)

Shortly after the state final win over Port Neches-Groves, the team rolled back into town early Sunday morning on December 19. That close to Christmas, and perhaps because winning was getting to be somewhat of an old habit, Stephenville decided not to have a parade that year. In its place, city officials went with a celebratory luncheon on the following Monday just outside of town where players, parents, and fans could attend and congratulate the team.

As Art sat and listened to stories, jokes, and those speaking from the heart, the coach knew in his own heart that he was out the door. In fact, before the event he agreed to take the job at Texas Tech to become the Red Raiders' running backs coach, although he was really hired to be their "Texas Connection" in recruiting. And that was fine with him. He was using this opportunity to further his career, with his sights set on becoming a collegiate head coach within five years.

In the meantime, he had another goal.

"I told myself I wanted to be the best assistant coach in America," Art recalled. "I said I would give this thing five years in college to see how it goes. I wanted to get into college and get on the road recruiting. I really enjoyed that. I enjoyed visiting with kids and their parents and the coaches. So I wanted to give it five years, and if it wasn't working out, I knew I could come back and get a good high school job. But I was determined to make it work in college."

Back in Stephenville, the news came out right in the middle of the Christmas break. Art never had the chance to tell his players he was leaving. He did visit with the coaching staff, but by then, the word had spread all over town like wildfire. Losing the coach was one thing, but the star quarterback, too?

Well, for a while, that part was up in the air. When Art initially took the job, his intentions were to keep his family in Stephenville and let Kendal finish up his senior season. He would stay with Jan and Staley. More than anything,

Art was keeping a promise to himself that he made some 30 years ago when his parents moved from Abilene to Rule. He told himself right then that he would never do two things: coach his own son and move his kids in the middle of high school.

The first one went out the window years earlier, and after the family discussed the situation for weeks, the decision was made that Kendal would leave Stephenville, as well, and move to a high school near Lubbock. He was actually allowed to make his own decision whether to round out his high school days with his Yellow Jackets teammates with whom he had grown up, or finish up at another spot. In the end, Kendal chose family.

"If I stayed, that was going to keep my parents separated for probably a year and a half until I graduated," he said. "If I didn't, they would move up, and our whole family would be in Lubbock. To me, that was the only factor in what I chose to do. My dad left it completely up to me."

Kendal might be one of the few athletes in history to be heavily recruited two years in a row. Plenty of high schools in the Lubbock area were trying to lure him to be their starting quarterback. Even Mike Lebby offered to return the favor and let Kendal live with them in Andrews.

But when he visited the area in January 2000, the three on Kendal's radar were Monterey and Coronado High Schools in Lubbock and Frenship in nearby Wolfforth, a team the Jackets barely defeated in the 1999 quarterfinals at Texas Stadium. Seeing the team in action during the game itself, in addition to meeting the coaching staff before and afterward, gave Art an immediate respect for the program. So when the time came to make a decision on a school for Kendal's senior season, Frenship ended up winning out, and he quickly left to be with his dad and participate in spring football. Meanwhile, Jan remained back in Stephenville so Staley could finish the eighth grade.

Ironically enough, after spending her first three semesters in college hurrying off every Friday to return home, Jancy now had her entire family coming to see her—permanently. She even moved from the dorms on the Tech campus into their four-bedroom house, reuniting the family once again.

But it was certainly a different dynamic for everyone. Kendal was a senior in a new school, trying to establish himself with a new set of teammates and friends. It didn't hurt that he was the reigning Class 4A Player of the Year and a superior athlete in all sports, of course. Making friends wasn't the hard part.

Leaving his old ones behind was. In fact, it was so difficult for Kendal that he never told his teammates he was moving, other than his good friend Kyle Easter, who only found out when Kendal called to tell him his textbooks were in his locker and ask if he could turn them in.

"I couldn't say bye," Kendal said. "They would've handcuffed me to the weight room. I wouldn't have gotten out of there."

With tears in his eyes, he did manage to call Coach Phillip Montgomery on his way out of town. Montgomery knew something was up when Kendal missed the after-school workouts. But following the good-byes, or rather lack thereof, the Briles family was ready to start a new chapter in Lubbock.

Another aspect that changed dramatically was Art's schedule. Moving from a high school head coach to a position coach in college meant he was on the road quite a bit recruiting. Because of that, Art remembers only attending about three of Kendal's games as a senior, even missing some of the playoffs.

The transition certainly wasn't ideal, but they were making it work. The Briles family was close enough to understand that this was what Art thought was the best move for him. And because of that alone, they all realized it was the right move for everyone.

★ ★ ★

As the Red Raiders running backs coach, one of the first recruits on Art's radar was an unheralded kid from an Oklahoma prep school. He was only 5′8″ and not particularly fast, but he was really quick. In football, he played running back and receiver with occasional quarterback snaps. He also punted and kicked field goals. He lined up at safety and returned kicks. And he played soccer, basketball, baseball, and ran track.

But to Oklahoma, Oklahoma State, and Tulsa, he was a slow kid who was 5′8″.

To Briles, he was something else. So much so he started calling this kid "the Natural" just from watching him on film. And even to this day, when Art scrolls through his iPhone, looking for five-time Pro Bowl wide receiver Wes Welker, he finds him listed simply as "Natural."

Nobody wanted Welker, and in the spring of 2000, Texas Tech wasn't convinced, either. Having coached at Oklahoma, Leach had heard about him, as well, but it was Coach Briles doing most of the legwork. So little was the interest in Welker that he didn't even take his first and only collegiate visit until the day after signing day. Tech had a spot open up at the last minute, which is when they extended the invitation for Welker and his parents to check out the school. If things went well, they were prepared to offer a scholarship.

So Welker flew in to Lubbock for his official visit, while his parents drove from Oklahoma City. They actually arrived at the campus first and found their way into Briles' office for a light, introductory meeting.

"So you're the Natural's parents, huh?" Briles said to break the ice.

"Umm, yes, we're Wes' parents," they replied.

"That's right. He's the Natural. You're the Natural's parents."

At this point, Shelly Welker was a bit confused. Remember, meeting coaches in their office wasn't something she was exactly used to. With her mind racing and wondering where Wes' birth certificate might be, she responded again.

"Yes coach, we are his *natural* parents."

Art laughed and explained his nickname for their son, telling them he was naturally gifted, playing several positions and a variety of sports. And not to mention the fact that he did them all well. The tables quickly turned from confusion to appreciation.

Art hadn't even met with Wes Welker officially just yet, but he had already won over his parents.

★   ★   ★

When the 2000 season began for the Red Raiders, not many in Lubbock knew what to expect from this team with a new coach in Leach and an offense designed to spread the whole field and score some points.

Art was obviously a new piece to the puzzle and came in with a nice pedigree, but he was one of many new faces on the staff. Still, it wasn't long before he stood out, especially to the players on the field.

Briles wasn't the same vibrant, energetic coach he was in Stephenville—he was double that. Because he was now a position coach, Art wasn't responsible for as many of the minor details that go with the territory of being a head coach. Focusing on the running backs with a voice in the offensive game-planning, he got to enjoy being more hands-on.

And that was evident in the weight room, too. Briles made a name for himself at Stephenville by simply lifting with his players, a rare practice among coaches at any level. But he lived by the theory of, don't ask anyone to do something you're not willing to do yourself, which included workouts.

His coaching style and methods didn't reach the entire team, but he made sure the running backs were in top shape. At the conclusion of each practice, Art would summon his group into the weight room for yet another round of lifting. Ricky and Shaud Williams, future NFL players, were like the rest of the backs who weren't too excited about post-practice workouts. But they bought in quickly, especially when they saw Art right there in the mix, doing old-school single-leg squats as he barked out names such as Peter Frampton or Jimi Hendrix to make sure the players knew that he knew who was singing the song on the radio.

Just like he did in Stephenville, he was building camaraderie, albeit within a more condensed, exclusive group.

But Art didn't just work out with his players. One of his favorite lifting partners was secondary coach Brian Norwood, who was also new to the staff. Norwood, who would later join Art at Baylor as defensive coordinator and then assistant head coach, calls Art the only person to ever "talk trash in the weight room," but in a way that made it fun for both.

"If he's getting a good lift in and does a hang-pull or squat, he'd throw the bar down and yell, 'Get you some of this, Norwood!'" Brian said. "But that's the way he was. Art just has some one-liners now and then. He was just competitive at all times. He was in there to get a workout in, but he wasn't about to let you push up more weight than him."

While he was listed as the team's running backs assistant, Art came to the school with a knack for coaching quarterbacks. He won four championships in Stephenville with four different passers, including his son. So even at Tech, the signal-callers gravitated toward Coach Briles. Leach was officially the quarterbacks coach, but as the head coach, he didn't always have the allotted time for one-on-one meetings. Over the next three years, quarterbacks would find themselves in Briles' office talking about anything from the game plan and Xs and Os to national sports, music, or life in general.

For the 2000 season, the Red Raiders welcomed back sophomore quarterback Kliff Kingsbury, who was a perfect fit for Leach's new offense. He had a big arm and was even better at distributing the ball to the right receiver. Picking apart the Big 12 over the next three seasons, he left the school as one of the most prolific passers, not only in Tech history, but also in conference record books.

Kingsbury recalled one of the first practices of the 2000 campaign when he kept hearing Coach Briles. Whether he was shouting words of encouragement or rattling off quirky sayings and phrases, his voice was being heard.

"I just remember him calling this freshman 'the Natural,' and if you looked at him, Wes was a short, white, frat-looking guy," Kingsbury said. "And the first day of fall camp, we kept hearing about 'the Natural,' and sure enough, he was that good. I just remember thinking [Art] had an eye for talent. Because if you say that little white kid is going to be that good the first day you see him practice, you know what you're looking for."

Welker started his career with the Red Raiders in the backfield, so he worked with Briles daily. While he later switched to a receiver role, Welker learned early on about the coach's attention to detail. Long before he got to Lubbock, Art always preached the importance of finishing the play. He would make his skill players, particularly the running backs, sprint toward the ball, regardless of where it ended up. At Tech, Briles told his new crew: "I don't care what the other positions do, the running backs in this room will run down and help our teammates."

At a practice during his freshman year, Welker picked up a blitzing linebacker in the hole and brought him to the ground, drawing quite a few "ooohs" from his teammates. Welker got up rather proud after having knocked down a bigger player and stood there admiring his hit.

Coach Briles wasn't so impressed. He got right in Welker's face and chewed him out, showing a side not many had seen to that point. "Quit patting yourself on the back and get your ass downfield.... You're going to watch as your teammates run down the field?"

Welker never stood and watched another play. Then again, he was making most of them. As a freshman, he had more of a backup role with the offense—although he still had 26 catches—but led the team in both kickoff and punt return yards.

Over the next few years, Welker was one of the most dynamic players in the nation, continually surprising opponents with his ability to get open, run by defenders, make them miss, and simply get the job done for his offense.

In 2000 the Red Raiders went 4–0 to start the season, and, believe it or not, one of the defining moments was a 13–7 win over North Texas, a team that had beaten Tech three consecutive times in Lubbock. And it was nearly a fourth straight before safety Kevin Curtis forced a fumble to prevent UNT's go-ahead touchdown in the final minutes.

"I just remember they had struggled with that team before we all got there," Art said. "And if we had lost that game, it could've been a lot tougher for us. That was a big turning point for that season and maybe the next few seasons."

Tech wasn't a consistent team in the Big 12 just yet, as they finished 3–5 in conference outings and 7–6 overall, which included a loss to East Carolina in their bowl game played in Houston. That marked the second straight year Briles walked off the Astrodome field to end the season. Winning a state title with his son as the star quarterback was one thing. Losing in something called the Galleryfurniture.com Bowl as a position coach was quite another.

The times were definitely different for Art. But then again, that was all by design.

★   ★   ★

While seeing a high school junior win state Player of the Year honors is rare enough, it's even more exceptional if he switches schools for his senior season.

Kendal Briles, however, was an extraordinary case, which matched his extraordinary talents. Frenship was lucky to have him, and without a doubt, he was about to make the Tigers a better football team. There was no question he would win the starting quarterback job—obviously that was one of the selling points in the first place. The thought process was to pair up Kendal with all-state tight end David Thomas, who would eventually play at Texas and later win a Super Bowl ring with the New Orleans Saints.

Kendal and Thomas were a formidable combination for the Tigers in 2000, which ended up winning the most games in school history. The biggest change was the explosive offense the team now enjoyed, thanks in large part to their new quarterback. In 1999 Frenship was good enough to reach the quarterfinals, but lost to a Kendal-led Stephenville squad at Texas Stadium. That group averaged 23.9 points per game. The following year, with Kendal behind center, the Tigers scored 38 points per game, including nine with 35 or more.

Ironically enough, Kendal had to face Andrews High School for a third straight year. With his good friend, Jeff Lebby, on the offensive line, and his dad's best friend and Jeff's father, Mike, still the Mustangs' head coach, they met again in a district game with Andrews this time pulling out a 36–35 nail-biting win.

Despite so much history and kinship between the families, one person not in attendance was Art, whose responsibilities with the Red Raiders prohibited him from making the game.

"I'm not sure if he felt this way, but for me, it was a little easier not to be there," Art said of Kendal's senior season. "I had watched him his whole life and coached him the last two years. Just sitting there watching was hard on me. When I wasn't there, I would call and find out what was going on."

Even without his dad in the stands, Kendal was still a dynamic playmaker with his arm and legs. The only concern he had was a recurring shoulder problem that he initially injured while skiing in New Mexico two years earlier. Against Snyder, the shoulder came out of socket again, forcing Kendal to wear a harness for the rest of the year while often dealing with enormous pain. He waited for the season to end before having reconstructive surgery.

After winning four playoff matchups, the 2000 campaign finally ended for Frenship in the state semifinals. Kendal ran for his life against a bigger, stronger, and much faster squad from Denton Ryan, but with the game at the all-too-familiar Texas Stadium, and in the middle of December, Art was able to see his son play.

He had been there from the very beginning, helping Kendal put on a Kansas City Chiefs football uniform one Christmas when he was six, and obviously he had a front-row seat for some of Kendal's most impressive performances. So with his high school career coming to a close, having Art there for the end was only fitting.

★   ★   ★

Kendal Briles had just won the Class 4A Player of the Year for the second straight season, earning the honor with two different teams. He was a do-it-all leader who was highly recruited by just about every school in the state, as well as many of the major programs nationwide.

Nebraska was one school that wanted Kendal to still be a quarterback. Others, like Texas specifically, preferred he line up at safety. There were some that even thought he'd be a better receiver because of his ability to make plays.

And then there was Texas Tech, the place his dad worked. The place he would often go to after his workouts at Frenship. He would have long talks with the assistants, including McNeil, who would occasionally pick up Kendal and carry him to his office where they would visit about all sorts of things. Norwood would run Kendal through defensive back drills in case he ended up signing with a school that coveted him as a safety.

While Tech was far from his first choice, Kendal realized it wouldn't be easy to say no. This wasn't just another school; this was his dad's school.

And it wasn't easy for Art, either. He was trying to figure out ways to beat Mack Brown's Texas Longhorns during the day while welcoming him into his home at night. But during the entire recruiting process, Art made one thing very clear:

"I told him he had to make his own decision," he said. "I didn't ask his advice when I left Stephenville, and so I wanted him to be comfortable in whatever he did. But I told him not to pick Tech just because I was there. If that's where he wanted to go, fine."

Even then, Kendal knew his dad's days in Lubbock were numbered. The plan all along was to become a head coach, and so picking the Red Raiders would've been simply a short-term decision.

For Kendal, the choice came down to Texas and Nebraska, which also meant it came down to safety or quarterback. Make no mistake, he loved to play quarterback. He loved having the ball in his hands on every snap and being able to dictate what happened every moment.

But he was a Texas kid with Texas-sized dreams. He grew up watching the Longhorns on TV every Saturday, and while he wasn't being recruited to be a passer, he also had a knack for safety, too. He called the position the "quarterback of the defense."

The race was a close one that needed a tiebreaker. And it just so happened that Kendal saw a few more familiar faces in Austin than he did in Lincoln, Nebraska. He stayed home and chose the Longhorns.

With his arm in a sling following shoulder surgery, Kendal signed with Texas during a ceremony at Frenship High School. Other than some epic basketball wars in the driveway, Kendal had always been on his dad's team. Now he was joining one of his biggest rivals.

★ ★ ★

Early in the 2001 season, Art and the Tech staff were in the office one Tuesday morning as they prepared for a Week 2 game against UTEP. The routine was the same: he spent a few hours at work reviewing film and preparing for practice; the coaches would take a break; and he would usually go grab a quick bite to eat. In the car was his time to get away for a few minutes and listen to some of his favorite tunes.

But this particular day, September 11, 2001, was anything but typical. Art was stopped at a red light not far from campus when a news bulletin cut off the music on the radio to announce that a plane had crashed into the World Trade Center in New York.

"Nobody really knew what was going on. Then they announced another hit a few minutes later," he said. "It's something you'll never forget. I just remember thinking right then, 'The world is different now.'"

As everyone else, Texas Tech football shut down that day and for most of the week. The UTEP game was cancelled and was not rescheduled. On the field, the Raiders went on to suffer tough road losses to Nebraska and Texas, the latter reuniting Art and Kendal, who was redshirting and didn't play a down that season.

Tech was 4–3 before a monumental win over Texas A&M. Unfortunately, the 12–0 shutout at Lubbock was perhaps memorable for what happened afterward when the Tech students not only tore the goal posts down at Jones SBC Stadium (now Jones AT&T Stadium), but proceeded to carry them up into the section of stands where some A&M fans had remained, prompting a near riot and igniting what turned out to be a heated rivalry.

The Raiders finished 7–5 in 2001, again losing in the postseason, this time to Iowa in the Alamo Bowl.

The next year, 2002, is considered a "breakout season" by Art. Tech finished 9–5, but experienced some wild games and lasting memories. They played in the famed "Horseshoe" at Ohio State, defeated Eli Manning and Ole Miss, 42–28, suffered a 51–48 overtime loss at home to North Carolina State, and celebrated a dramatic 48–47 win over A&M in College Station.

The Red Raiders found themselves in the hunt for the Big 12 title after winning two straight games to improve their record to 7–4. Up next was rival Texas, the No. 4–ranked team in the country. An opponent that always amped up the excitement on any campus.

For Art, this was different. This was personal. He coached his running backs to get low and power through any defenders, typically the safeties. Now he'd be telling them to run over his son.

Without a doubt, this was not just another game. Art and Kendal always talked during the week, sometimes more than once. But this time, there would be no chatting. They didn't visit on the phone prior to the matchup and only briefly had a word before the game, with the gist of the conversation centering on Kendal's expected playing time.

"I tried not to talk much because I thought it was sort of a violation of a coach/player credo," Art said. "You don't show your cards to somebody trying to beat you. And as much as he loved me, he wanted to win. It was strictly business before the game."

Even to this day, Art says he doesn't remember much because he admitted trying to block out that game.

For Tech, it was a great one, as the Raiders rallied from 14–0 down to win 42–38 at home on a late touchdown catch by one of Art's running backs, freshman Taurean Henderson. Afterward, the ABC cameras focused on Texas quarterback Chris Simms, but the corner of the screen caught a big hug between Art and Kendal. Despite his disappointment, Kendal stuck around long enough to pose for a family picture, which included mostly Red and Black gear, although rumor has it that some family members donned Longhorns socks to support Kendal.

The win over Texas gave Tech a chance for a share of the Big 12 title, but a 60–15 loss to Oklahoma the next week dashed those hopes. The defeat was a bitter pill to swallow for a team that entered the game with visions of winning the conference. Still, the Raiders had an invitation to Orlando, the site of the Tangerine Bowl.

While the Red Raiders would go on to blow out Clemson in that final game, 55–15, the team set sail for the land of Disney World without their running backs coach. Art Briles had paid his dues as an assistant. His goal all along was to be a head coach at the college level. And that was about to become a reality.

23. Following Jancy

"Can't score unless you're trying to."

IN AUGUST 2002 Art Briles' oldest daughter Jancy was ready to be out on her own again. After two years of living back at home while she finished her third and fourth years of college, she was just six hours short of graduating when she got accepted into pharmacy school.

Since the pharmacy school at Tech would've required her to move to Amarillo, she instead found a program at the University of Houston. While Jancy has always been family-oriented, she wanted a new career path, a new apartment. She needed a fresh start.

That lasted all of four months. By the end of the fall semester, Art had followed his daughter once again.

In 2002 Houston had a long list of needs when it came to Cougars football, beginning with a head coach. Briles knew he was the right man for the job. He had Houston ties, having played there in the 1970s. He had support from many alums and other local figures, such as former coach Bill Yeoman. More than anything, though, Art had the passion to take over a struggling program and accept a job no one else wanted.

Soon after Texas Tech finished up the 2002 regular season, Briles threw his hat in the ring for the vacancy in Houston, which had just fired Dana Dimel after he went 8–26 over three years with a 0–11 campaign in 2001.

During his interview, held at the Four Seasons Hotel in downtown Houston, Art went to a meeting on the top floor where he sat in a room with about eight to 10 members of the search committee, including Yeoman. That's where he first met Ken Bailey, a quarterback for the Cougars in the late 1960s who later became one of the nation's most respected lawyers. More than just an influential voice in his hiring, Art considers Bailey a great friend to this day. The room also consisted of attorney John O'Quinn and Dave Maggard, the UH athletics director at the time.

After two hours of fielding questions on everything from philosophy and schemes to his family life, Art returned to Lubbock and continued his recruiting duties at Tech. About four days later, while working late in his office, he received Maggard's phone call telling him the job was his.

He accepted quickly—time already wasn't on his side with signing day fast approaching. He knew he could put together a quality staff, including two of his former coaches at Stephenville, Randy Clements and Phillip Montgomery, the latter having left to become offensive coordinator at Denton High School. Art also hired Alan Weddell, the former head coach at La Marque who faced Stephenville in both the 1993 and 1994 state title games. He would assist as the Cougars' linebackers coach and eventually move up to defensive coordinator. A few months after getting the position, Art would then bring on Colin Shillinglaw, the athletics trainer at Stephenville, to serve as director of football operations in Houston.

Things were moving fast, but that was the only speed to go. These were decisions that not only needed to be made, but were ones that Art had always dreamed of making on this level. How this job was perceived from the outside didn't matter.

"More people turned it down than applied," Art recalled about the position. "The ones who turned it down weren't even seriously considering it. When I got on campus, they were actually talking about dropping the program."

In 1998 Houston moved its football games from the Astrodome to its own Robertson Stadium, hoping to create more of a buzz with the students and faculty. But during that time, any gridiron talk around the city centered on the NFL. The Texans had jumped onto the scene and would play their inaugural season in 2002. And after a shocking win over the already hated Dallas Cowboys in the team's first game, Houston was a football town once again.

The problem was, all that excitement had nothing to do with the Cougars.

But none of that concerned Art. Turning around programs was something with which he was already familiar. He oversaw culture changes in Sweetwater and Hamlin, and definitely Stephenville, where the program hadn't seen a playoff game in 36 years when he took over in 1988. He left the school 12 years later with four state titles.

So not only was he unfazed about taking a less-attractive position, Art actually thrived on it. He believed in his style of coaching. He believed he could overcome long odds through hard work.

All he wanted was a chance.

"This is what I tell my players today: 'You never get a second chance to make a first impression,'" Art said. "I acted right, did right, didn't get in trouble while I was there [at Houston from 1974 to 1977]. Those people who knew me then when I was going to school there, all of a sudden were there making decisions."

Briles wasn't worried that he was one of the 10 lowest-paid coaches in Division I when he took the job, making about $250,000 annually. When it comes to money, he has always been a believer that results produce raises—at that job or another. Either way, if you succeed, you'll be rewarded.

Art and Jan flew back to Houston to officially accept the position on December 6, 2002. Art thought he would sign some paperwork and maybe, depending on the time of day, do an interview or two with the local TV stations. With that in mind, one of the last things he did in Lubbock was purchase a suit from a department store close to campus.

He actually arrived in Houston with mixed feelings. While excited about getting his first head coaching job at the collegiate level and returning to a familiar place where he once played, Briles also remembered Houston as a devastating time in his life. Not a day goes by that he doesn't remember losing his parents and aunt due to the tragic accident in 1976. When he thinks of his playing days with the Cougars, having those horrific memories surface is only natural.

When he got to the campus that first day, Art was still unaware of the schedule of events. He shook hands with Maggard and signed the necessary papers. From there, he was ushered into a room with supporters in Cougar Pride, a fundraising group of big-time donors who were given the first chance to meet and greet the new coach.

Afterward, he was told there would be a press conference with the media. Don't forget, Art was a head coach at Hamlin, Georgetown, and Stephenville, not exactly metropolitan hubs. And while Texas Tech is a Big 12 school, there weren't many media requests for the running backs coach.

"So I'm thinking I'm going to talk to maybe two or three sportswriters with caps on and a pencil behind their ears," he said.

But when he walked out of Maggard's second-floor office and peeked over the balcony down into the large meeting room, he was blown away.

He saw the Houston Cougars marching band, the cheerleaders, and many of the players, whom he had never met. Overall, there were more than 300 people crammed into the area, among them Art's favorite member of the student body, Jancy, who was sitting right near the front.

"I knew right then and there that this was the right thing and this was the right time," he said. "The people here were hungry to win and they were excited."

Not nearly as excited as the person they were waiting for.

★   ★   ★

Most coaches will tell you they'd be nothing without great players. Then again, at the college level, it's the head coach's top priority to go out and find those guys. Not just the best players, but the right players, the ones who fit the system, both in scheme and personality.

As an offensive-minded coach, Art's first order of business in recruiting was to get a quarterback.

By early December, most of the top prospects have either committed or have at least narrowed their choices down to two or three finalists. But there are always exceptions to the rule. Art and his staff were hoping Kevin Kolb would be that exception.

Kolb moved to Stephenville in 1999 and played on the varsity team as a freshman, backing up Kendal Briles before then taking over as a starter when Art and his family moved to Lubbock. He not only had the look of a quarterback, standing 6′2″ and pushing 200 pounds as a sophomore, more importantly, he had the strong arm to match. Kolb broke his collarbone just two games into his sophomore season, but when he returned as a junior, he lived up to the expectations, leading the Jackets into the playoffs two straight years and posting a 12–2 record as a senior.

While Coach Briles had been pushing hard to land Kolb in Lubbock, Tech had more interest in Phillip Daugherty, a passer from Bridgeport, who ironically was an offensive lineman with Kolb at Decatur High School before they both moved. Kolb still could've picked Tech but wasn't feeling the vibe. He was more excited about moving up to Stillwater, and he committed to Oklahoma State, where Mike Gundy was the offensive coordinator and still two years away from becoming the head man.

But the reunion of Coach Briles, Montgomery, and Clements in Houston was intriguing to Kolb. Throw that in with the chance to play as a freshman, and the opportunity was simply too hard to resist. Deciding to switch commitments from Oklahoma State to Houston was easy. Informing Gundy wasn't.

"He told me, 'These are high school coaches trying to play at the D-1 level,'" Kolb said. "He tried everything in the book. He was upset, and to his defense, he thought I was going to be a good player. So he was taking his shots pretty good, but I had to stick to my guns. With Coach Briles and his staff all going to Houston, there were just too many good things lined up to pass up."

While Art had to lure Kolb away from a Big 12 program, he didn't have to do much convincing to land the kid who would eventually become Kolb's go-to receiver. Donnie Avery had one scholarship offer heading into the 2003 signing day. Unless something changed dramatically, he was going to attend Arkansas State. Avery could definitely run, but that's basically the only thing college recruiters had seen him do. Therefore, most schools wanted him to play defensive back as a walk-on.

Avery was a star athlete at Hastings High School in Alief, a community that lies primarily within the city limits of Houston. As a receiver, he only caught two touchdowns as a senior, but one of them just so happened to occur in the brief moments Coach Briles was watching his tape.

On the film, Art saw Avery take a slant over the middle, split the defenders, and go 80 yards untouched, blazing past everyone to the end zone. "Offer him," Briles told wide receivers coach Jason Phillips. "Offer him. We've got to have this guy. He's different."

Some of the players Houston recruited, like Avery, came down to a simple hunch. In his second season with the Cougars, Art took a chance on a German-born tight end who weighed 245 pounds but spoke very little English. Now Sebastian Vollmer is a starting offensive tackle with the New England Patriots.

In 2004 they signed a kid from Fort Worth Dunbar High School named Phillip Hunt, who barely had any offers. After redshirting his first year, he was named to the Conference USA All-Freshman Team in 2005 and garnered first-team honors in both 2007 and 2008. He also earned the conference's Defensive Player of the Year award as a senior.

While some of the players may have been rather unfamiliar to the Houston coaching staff, there was one in particular who knew a thing or two about the coaches. Kendal Briles' first two seasons at Texas weren't exactly what he envisioned. After redshirting as a freshman, he battled injuries in 2002 and then had to fight for playing time, rotating in and out of the starting lineup. And when his nagging shoulder injury revisited again, requiring a third surgery, Kendal started thinking Austin might not be the best place for him.

His father getting the Houston job only heightened his thoughts about transferring. In fact, when he signed with Texas, Kendal had a verbal agreement with head coach Mack Brown that he could get out of his scholarship and join his dad if he so desired. While the arrangement was more of an afterthought before, now it was a reality.

Brown was hesitant about giving him a release, only because he didn't want to lose a good player. Then again, he remembered going into the Briles home during his recruiting visits and realizing how Art and Jan had little influence in Kendal's decision. So he wasn't about to do the same two years later.

After the Longhorns granted his official release, he was off to Houston to reunite with his family again. Kendal's initial plan was to play quarterback once again for his dad, and although he had to sit out the 2003 season as a transfer, he expected to compete with Kolb for the starting job heading into 2004.

And when Kolb first heard the news, he admitted there was an "Are you kidding me?" moment. Here he had stiff-armed Oklahoma State for Houston, and now he might have to sit behind the coach's son?

But that never materialized. Houston started to win earlier than anyone expected, and Kolb was one of the biggest reasons why.

★ ★ ★

In the days leading up to the 2003 season opener, a decision needed to be made regarding the starting quarterback. Talent-wise, Kolb was better in practice than sophomore Blade Bassler. He was even more consistent with his reads and accuracy. Alas, Kolb was also a freshman.

In his mind, Art knew all along Kolb would probably get the nod, but he waited until the Thursday before kickoff against Rice to name him as the starter. Now, this wasn't just any season opener; this was against their crosstown rivals in a game known as the Bayou Bucket Classic.

But Art thought Kolb was ready for the challenge. He had been a head coach before, albeit in high school. Kolb had been a starter before, also in high school. The time had come for both to step up together.

And against Rice, the Cougars were dominant, thanks to their new quarterback, who resembled anything but a freshman. Kolb torched the Owls, completing 17 of his 22 passes for 246 yards and no interceptions. He threw two scores and ran for two more in a 48–14 rout at Robertson Stadium.

What a way for Houston to start. In the past, the team had not only struggled to win games but did so with a rather boring offense. In the debut of the Briles era, the Cougars came out with a spread-out attack featuring a quarterback who just might be the real deal.

But the excitement of the 1–0 record crashed in a hurry the next week. Houston made a trip to "the Big House" at Michigan and found out right away how much work was still to be done. A 50–3 defeat at the hands of the Wolverines was a major setback, but obviously didn't deter the Cougars in any way. After the loss, the team reeled off four straight wins, including a 42–35 victory over Mississippi State, coached by Jackie Sherrill. Kolb was magnificent again, going 20-of-29 for 321 yards with four touchdowns and no picks.

One year removed from being 5–7, Houston was now 5–1. They weren't just thinking about any old bowl; they had their sights set on a premier postseason game.

While the campus was fired up beyond belief, Kolb took the success in stride. He really wasn't sure what the hype was all about. At Stephenville, being 5–1 meant the chance to go undefeated was already over. Sure, things were different in college, but he expected to win. And that stemmed from his head coach.

But 5–1 turned into 5–2, then 5–3, followed by 5–4 after three straight home losses to Memphis, Texas Christian, and Southern Mississippi. Three weeks earlier, the Cougars envisioned a possible New Year's Day game, and now they were just fighting for that sixth win.

"I remember thinking how hard it really is to get bowl eligible at Houston," Art said. "But we kept fighting through it. We knew we just had to get over the hump."

The hump came in West Point, New York, during a road game against Army, where Bill Yeoman—often considered the "father of Houston football" after having coached the Cougars for 25 years—had been a former team captain as a center for the Cadets. Army welcomed back Yeoman, who still traveled to all away games as an honorary consultant, with several honorary events, including a celebratory breakfast that morning.

Once the game got started, Army grabbed an early 7–0 lead on a 60-yard touchdown pass. After that, Houston dominated both sides of the ball. The Cougars scored 34 straight points over the next three quarters before Coach Briles called off the dogs. He had the upmost appreciation for Army and he wasn't about to go into their house and run up the score. They only thing he ran was the ball, handing off 70 times as Houston held possession for more that 39 minutes of game clock.

They were respectful in beating Army, and so the excitement on the sideline about becoming bowl eligible was evident, but went to another level in the locker room, thanks to their head coach, who had a knack for stepping out of character when the moment was right.

With his players chanting, Art jumped up on a table, slung off his coach's shirt, showing just a white T-shirt underneath. In a move that would've made wrestler Hulk Hogan proud, he ripped his shirt down the middle, tearing it off to reveal a huge No. 6 painted in blue on his chest. In fact, he had painted on that 6 before each of the last three games, only to come up short every week. Briles would either shower in private or leave it on until he got home.

The locker room completely erupted. And not just because of the numerical, bowl-eligible reference. The cheers were also for a guy who preaches weight-room consistency. Seeing their coach with his shirt off for the first time was impressive to a bunch of 20-year-olds.

"He's pretty jacked," Kolb said. "He would work out with the kids, and they knew he was strong. But when he did that, everyone went crazy."

One of Houston's most recognizable alums is longtime CBS broadcaster Jim Nantz, who is well known for his calling of NFL and NCAA basketball tournament games, as well as golf coverage that includes the Masters. Despite a busy schedule, in 2003 he was fortunate enough to make the game at Army, where he watched from a club suite.

As he came out of the elevator, Nantz was stopped by a retired four-star general who appeared to be in his late seventies. Leaning on a cane, the man recognized Nantz in his red Houston attire.

"Let me tell you something. I've been coming to games here at Army for over a half-century. That's the classiest bunch of kids. And that coach is unbelievable. I can't tell you how well they treated our team. We know the score could've been a lot worse than 34–14."

Nantz has followed the Cougars closely over the years, but that moment sticks out more than any other in regards to the Art Briles era.

"It just made me really proud that we went up there and made an impression on an old Army general," Nantz said. "Houston was a group that had it together, led by this remarkable coach."

The Cougars finished the regular season at 7–5 and were headed to their first bowl game in seven years, accepting an invitation to the Sheraton Hawai'i Bowl. Nearly 12 months earlier, Art took a job that few people wanted. Now, he was taking his team to paradise.

★ ★ ★

Briles realized one of the reasons he was offered the Houston job in the first place stemmed from his ties to the school as a former player. So he made sure to embrace that as much as possible. One of the first calls he made was to Danny Davis, the quarterback of the Cougars in 1976 when they won the Southwest Conference title. Davis was now a prestigious pastor at Jordan Grove Missionary Baptist Church, located in Houston's Third Ward. Art reconnected with Davis, even attending a few sermons, and asked him to serve as the team chaplain.

"I told him, 'You handle the playing, I'll do the praying,'" Davis said.

In that first season, the pastor made every home contest and most of the road trips but knew if the Cougars earned a bowl appearance, breaking away from a Sunday service that close to Christmas would be difficult. Knowing how superstitious coaches can be, and Art was certainly no exception, Davis made sure to remind his friend several times during the season that he wouldn't be able to make the bowl game. But Art always told him he understood and even appreciated his concern.

The day the Cougars got the call to play the Hawai'i Bowl, Art phoned Davis one more time.

"Double D…. Hey, I know you can't go with us. We're going to miss you at the bowl game."

"I know, coach. I wish I could make it. You know, Christmas is a sacred time here at the church. But good luck to you. By the way, what bowl game are you going to?"

"We're going to Hawaii, Double D."

"Yeah, my church will understand! Count me in!"

With Davis in tow, upon arrival, Art recognized right away that this wasn't exactly a normal bowl setup. In fact, it was nothing short of a road game for the Cougars, having to face a University of Hawaii team that used its own dressing room and played in its home stadium.

"It was the first time I had ever been over there," Art said. "I didn't realize how strong the culture and pride was by the people living there. They're part of the U.S., but they also have their own traditions. I got to witness it first-hand. In the bowl games, it's usually 50-50 from the hosts as far as how they treat both teams. This was 100 to zero."

Despite being the visitors, the Cougars seemed to feel at home early, leading 10–0 in the first quarter and 20–10 in the second quarter. But led by June Jones, a former NFL head coach with the Falcons, Hawaii rallied back behind star quarterback Timmy Chang, who threw for 475 yards. The Warriors took control in the second half and appeared to have the game won before Kolb hit speedy receiver Vincent Marshall over the middle for an 81-yard touchdown to tie the game, 34–34, with 22 seconds remaining.

Had he known three overtimes were on the horizon, Art would've gone for the two-point conversion right then, a move he contemplated before kicking the extra point.

In the third overtime, Hawaii led 54–48 when Kolb's fourth-down pass to the end zone fell incomplete, the Cougars coming up short. But while the game might have come to a conclusion, the fireworks had barely begun.

On the final play, Kolb rolled to his right and threw the ball just before he got to the Warriors sideline. As the Hawaii team celebrated, many of them heckled the freshman quarterback, who realized he was largely outnumbered on that side of the field, and after four quarters and three overtimes, had little energy to do anything, anyway.

Surrounded by a handful of Hawaii players, Kolb was bailed out by Warriors defensive tackle Isaac Sopoaga. The two had met at a hospital visit earlier in the week as part of the pre-bowl festivities. But as Sopoaga grabbed Kolb to protect him, it didn't sit well with the Houston offensive linemen, who thought their quarterback was in trouble.

That's when things turned from ugly to nasty. In one of the worst on-field football fights in memory, helmets were swung as weapons, and players on the ground found themselves kicked and kneed in the head. Bloody lips and noses were plentiful as both teams slugged it out for nearly eight minutes before coaches and policemen could finally separate both sides.

Meanwhile, Kolb got bear-hugged by Maggard, who wasn't about to let his freshman quarterback mix it up in such a scary scene. Art recalls the incident as "total chaos" and still is amazed there weren't any serious injuries that came from the scuffle.

As Briles walked off the field, he was obviously disappointed in the score and embarrassed to be a part of such a dangerous scene. But what he already recognized about this bunch of kids was reiterated in those final frenzied minutes.

"I knew it beforehand...don't call us out because we'll show up," Art said. "We're never going to back down from any situation."

If the Cougars proved anything in Briles' first year with the team, they were certainly prepared to put up a fight.

24. Making Shasta Smile

"Live mild, play wild."

ART BRILES HASN'T met many one-liners he didn't like. If he has a trademark, it's his quick wit to come up with a catchy phrase or nickname—to personalize an individual or even the moment. During his initial press conference at Houston, Art told the welcoming crowd one of his goals was to "put a smile back on Shasta's face."

Shasta would be the school's official mascot, a menacing Cougar with an intimidating scowl that's honored with a campus statue and is portrayed in logos on T-shirts, bumper stickers, and other Houston memorabilia.

When Art made his comment in 2003, it was the 14th year in what turned out to be a 23-year absence of the real-life cougar. From 1947 to 1989, Shasta's lineage was passed down through five of the big cats. When Art was a student, from 1974 to 1977, he recalled seeing Shasta III as a visible symbol around campus. In 2012 the school brought back another real-life mascot, adopting a cougar cub, Shasta VI, who now resides at the Houston Zoo and appears via webcam during sporting events and various school functions.

Art's comment in this case was more generic. In fact, he didn't even realize the tradition of having a live cougar had gone away. But his point was well taken. He knew there wasn't a lot to smile about when it came to Houston football, and that was something he wanted to change. From the president of the university to the big-money donors to the diehard fans to, yes, the mascot that didn't even exist, his goal was to bring some excitement back to the campus.

In his first year, he was able to do just that, winning seven games and leading the Cougars to the Hawai'i Bowl.

But all the smiles after that 2003 campaign were turned upside down again in 2004. Everything the Cougars had done to change the culture the year before took a major hit the following season.

Kevin Kolb returned as a sophomore, and Kendal Briles was now eligible to play. While he initially transferred from Texas to possibly play quarterback, unseating Kolb wasn't going to happen. Kendal was better suited to be an inside receiver, and he went on to post 25 catches that season. He did occasionally line up behind center, although mostly to run.

The schedule was challenging to say the least, but then again, that was the plan. Houston's football program was not in great shape financially. The Cougars needed to play the "money games" such as Michigan in 2003 and Oklahoma in 2004. Those revenue-collecting matchups often give schools up to $1 million, a figure that's simply too much to pass up for a program like Houston, which contemplated dropping football just two seasons earlier.

But while it might be good for the school, a 63–13 loss to Oklahoma was tough to swallow for Art, the ultra-competitor who doesn't like to lose a game of spades, much less take a 50-point drubbing.

"You could tell that 2004 season was hard on him," Kolb said. "There would be days when we knew he hadn't slept a wink the night before."

But worse than losing to Oklahoma or Miami (Fla.) at home was the close defeats in conference play that Houston had found a way to win the previous season. The Cougars wound up going 3–8 in 2004, but Art wasn't discouraged.

"You could tell we were getting better," he recalled. "We had some tough losses that year, but I thought we were still able to compete. We went 1–6 and then won two straight, so we never stopped fighting. We left that season thinking we were still going in the right direction because we had some really talented players."

One of those was Donnie Avery, a redshirt freshman in 2004 who possessed big-time speed but was still raw as receiver, having come from a high school program that rarely threw the ball. He finished with just 18 catches, which turned out to be the lowest in his four-year career. And while the Cougars' three-win campaign was hardly memorable, Avery considers a three-day span during that season a period he'll never forget.

Knowing Avery was about to become a father, Briles excused him from Friday meetings at the team hotel the night before Houston played host to East Carolina. Avery's daughter, Dionna, was born in the early hours Saturday morning before the afternoon kickoff.

Filled with adrenaline and excitement but lacking sleep, Avery joined his teammates at the stadium and was quickly met in the locker room by his head coach.

"D.A., this is going to be special for you," Briles said. "We're going to make sure you remember this day, and this game."

Avery recalled Coach Briles doing everything in his power to get the ball in his hands. The receiver hauled in two passes for 58 yards, including a 48-yard bomb that set up a touchdown, and had a few more thrown in his direction, although he wasn't able to capitalize on them with a catch. Still, the gesture by his head coach, whose team had won only twice all year, to make sure a redshirt freshman had a memorable game on the same day his daughter was born is something Avery will always cherish. The Cougars came out on top 34–24, to improve to 3–6, but wouldn't earn another victory that season.

In the spring of 2005, Avery was overwhelmed with trying to play football, help raise a newborn, and go to class—in that order. So by the end of that semester, he learned his grades were too low to remain eligible for the next season. His scholarship would be revoked unless he retook a few courses during the summer. With the baby, taking "extra" courses wasn't on his agenda. While he was coming off a promising year, thoughts of giving up on football and school altogether seemed to be the easy route.

Avery entered Briles' office one morning and told him of his plans to quit. Being a dad and a student was too difficult for this football player, so he was prepared to walk away. He just wanted to tell his coach first.

Art wasn't about to let that happen. "D.A., don't be a quitter," he said. "I promise you'll regret this later in life. Hang in there. I'll help you. But do it for your daughter so you can show her an example of what you went through. Whatever you need, I'll be here for you."

Right then and there, Avery became an adult, one who could face his problems head on and lean on others when help was needed. After going to summer school and making his grades, he went on to play three more years as one of the best receivers in school history. (Avery was the first receiver taken in the 2008 NFL Draft, selected by the St. Louis Rams with the 33rd overall pick.)

Avery certainly wasn't the first or last player whose course of life was changed by just a simple conversation with Coach Briles. Teaching kids to be great players on the field was only the half the battle. Preparing them to be men was another.

★ ★ ★

If the 2005 season could be summed up with a two-word phrase, it would be one that Art Briles repeatedly said to his offensive players throughout the 12-game schedule: ever-changing.

He told his team all season long that they wouldn't be doing the same things over and over. If they were pass-happy one week against Tulane, they might then run the ball 56 times to shake off Memphis. If they threw two deep passes during the entire game at UTEP, they might throw two on the first two plays of the next week's matchup in Tulsa.

Briles knew all about tendencies. He knew most college staffs have quality-control coaches who chart nothing but trends—what a team typically runs on third-and-long or how many times they run to the short-side of the field on first down. Well, Art didn't want anything to do with that.

For the scouting report on his team he wanted: there is no scouting report. He needed his offense to be ever-changing. And in 2005 the Cougars managed to sneak into another bowl game with a 6–5 record, thanks to a 35–18 win over Rice in the regular season finale. Houston was also the only Conference USA team that year to defeat a member of the powerhouse Southeastern Conference when they took down Mississippi State 28–16 in Starkville.

Overall, the season could've actually been much better, but the Cougars were too often tripped up late in games, including a 44–41 overtime loss to UTEP and a 31–29 defeat by Central Florida in Orlando.

One of the craziest moments of Briles' coaching career occurred early in the 2005 season. Hurricane Rita was one of the more damaging natural disasters to ever hit the Texas Gulf Coast. On Thursday, September 22, the storm forced millions to evacuate Houston, creating memorable images of cars trying to exit the city. Coach Briles and the university made the decision to have the team stay in Houston and wait for a flight that could get them out of town. That Saturday's scheduled home contest against Southern Mississippi was canceled, but the Cougars were already thinking about how they would get to Tulsa, the site of their next game in nine days. Unfortunately, their thoughts of acquiring a charter flight hit several snags.

Meanwhile, by mid-afternoon, panic was starting to creep in. Some players were fleeing the scene like the rest of the city. Others decided to stay, which didn't sit well with a few parents. One father even called the campus police to report that his son was being held hostage. When the officer arrived on the scene, he was informed the players simply had no choice but to stick it out.

The plan shifted instead to traveling by bus to Tulsa, but Briles soon realized that couldn't happen until Friday morning. So unlike the majority of the 2.1 million who called Houston home, the Cougars football team remained in the city. The entire group spent the night at the field house, with players sleeping on training tables, the locker room floor, or anywhere else they could find a spot. With food scarce, the campus police tried to help, offering candy bars and snacks, but needless to say, there were some hungry young men.

"We called it the last night on earth," Briles said. "It was one night you'll never forget. Houston was a ghost town, but we had no way of getting out."

Fortunately, the Cougars eventually found busses from Tulsa to pick them up that next morning. Once the team finally arrived in Tulsa that Friday evening after a 14-hour journey, the players were then crammed into a hotel for eight full days before the next game.

Despite the less-than-ideal situation, the Cougars rallied and took out a week's worth of frustrations by beating the aptly named Hurricanes 30–23. Flying to Houston afterward, there was no doubt the team was now returning home more united than when it left.

But more than any win, what started to differentiate the Cougars from the average collegiate offense was their weekly game plan.

"Anyone can say what they want to say, but we were the first ones to run that zone-option or throw the bubble to inside receivers," said Kolb. "The two-by-two formation…we were doing that, that year. That stuff all evolved that season. Now you see everyone doing it."

Just like he had learned as a head coach in Hamlin, Texas, 20 years earlier, Coach Briles wanted to use every inch of the field. The wider the offense, the thinner the defense, which would create more room to exploit mismatches. One who perhaps benefited the most was Kendal, who finished as the Cougars' second-leading receiver with 45 catches in 2005, becoming a true possession guy while averaging 8.2 yards a reception.

With that kind of innovative thinking, the Cougars were going bowling again, facing Kansas in the Fort Worth Bowl. Unfortunately, Briles' potent offense struggled against a Big 12 foe that outmuscled the team for a 42–13 win, evening Houston's final record at 6–6.

The loss proved to be the last game for Kendal, whose collegiate career obviously didn't turn out the way he had planned. He won two state championship rings as a sophomore and junior and also earned two Class 4A Player of the Year awards at two different schools. But college was a different story.

Having undergone two shoulder surgeries, not to mention changing schools and positions, Kendal was tired, beat up, and mentally exhausted by the end of the 2005 season. He had given everything he could to a sport that had been good to him. And truth be told, Kendal was pretty good for the sport, too.

★ ★ ★

By now, Briles' oldest daughter, Jancy, had graduated from Houston with a communications degree, having switched majors from pharmacy school. The year before marked the first and only time all three of Art and Jan's children were at the same school, as Kendal had transferred from Texas and Staley was a freshman after graduating Frenship High in only three years to avoid having to change schools yet again as the family settled in Houston.

Jancy, meanwhile, landed internships with the Houston Texans and Fox Sports Southwest, experience that led to a paid internship as a public relations assistant with the Dallas Cowboys for the 2005 season.

During a break in preparations for the Fort Worth Bowl, Art made his way to the Cowboys' headquarters in Valley Ranch to have lunch with Jancy. He also got a chance to sneak out to practice as the team was trying to make a run to the NFL playoffs. That's where he caught the eye of then–head coach Bill Parcells, who had an old-school fear about football spies. Any person on the sideline with whom he wasn't familiar caught his attention, and the head coach at Houston was no different.

He motioned Art over to speak with him and quickly realized not only what team he coached, but whose father he was. Parcells, who had three daughters of his own, took an immediate liking to Jancy, and the two have remained friends long after he retired. Parcells admired the relationship Jancy had with her dad, considering the time restraints coaches have with their families.

Kevin Kolb (below, with Art Briles) won the
2006 Conference USA Offensive MVP.
Texas Tech's Wes Welker (right) was one of Art's
first recruits in Lubbock. Houston's Donnie Avery
(bottom) was the first wide receiver taken in the
2008 NFL Draft (St. Louis Rams).

At Houston, Art Briles (left) led the Cougars to four bowl games in his five seasons, along with a 2006 Conference USA Championship win over Southern Miss. On Senior Day in 2005 (below), Kendal played his final collegiate game and handed out roses to his sisters Staley (left) and Jancy (middle) and mother Jan. The family poses for a postgame photo against crosstown rival Rice. The Cougars won 35–18 to improve to 6–5 and become bowl-eligible.

*(Clockwise from top left)
Branndon Stewart led
Stephenville to a 1993 state
title; Kelan Luker had a record-
setting year in 1998; RGIII
won Baylor's first Heisman;
Nick Florence broke Griffin's
Baylor passing record in 2012;
and Case Keenum is currently
the NCAA's all-time leader in
yards, completions, and TDs.*

Art Briles (above) is introduced as Baylor's 25th head football coach in a press conference held on November 28, 2007. Baylor's first three first-round picks under Art Briles (below, from left): Jason Smith (No. 2 overall), Danny Watkins (No. 23), and Phil Taylor (No. 21). In 2012 Robert Griffin III and Kendall Wright (not pictured) were also first-round picks.

Terrance Williams (above), a third-round pick of the Cowboys in 2013, breaks away against Texas in a 30–22 win in 2010. Baylor's first win in Austin in 19 years ignited quite a locker-room celebration with Art and his joyous players (below).

(Clockwise from top left) Art Briles and former high school foe/ then–Chicago Bears head coach Lovie Smith share a laugh as they take in Baylor pro day workouts in 2012 in Waco; Art and Bob Simpson; Art and singer/ songwriter Amos Lee; Art gets a celebratory bath after his first bowl win—a 67–56 win over Washington in the 2011 Alamo Bowl.

Terrance Ganaway (above left) is the only player to suit up for Art at both Houston and Baylor. Kendall Wright (above right) breaks free in a 45–38 win over Oklahoma in 2011. Waco-product Ahmad Dixon (below left) is one of Baylor's highest-rated recruits. After his sixth year at Baylor, Kaz Kazadi (below right) was named the 2012 Samson Equipment Strength and Conditioning Coach of the Year.

Art and RGIII (above left), now the QB for the Redskins, talk prior to his game against the Cowboys in D.C.; the Briles clan (above right) in May 2013 (from left): Staley, Jeff Lebby, Jancy, Kendal, one-year-old Kinley, Jan and Art, Sarah Briles (kneeling) with Jaytn. (Below) Big wins have become the norm in Waco, suggesting Baylor football is indeed, looking up.

Once during a media-filled press conference at the Cowboys' facility, Jancy accidentally unplugged a cord used by a local radio engineer, who was feeding the audio back to his station on a live feed. Frantically, the engineer started yelling at Jancy, causing awkward and unexpected tension. That's when Parcells gave a steely glare at the board-op and told him and everyone around his thoughts on Miss Jancy.

"See this girl here?" Parcells said, pointing to the now-red-faced intern. "She can do no wrong!"

The young girl who grew up shaking her Folgers Coffee can filled with nails, who made the high school cheerleading squad but admittedly turned her back to the crowd and missed routine fourth-quarter cheers because she was too busy shouting instructions, and who would leave college every weekend to see her dad coach and her brother play, was fitting in nicely with America's Team. And she had become a favorite of a future Hall of Fame coach.

★ ★ ★

By the time Kolb reached his senior year, he was more than just on the same page with Coach Briles and the Houston staff, although you couldn't say he knew the playbook inside and out—only because there was no playbook.

Art doesn't have a folder somewhere that has a list of plays. He doesn't have a notebook that the team takes home to study. The coaches have grids to pass out to the quarterbacks but for the most part, the offense is learned through repetition in practice. Art believes players learn better through visual aid and watching tape, rather than reading and memorizing formations and calls.

At Stephenville, Art never had a quarterback start more than two years, so it was a big deal for Kolb to enter his fourth consecutive season as a starter. And right away, he looked every bit the part, helping Houston cruise to 4–0.

The fourth of those wins was definitely the sweetest for Kolb, who spurned Oklahoma State to sign with the Cougars and had to listen to Mike Gundy take shots at Coach Briles and his inexperienced staff. Gundy was offensive coordinator at the time under Les Miles, who had to read about Kolb's change of heart in the newspaper because Gundy said he couldn't break the bad news in person. When Miles went to LSU in 2005, Gundy became head coach, which even further enhanced the drama for this showdown.

To beat Oklahoma State 34–25 in Houston was satisfying enough for Kolb, but to have a near-flawless day was even better. He threw for 313 yards with no picks and four touchdowns, including a scoring toss to receiver Biren Ealy in the fourth quarter to seal the win.

While there were plenty of stories regarding Kolb and Gundy, the quarterback's own head coach praised him during the on-field postgame TV interview: "Kevin brings a lot of courage, a lot of intelligence, and a lot of guts. Those are certainly three characteristics you want in a guy, and he's got them all."

Kolb was suddenly on the radar for the Heisman Trophy, but that ended with three straight losses by a combined eight points. A 14–13 heartbreaker at Miami (Fla.) was followed by a 31–28 defeat by Louisiana-Lafayette and a 31–27 setback against Conference USA rival Southern Mississippi.

After that road loss to the Eagles, Art saw a group of frustrated young men. Three weeks ago, they were 4–0, and now the wheels were coming off at 4–3. Always staying positive, Coach Briles told them to keep their heads up and offered up a poignant message: "If you guys stay focused and keep working hard, we'll be all right. If we take care of ourselves, we'll see them again."

He was referring to the Conference USA Championship Game.

Inspired by their coach's vote of confidence, the Cougars reeled off three straight victories to improve to 7–3 heading into an all-important clash with Southern Methodist in Dallas. At 5–1 in conference play, Houston needed one win to clinch a spot in the C-USA title game for the first time in school history.

But winning in Dallas wouldn't be easy. Playing at the relatively new Gerald J. Ford Stadium, which opened in 2000, Houston found itself down 27–23 to the Mustangs and facing third-and-21 from its own 5-yard line midway through the fourth quarter. That's when Kolb hit Avery for a 28-yard gain to extend the drive, the Cougars eventually crossing the goal line on the quarterback's two-yard touchdown run with 6:52 to play, giving Houston a 31–27 lead. After a turnover and a 61-yard score by Jackie Battle, the Cougars were going to the championship.

As the final seconds ticked off, Kolb and Briles shared a moment on the sideline that seemed bigger than football. The quarterback put his arm around the head coach and offered some sarcasm: "What did you expect, coach? Of course, we'd go 94 and win this."

But Art wasn't ready to celebrate just yet. "This is different, 'Kabo,'" as he pointed toward the crowd. And that's when it hit the senior quarterback, who knew some of Briles' story about his parents, but certainly not from having had a conversation with the coach. To his knowledge, it was a topic no one talked about.

That didn't mean it wasn't on Art's mind. With Houston playing at SMU in 2006—30 years since the tragic October 16, 1976, game when Houston defeated the Mustangs at the Cotton Bowl—the memory of his parents being tragically killed en route to the stadium was surfacing.

His quarterback understood. He hugged him, told him he loved him, and patted him on the butt. Coach Briles wiped away a forming tear, regrouped his thoughts, and carried on. His team was headed to a championship.

The two individuals he was thinking about the most would've been so proud.

★   ★   ★

Just as Coach Briles predicted, his Cougars would see Southern Miss again in the Conference USA Championship Game. Because Houston owned a better overall conference mark at 7–1, the Cougars hosted the showdown at Robertson Stadium.

Seeking its first conference championship in 10 years, Houston played in front of a packed house of more than 30,000 fans and needed the support of every one of them to rally in the third quarter. Never considered the fleetest of foot, Kolb gave the Cougars a 20–17 lead on a 46-yard touchdown run. A pair of scoring passes from Kolb to Ealy then put the game away, earning Houston a title they hadn't heard around campus in a decade: champions.

At the trophy presentation after the game, both Kolb and Briles went to the podium on the field. The quarterback was named Offensive MVP, while the coach was there to accept the conference trophy. Once both awards were given out, Art turned and looked right into Kolb's eyes: "We earned this one, brother!"

Those eyes of Kolb's quickly moistened as the emotions simply caught up with him. Kolb went to Houston because he believed in his coach. And that coach believed Kolb was good enough to get the job done. They did it their way and they did it together.

And together, they racked in some hardware, too. Kolb was named consensus C-USA Offensive Player of the Year, ending his career ranked third in NCAA history for total offense and fourth in passing yards. Briles earned Sportexe Division I-A National Coach of the Year honors and was named 2006 Conference USA Coach of the Year.

Riding a six-game winning streak, Houston advanced to the Liberty Bowl in Memphis, where Art would square off against "the old ball coach" Steve Spurrier, who was in his second season at South Carolina. He had won a national championship 10 years earlier at Florida and had a brief stint in the NFL with the Washington Redskins. As the creator of an offense often described as "Fun & Gun," Spurrier was in the process of turning around the Gamecocks program.

Fireworks were expected, and neither offense disappointed as Houston led 28–27 at the half. Making his 50th and final start for the Cougars, Kolb threw for three touchdowns and 386 yards, including 201 to wide receiver Vincent Marshall.

But in the end, South Carolina continued to score, as well, and survived a wild 44–36 win over Houston. Alan Weddell, the defensive coordinator who seemingly had few answers for Spurrier's offense, recalled his disappointment entering the locker room afterward. He felt partially responsible for his team's heartache.

But his head coach did what he always did and fell on the sword. Art told the players and coaches the loss was his fault. He said the offense didn't score enough points and as the play-caller and offensive coordinator, the finger should be pointed right back at him.

"I remember thinking we should've won this game," Weddell said. "We just needed more stops. But Coach Briles is up there saying, 'The offense didn't get it done.' I'm just thinking to myself, 'Coach, we gave up 44 points. I think the defense let us down.' But that's just who he was. He never blamed anyone. It just shows his humility."

★   ★   ★

Before the 2007 season opener at the University of Oregon, the mood was festive and light on the team charter. Houston had turned things around with three bowl appearances in four years, and Art was feeling confident about the direction of the program.

During the flight, he saw a true freshman tailback walking down the aisle. Always one to give some encouragement, the coach stopped young Terrance Ganaway, an 18-year-old from DeKalb, Texas.

"Hey, DeKalb, are you ready for this?

"Yes, sir," the young freshman replied.

"Well, good. You're going to play. And you're going to score the first touchdown of the season tomorrow, so be ready."

Houston didn't win the game, losing 48–27 to the sleek Ducks, but true to form, Coach Briles was spot on with his prediction. Anthony Alridge ripped off a long run to the 1-yard line before Ganaway finished the job on the next play to get the Cougars on the board.

Ganaway was the power back, while the explosiveness came from teammate Anthony Alridge, who was aptly named "Quick 6" for his home run–hitting speed.

With Kolb gone to the NFL in 2007, the Cougars balanced a pair of quarterbacks in Case Keenum and Blake Joseph, often rotating them in between series. Keenum actually lived down the street from the Briles family in Stephenville when his father, Steve, coached at Tarleton State.

Facing Alabama and first-year head coach Nick Saban in its fifth game of the season, Houston was knocking at the door in the final seconds before Keenum threw an interception in a 30–24 loss to the Crimson Tide. The next week against Rice, Joseph got the nod, and the Cougars came out blazing as Avery set a school record with 205 receiving yards in the first quarter. Joseph passed for 318 yards and three touchdowns with one interception in the first half...only to get benched for the second.

Art was frustrated with a fumble just before halftime that prevented the Cougars from taking a lead, so he went with Keenum after the break. While his numbers weren't as gaudy—15-of-18 for 156 yards with an interception—he did run for a score early in the fourth to begin Houston's comeback from a 48–35 deficit. More than anything, Keenum knew how to distribute the ball, as the Cougars became the first team in NCAA history to have a 300-yard receiver and 200-yard rusher in the same game. Avery caught 13 passes for 346 receiving yards and two scores while Alridge rushed for 205 yards and four touchdowns.

The Cougars outlasted Rice in the end, winning 56–48 to pull Houston to a 3–3 mark. Winning the Bayou Bucket ignited the Coogs to four straight wins, setting up a chance to play for another C-USA title. But a tough loss at Tulsa the next week ended those hopes, although Houston still had another bowl trip in its sights.

The question buzzing around campus, though, was if Briles would be on the sideline to coach it.

After wins over Marshall and Texas Southern, Art's name was being mentioned yet again for other coaching vacancies. The year before he interviewed for the Iowa State position, although he was passed over for Gene Chizik, who would go on to win a national championship with Auburn in 2010.

While Art was getting high praise from the fans, media, and boosters, his relationship with athletics director Dave Maggard was starting to sour, and he wasn't sure why. Art had dealt with superintendents, principals, and even head coaches while he was an assistant and never had any major problems with his superiors. Despite seeing his salary more than tripling and reaching nearly $900,000 by 2007, Houston's head coach and AD weren't always on the same page.

"It deteriorated," Art said of his relationship with Maggard. "His people skills and the way he handled personnel—not just me, but my coaches and some of our student-athletes—differed from some of my beliefs. But I'll always be indebted to him for giving me an opportunity. That's all I ever wanted, and he gave me that chance."

Many of those close to the football program believe the differences between the two stem from Briles' interview with the Cyclones, or perhaps his reported interest in the Minnesota job before the 2006 season. While Art played for the Cougars and was considered a "Houston guy" around town, he's always been a competitor first. Conference USA had exciting football, no doubt, but just couldn't compare nationally to the likes of the Big 12, SEC, Big Ten, and others. He knew it was time to start seriously entertaining other offers.

He was happy in Houston. His family was happy there, as well. But he knew there was a bigger stage out there with his name on it.

25. Baylor Nation

"You change attitude, but you can't change ability."

IN NOVEMBER 2007 Baylor athletics director Ian McCaw had never met Art Briles. The name was familiar, but he admittedly knew little about the head football coach at the University of Houston.

Although their first encounter was a lengthy sit-down meeting, it only took five minutes for McCaw to realize he was talking to the next head football coach at Baylor.

The Bears had just wrapped up another 3–9 campaign and for the 13th straight season were not eligible for a bowl. With Guy Morriss having just resigned, ending a disappointing five-year tenure in Waco, Baylor was once again in need of a new coach.

Fifteen years had passed since the legendary Grant Teaff retired as the Bears head coach following the 1992 season. He was the greatest Baylor had ever known, roaming the sideline in Waco for 21 years, which earned him a bronze statue just outside of Floyd Casey Stadium.

Since Teaff's departure, Baylor had been unsuccessful in its attempts to replace him. Chuck Reedy, Dave Roberts, Kevin Steele, and now Morriss had all failed to lead the program back to being respectable or even competitive, much less successful.

So now the Bears were at it again, and this time they wanted to make a splash. The boosters and alums knew exactly who they wanted. To them, there was only one man for the job: Mike Singletary.

The former Baylor All-American and 10-time Pro Bowl linebacker of the Chicago Bears had been in San Francisco, serving as the 49ers linebackers coach and assistant head coach. The alums just knew Singletary would be a great fit. He wasn't just a Baylor guy. He also had a hard-nosed, workman-like mentality that earned him the nickname "Iron Mike" during his stellar playing career. And if that wasn't enough, Singletary's son, Matt, had just finished up his freshman season on the Baylor football squad.

McCaw admits he wasn't sure from the beginning if Singletary was the right fit for the school, but the pressure to at least speak to the NFL great was overwhelming. So McCaw flew to San Francisco in late November for a quick interview, although soon enough both sides realized this wasn't the best option for either party.

"After meeting with Mike, it just seemed like he was on the NFL track and really wasn't what we were looking for," McCaw said.

Singletary remained with San Francisco and eventually became interim head coach of the 49ers later in the 2008 season before the position became full-time the next year. He was let go with one game left in the 2010 schedule and is currently the linebackers coach for the Minnesota Vikings.

After Singletary's interview, McCaw then turned his attention back to the search, which at the time was being run by Eastman & Beaudine, a firm based in Plano, Texas, that helps find candidates for high-profile openings in the sports and entertainment industries. Led by Bob Beaudine, the consultants came up with a short list of possibilities.

What McCaw and Beaudine immediately found was their research had something in common. "The one name, in his homework and my homework, that kept rising to the top was Art Briles," McCaw said. "I hadn't met Art before, nor had Bob, but we kept hearing glowing things. They kept saying he'd be a great coach at Baylor and a great fit at Baylor."

Those recommendations were coming from Big 12 coaches and administrators, as well as Teaff, who continues to stay close to Baylor athletics and has even served on a few search committees to fill certain prominent positions within the school.

After Houston's final regular season game in 2007 against Texas Southern, McCaw arranged a meeting with Art in Dallas on Monday, November 26. They spoke for three hours, which McCaw said felt like 15 minutes.

"He has a PhD in relationship skills," McCaw said of Briles. "He makes you feel very comfortable, and you feel like you've known him your whole life after a short period of time."

McCaw said they discussed coaching philosophy, recruiting, and putting a staff together, as well as everything else that goes into a normal interview. He knew Briles was the right leader for the Bears football program.

Of course, Baylor isn't for everyone. Sitting firmly in the Bible Belt, the proud Baptist school wouldn't work for many football coaches trying to climb the collegiate coaching ladder. High Christian values are a must. A squeaky clean past is also very favorable.

Briles had both, not to mention a history of turning around programs, something he'd done his entire life in stops at Sweetwater, Hamlin, Stephenville, and Houston. From Baylor's standpoint, this was the right man for the job.

And for Art, Baylor was also perfect for several reasons, first and foremost because of the opportunity to advance his career. "I always wanted to get into the Big 12," he said. "You have the chance to play against the best, coach against the best, and beat the best. It was such an attractive job because I grew up a Southwest Conference guy, and I viewed the Big 12 as an extension of the old SWC. I had coached in Texas all my life and had no plans to coach anywhere outside the state."

Two days after his appointment with McCaw, November 28, 2007, Art Briles was officially announced as the new head coach of the Baylor Bears in an evening press conference, wrapping up a wild day that saw him meet with his Houston players earlier in the afternoon.

The decision for Briles not to lead the Cougars against TCU in the Texas Bowl, played in Houston, was a mutual one between the coach and athletics director Dave Maggard. "I remember the guys being upset about him leaving," said running back Terrance Ganaway, who was a freshman at Houston in 2007, but later transferred to Baylor, where he played three seasons. "The guys were upset to lose him. He was a great coach for us. But when he talked about having to go and take care of his family, it's hard to be mad at that."

More than just a great opportunity to coach against better competition, the move to Baylor also meant financial gain. To show its commitment to Briles, Baylor gave the new coach a seven-year deal, which paid him about $1.4 million annually, a more than 50 percent increase over what his final salary was at Houston.

John McClain, a longtime sportswriter for the *Houston Chronicle*, followed Art's career with the Cougars, although he mainly covered the NFL. But McClain was also a Baylor alum, and so he remembers initially scratching his head when learning of Briles' move from a now-cushy Houston job to the one in Waco, which seemed to be a dead-end opportunity that would end in failure as it had for the three coaches before him.

Then again, McClain remembered thinking the exact same thing about Art's decision to come to Houston five years earlier when the Cougars were considering dropping the football program altogether. Briles accepted the job without hesitation and eventually took them to bowl games in four out of his five years with the school. Needless to say, when his longtime Baylor buddies called him up, McClain had nothing but glowing reviews for the new coach. To this day, McClain believes three of the smartest things Art ever did occurred in his opening press conference at Baylor, held in a suite at Floyd Casey Stadium.

For starters, he mentioned Teaff in the first two sentences of his introductory statement, paying him the necessary respect. He then pointed out Dave Campbell. The editor of *Dave Campbell's Texas Football*, as well as the Baylor alumni publication at the time, Briles made sure to recognize him and pose for pictures with him and Teaff afterward. He also mentioned Frank Fallon in his initial speech, remembering the longtime radio voice of the Bears.

"That was the hat trick right there," McClain recalled. "No other coach Baylor has ever hired either knew Fallon or was smart enough to look him up. But to shake hands with two of the biggest icons for Baylor and the state was a very smart move, and then to say that about Frank was great. I don't know if that was calculated or just the way Art is, but it was a genius move because it showed his respect for the position. It was a great start."

And Briles didn't just pay respect to those individuals. He also addressed the crowd on hand, which included boosters, members of the alumni association, current players, and a few fans.

"With people like you helping us, when those guys arrive on campus, and they see the support and the love, then we can make it happen. And we are going to make it happen. So let's get in this thing together. Let's not worry about what happened yesterday. Let's work today and make sure it's a great tomorrow for the Baylor Bears. Sic 'Em, Bears."

★ ★ ★

When a coach takes over a new position, he immediately has two very important jobs that must be done thoroughly, but also promptly if possible:

1. Formulate a coaching staff.
2. Tackle recruiting with full force.

These two responsibilities are connected because the assistant coaches need to reach out to the recruits—in this case, both the ones committed to Baylor, along with some of the players who were set to play for Art and his staff at Houston, including a certain quarterback from Copperas Cove.

Robert Griffin III was Art's prized recruit for the Cougars heading into the 2008 season. The dual-threat quarterback was an electrifying player and was one of the few whom Briles made a point to call himself after he moved to Baylor.

Griffin took a couple of days to rethink his options, but the fact Copperas Cove was only 70 minutes from Waco, and his parents actually wanted him to look closely at Baylor all along, made the decision easy. Still, the biggest reason wasn't proximity to his hometown. Griffin was committed to Briles first, not Houston.

Not long after Griffin made the switch, Art continued to call the house to speak to not only Robert, but also his parents, Robert Sr. and Jacqueline. Finally, Jacqueline was honest and told Art not to waste his time. "Don't worry about Robert," she said. "He's going to Baylor. Just worry about the other recruits and get him some help."

But before he could do that, his assistants had to be finalized. Luckily for Briles, he had a solid supporting cast around him at Houston. He knew if he ever took another job, he'd have certain coaches follow him. Sure enough, Randy Clements, Phillip Montgomery, and Colin Shillinglaw, all of whom had been with him in Stephenville, as well, joined the staff at Baylor.

Kendal Briles had already established himself in Houston as an assistant project manager at Perry Homes, one of the nation's largest home-building companies, which was owned by Art's good friend, Bob Perry. Kendal actually took a pay cut to join his dad's staff as an inside receivers coach at Baylor. His childhood friend, Jeff Lebby, the son of Art's good friend and coaching colleague, Mike, was also added as a graduate assistant.

While Art kept a few holdovers from the Bears staff, one of the most important additions he made was the hiring of Kaz Kazadi as the team's strength coach. The ultra-intense Kazadi, who had been an assistant strength coach for the 49ers, helped Briles change the culture at Baylor right away.

Hired when most of the student-athletes were away on Christmas Break, Kazadi worked long hours during the holidays to reorganize the weight room, which at the time was located at Floyd Casey Stadium. He wanted the players to return for the spring semester with a different attitude, mindset, and work ethic.

He arranged the weight room with different motivational signs hanging on the walls, along with more Baylor memorabilia. There was only so much he could do in a few weeks, but Kazadi wanted to show them things were going to be different.

"I wanted them coming in here ready to work," Kazadi said. "Coach Briles had a vision. He had a plan to get this turned around and knew it started here. I was excited about being a part of it. And we hit the ground running right away."

Briles named Brian Norwood as his defensive coordinator. Norwood spent just one year with him at Texas Tech in 2000, but the two immediately hit it off as good friends with similar personalities and lifestyles. Norwood's latest stop had been with Penn State, where he coached under Joe Paterno, and he was driving to a recruit's house in Texas when he heard on the radio that Briles got the job.

He was calling on a player from Celina, a powerhouse 3A school that was preparing for a big playoff game. Norwood was there to visit, but the focus for the youngster in question was on the Bobcats' upcoming regional matchup against Pittsburg. In fact, the recruit's family even watched tape of the upcoming opponent while he was there, both to get ready and to possibly show Norwood how serious football was in their household.

Norwood glanced up at the tape a few times, but the quarterback from Pittsburg was who he kept noticing. Even though he wasn't tall and wasn't a true pocket passer, he was making people miss left and right. Norwood never said anything, but in his mind, he kept wondering about this opposing player Celina was about to face. In the end, the Bobcats dominated Pittsburg on their way to another state title that year.

But a few weeks later, when he got the call from Briles to come down and run Baylor's defense, Norwood quickly mentioned the Pittsburg quarterback to his new boss, who responded quickly: "Oh you, mean Kendall Wright. Yeah, we're all over him. We're working on it."

Wright was recruited as an "athlete" for his blazing speed and ball instincts. Whether he played quarterback, receiver, tailback, or perhaps defensive back, Briles knew they wanted him. And they wanted him at Houston, too.

"I remember Coach Clements came up to my school every day wearing a red [Houston] shirt," Wright said. "Monday, Tuesday, Wednesday, and Thursday…red shirt. Then on Friday he's got a green shirt. That's when I knew they all went to Baylor."

Not long after that, Wright committed to play for the Bears.

Which was exactly what Mrs. Griffin wanted.

★   ★   ★

Inheriting a team that had won three games the previous season, suffering through eight straight losses to end the schedule, Art Briles knew he had many big tasks ahead of him. Talking a player out of leaving early for the NFL was not one he expected right away.

But that was the case for offensive tackle Jason Smith, a big-bodied, light-footed mammoth with a personality that lit up the room. Strong, gifted, motivated, and tough, after three seasons of watching Baylor win 12 games, he was frustrated.

Smith was about to be a senior, and everything he thought would happen at Baylor hadn't so far. He could count all of his Big 12 victories on his two gigantic hands. Now, with a new staff in place, the timing seemed right for him to head off to the pros, where he was expected to be a mid-round pick, possibly as high as the second.

Just as he did back when coaching high schoolers, Art knew the key to having a successful team starts in the trenches. Any offensive lineman with NFL ability was needed in a bad way at Baylor, and so if Smith was wavering at all in his decision, Art wanted to make sure he did his best to keep him.

So he started asking around about Smith, including the holdover coaches and trainers, and found out a few interesting details. Briles learned he was big into horses and ranching and even visited a friend's nearby spread nearly every weekend.

Knowing he would soon have to make his decision on whether to return to school or leave early, Smith timed it just right, finding Briles in the weight room working out. He wanted to hear more about this coach.

"I remember thinking, *I want him to tell me the truth, or I'm out of here*," Smith said.

They chatted for about 45 minutes as they ran side-by-side on treadmills. The conversation consisted of everything from the offensive scheme to family to players on the team.

Finally, Coach Briles put Smith's decision in simple terms for the offensive tackle: "Jason, if you leave right now, you'll be drafted. You're that good. Someone will take you in the middle rounds, and you'll make a team. But you're only going to make so much money. If you stay, I'll guarantee you this: there's a big difference between visiting the ranch and owning the ranch."

Smith's eyes got wide, and his ears perked up as the coach continued to analogize his way into the big lineman's heart: "You can either buy your grandma a car or a Cadillac."

Sold. Smith was all-in. He was blown away by Coach Briles' speech and the fact that he had obviously taken the time to know more about him. That was good enough for Smith, who to this day says Art was the difference-maker in his professional career.

"I compare it to a person out at sea. I just wanted off the boat. Just let me out. I'd rather just figure it out because I wanted no more part of losing," Smith said. "But when coach came along, he was my Coast Guard. He was the savior that came along and said, 'Take my hand, jump in my boat. I have a plan. Just grab this paddle, and we'll make it work. We'll keep paddling and won't worry about anything else.' And that's what we did. We went to work. We didn't worry about the draft. We just focused on the season and let everything take care of itself."

Smith anchored the Bears offensive line at the left tackle spot and was named an All-American. That next April, he was drafted No. 2 overall by the St. Louis Rams, signing a six-year, $33 million contract.

His first two major purchases? A Cadillac for his grandmother and a 1,000-acre horse ranch that he operates near Fairfield, Texas.

★ ★ ★

That initial Baylor press conference was the first opportunity for the Waco media to hear Art's dry humor and quick wit. A larger audience witnessed his personality for the first time at the Big 12 Media Days in Kansas City in late July 2008.

Dressed in a black mock turtleneck—long sleeved, of course—Briles had some fun with the reporters, throwing out a few one-liners and using his Texas drawl to emphasize a point here and there.

Covering media day is always a spectacle, and never easy for a writer who is used to hearing the same coach-speak that typically includes their tough upcoming schedule, the recruits the coach is excited about, and the usual optimism about the season, assuming the ball bounces their way. Reporters are always looking for a different angle, and Briles gave them one. Every media market planning to write a Baylor story seemingly ran with it.

In the middle of explaining his reasoning for taking the Bears job, Art recalled a family conversation he had, weighing the pros and cons of leaving Houston. He then shared what his oldest daughter, Jancy, had said in an attempt to play devil's advocate. "She said, 'Why would you do that, Daddy?' Nothing's gray with her. It's black or white. But there's a lot of gray in me."

Art wasn't talking about hair color. He could see through some of the reasons not to take the Baylor job. Then again, he saw past the obstacles that might have deterred him from taking over at Stephenville or Houston, whose programs were often described as "rock bottom" before his arrival.

That kind of talk was all relative for Art. Losing his parents that fateful day in 1976 at the age of 20 is his definition of rock bottom. Nothing else is comparable.

"That's what my journey in life has done to me," he said. "When you've been on the ground floor, you're not afraid to go back there. When you've survived what I survived on October 16, it's hard to be afraid of situations."

As for the reporters, they had their lead. Stories surfaced the next day in papers across the country with quips about Jancy's question. While they were all written differently, the message was the same: Is Art Briles crazy to take the Baylor job? His own daughter seems to think so.

The final sentence of one story published in the *Dallas Morning News* read: "And if it sounds impossible to turn around Baylor, get in line right behind Jancy."

Everyone felt the articles were all light-hearted fun—everyone except Jancy, who thousands of miles away in California started getting wind of the comments and the stories that were emerging. Now a full-time public relations assistant for the Dallas Cowboys, Jancy was on a bus from the airport to the training camp location in Oxnard, California, when she realized she was being portrayed as someone not on board with her dad's decision.

Mortified. Humiliated. Embarrassed. Demoralized. You name it. Jancy felt a wave of different emotions as tears rolled down her cheeks. The last way she ever wanted to be depicted was as someone unsupportive of her father, whom she has idolized since the time she could walk and talk.

But her parents have always treated her on their own level. The Briles make "family" decisions, and Jancy's opinion is not only asked, but valued. In this case, she was weighing the negatives and wanted them on the table just like everything else. Don't forget, she lived in Dallas now, so having her family 90 minutes from her house, as opposed to four hours away, was a big plus. But her role as the oldest child was to make sure all points were made. Once going to Baylor was clearly the right move, Jancy was just as excited as anyone, cutting out of work early on the day of the news conference to be there for her father.

Every story dies down over time, and this one was no exception. But even now, Jancy wishes those articles could be removed from newspapers' archives and online search engines. There were already enough people doubting her dad's decision to go to Baylor. In no way did she want anyone thinking she was, as well.

26. A Kid Named Robert

"You can't tackle what you can't touch."

IN FOUR YEARS at Baylor, Robert Griffin III ran 2,254 yards moving forward. However, it was the one yard he stepped back that put him on the map.

The new chapter of Baylor football opened with a Thursday night game in Waco against Wake Forest, televised on FSN. The Art Briles era was underway, and although it wasn't being publicized as much, the Robert Griffin era was about to begin, as well.

Griffin didn't even start the game, as Briles went with an experienced senior at quarterback, Kirby Freeman, who had transferred from Miami (Fla.). Freeman's father, Steve, coached under Art his first two years at Stephenville and eventually became the head coach at Brownwood High School. But that wasn't the reason why Freeman was behind center for the opener versus the Demon Deacons.

Art knew Griffin was good. He knew he was going to be great. But in the first game, with the world watching, he wanted a little more experience. He wanted to ease his freshman onto the big stage.

As it turned out, the entire Baylor squad had trouble getting into the flow that night. With an energetic crowd on hand to see their new coach and new team, the Bears couldn't use the momentum to their advantage. Wake Forest built a 17–0 lead that ballooned to 34–6 late in the third quarter, which sent many of the fans to the exits early, something Baylor folks were all too familiar with.

After the game, with Wake Forest claiming a 41–13 victory, Coach Briles was extremely dejected in his postgame press conference: "Certainly not the way we drew it up. The thing that's really painful for me and the staff is you want to give people a reason to believe. I feel like we let a lot of people down."

If there was one spark that came out of that disappointing debut, though, it was the play of Griffin. The freshman was far from perfect, but he had his moments of dazzle. In fact, who knew that game would provide one of the more memorable highlights of Griffin's career?

Shortly after being inserted into the lineup during the second quarter, Griffin took a designed quarterback sweep to the left side and turned upfield for what looked like a simple four-yard run, as a defender prepared to meet him at the sideline. But that's when Griffin's natural ability and uncanny instincts took over. The freshman hit the brakes and hopped backward a yard as a Wake Forest defensive tackle flew by him and into the Baylor bench. Griffin then put the gear back into drive and darted up the sideline for what turned into a 22-yard gain.

"Honestly, I didn't even know the guy was coming," Griffin said. "For some reason, something told me to stop, and I stopped, and then I took off. The whirlwind behind that play was unbelievable. The buzz turned into a lot of hype."

At the time, the run was an exciting effort for a Baylor team in need of a lift. Looking back, Griffin's move was the start of one of the most glorious careers in college football history.

Ahmad Dixon was considered a top recruit among Texas high school juniors, but despite living in Waco, he rarely went to Baylor games—"Unless," as he put it, "we wanted to see someone like a Vince Young at Texas." He was in the stands for Briles' first game, however, after he agreed to make a visit, thanks to the encouragement of defensive coordinator Brian Norwood, whose son Levi was a teammate of Dixon's at Waco Midway. Dixon hadn't been across town to see the Bears in four years. Even today, he is mesmerized by what he refers to as "the play."

"Everyone went deep and Robert takes off down the sideline. He was probably five yards away from where Coach Briles was standing. I see him stop, drop on a dime, and the whole stadium goes crazy. It was a play you would see in a video game."

For Dixon, who, when he committed two years later, wound up being the highest-ranked recruit ever signed by Baylor, the play was a convincing influence.

"Honestly, I didn't look at Baylor like that," Dixon said. "I didn't think they had players who could do things like that. When I saw that, I instantly changed my perception of Baylor and realized the type of guys Coach Briles was bringing in."

But highlight plays were nothing new for Griffin. As a high school senior, he was considered a top 100 recruit and was listed as the No. 3 dual-threat quarterback available. He led Copperas Cove to the Class 4A state championship game, only to lose to Lamar Consolidated, who was carried by future NFL tailback Jacquizz Rodgers.

When Briles and coaches Phillip Montgomery and Randy Clements raved about "this recruit we have coming over from Houston," many of the locals in Waco, holdover coaches, and even Baylor athletics director Ian McCaw were already well aware of who this Griffin kid was. He had played in district games against Waco teams, and Copperas Cove often had postseason matchups at Floyd Casey Stadium.

Before his junior year, Griffin attended Houston's summer football camp, and that's when his interest in Briles and the Cougars initially took hold. He was on the radar for just about every school, but not all of them saw him as a quarterback. Griffin was already one of the fastest high school kids in the state, and because of his speed, many colleges were recruiting him as a wide receiver or safety. A few wanted to see how he might develop as a quarterback.

Montgomery, Houston's quarterbacks coach, eventually became the go-to recruiter for Griffin, making routine visits to Copperas Cove, where he would meet up with Robert and his parents, Robert Sr. and Jacqueline, at a local restaurant. During the 2006–2007 season, Montgomery often ate with the Griffins more than he did his own family. But he said that initial camp was the turning point.

"I remember watching tape with him at that camp and his parents were with him," Montgomery said. "Just listening to him talk and watching him soak up all of the coaching he was getting, you knew he was different. And then he went out there and threw the ball, and it was a no-brainer to us. We knew other schools were looking at him as something else, but he was a quarterback from day one with us."

After only a few throws, Coach Briles pulled Robert aside for an important question.

"So how many camps are you planning on going to?" he asked.

"Not many, coach. I'm really not a big camp guy. I don't like going to a lot of these."

"Good. That's good. You don't need to go to any more."

Houston offered him a scholarship, and before too long, Griffin was committed to the Cougars. Or rather he was committed to Art Briles.

"From the very beginning, I just trusted him. I had a good feeling about him," Griffin said. "With other coaches, it's not that they're bad coaches. It just wasn't what you wanted. At Houston, I felt like I had a chance to start. Coach was real honest about that, about me being in the race to start at Houston."

When Briles made the move to Baylor in late November 2007, he didn't immediately phone Griffin. And during that time, the quarterback somewhat opened the door for other recruiters. He looked again at Stanford, Kansas, and Oregon.

Two days after the announcement, Briles called. "Robert, I'm sure you've heard by now I'm going to Baylor," he said. "I want you to come with me. I think you'll have a chance to play right away. It's closer to home for you. We're going to the Big 12, where the elite players are. And you're an elite player."

All of that sounded great to Robert, who was sold by the words "come with me."

★   ★   ★

National Signing Day is perhaps the most nerve-racking time of year for a college coach. The first Wednesday in February has now turned into a made-for-TV event with some of the big recruits announcing their choice of school during live press conferences. Even for the lesser-known players, holding a ceremony in the high school's auditorium in front of their peers is still a cherished moment.

Coaches sweat out each potential recruit until that fax comes through with the necessary signature. Until then, minds can always change. But there's a surefire way to avoid those nervous feelings about a star recruit—get him on campus a month earlier.

Art never worried about Griffin changing his mind because he was already enrolled at Baylor for the 2008 spring semester. As great an athlete as he was, Griffin might have been an even better student. He graduated with honors midway through his senior year of high school, which allowed him to get a head start on his three main goals: getting a college degree, winning the starting job at quarterback, and trying to qualify for the 2008 Summer Olympics.

For all the accolades Griffin earned on the gridiron in college, the first uniform he ever wore in live competition was Baylor's sprinter suit, running hurdles for the Bears that first spring. In 2007 Griffin was named the Gatorade Texas Track & Field Athlete of the Year after setting state records in the 110-meter hurdles (13.3) and the 300-meter hurdles (35.33), just missing what was then the national high school mark of 35.32.

As soon as spring football ended, where he finished practices as the No. 1 quarterback on the depth chart, he started turning heads in track. Griffin won the Big 12 gold medal in the 400-meter hurdles with the third-fastest time in school history, 49.22. Soon afterward, he won the NCAA Midwest Regional in the 400 hurdles with a meet-record of 49.53. And then in the NCAA Outdoor Championships, he placed third with a time of 49.55. Not bad for an 18-year-old who should have been going to his senior prom. Instead, he was outrunning 21- and 22-year-olds who had trained several years for these events.

Those times were good enough to qualify him for the U.S. Olympic Trials with a chance to compete in the 2008 Summer Games in Beijing. The trials were held in Eugene, Oregon, that June with thousands of onlookers in the stands. Among them were Art Briles and his entire family. They had been vacationing in Vancouver, but purposely timed the trip to come through Oregon and watch this quarterback of the future compete against the best track athletes in the world.

"It was awesome to see him. It was just a special moment," Griffin said. "I was an 18-year-old kid, getting ready to run in the Olympic trials against guys who are world record holders and have won gold medals and all that stuff. For him to come over and watch me do the thing that I love, it showed me a lot about him. That it wasn't just about the football or the track, it was about the person."

Griffin finished 11th, one spot short of making the finals.

"In track, you never know what's going to happen once you make the finals," Griffin said, "but it really wasn't meant to be. Who knows? Had I qualified for the Olympics, I might not have ever played football."

★ ★ ★

The step-back play against Wake Forest made the ESPN *SportsCenter* highlight reel that night, so officially Robert Griffin was on the scene.

He started the next week against Northwestern State in a 51–6 romp, but his true arrival occurred the following Friday against Pac-10 foe Washington State. Griffin set a Baylor single-game rushing record with 217 yards and scored twice as the Bears dominated the Cougars 45–17.

Baylor made it back to the national TV scene the next week at the University of Connecticut in another Friday night game, one in which Griffin endured some of the hardest collisions of his collegiate career.

"I can still feel one of those sideline hits today," he says.

The Bears lost 31–28, but Griffin and receiver Kendall Wright, a fellow freshman, gave Baylor fans and the entire nation something to be excited about. Overall, the entire 2008 season had its share of moral victories. For a team that won just three games the previous year and only had 15 wins in the last four, just being able to compete with Big 12 schools was a good start.

Baylor hung with Oklahoma for a while before the Sooners pulled away for a 49–17 win in their conference opener, with Art then earning his first Big 12 win against Iowa State, whipping the Cyclones 38–10 in Waco. One of Griffin's favorite collegiate memories occurred in that game when good friend Mikail Baker returned a kickoff for a touchdown, a play he knew was needed for Baker's confidence.

After the Iowa State victory, Baylor lost four straight, yet at the same time, the Bears were earning respect. The losing streak included a 32–20 loss to Nebraska in Lincoln and a 31–28 defeat by Missouri at home. Against Texas in Austin, Baylor was hanging tough late in the second quarter, 14–14, before the Longhorns exploded for a 45–21 rout.

That game was one of the first times Griffin realized just how competitive his head coach could be. The wheels were coming off in the second half as Texas had now built a three-score lead, and Griffin was extremely frustrated that he couldn't get the offense on track. Coach Briles grabbed his freshman quarterback by the helmet and ripped into him.

"What are you doing? Are you giving up?" he said.

"I'm not giving up, coach. I feel like I'm the only one out there fighting."

Even though Griffin was a freshman, Art viewed him as his star. And sometimes, even the star suffers the coach's wrath…just because.

"Constantly, throughout my college career, we would have little moments like that, but he'd come back the next day and say, 'You're right, but I had to show the team that I was going to challenge you,'" said Griffin. "And I understand, but in the moment, I'm not thinking that. He'd do that constantly. He'd do that in practice and in the games. So the team would see I'm not getting any free passes. It's funny to me that he could be dead wrong, but in that moment everyone thought he was right."

The signature win of 2008 came against Texas A&M, as Baylor rolled through the Aggies 41–21 on Senior Day. For a player like offensive tackle Jason Smith, who because of Coach Briles had decided to stick around for one more year with the Bears, the sendoff from Floyd Casey Stadium was perfect.

That left just one more game on the schedule. Lubbock will always hold a special place in Art's heart. That's where he got his life back on track after his parents' accident. He graduated from Texas Tech. The road to his first high school coaching job came through a connection there. His initial opportunity as a collegiate assistant came with the Red Raiders staff. Briles even married his wife, Jan, while still attending the school.

So no matter the records or circumstances, playing in Lubbock will always be special. And the 2008 finale certainly was, as Tech was 10–1 and fighting for a share of the Big 12 title. Baylor led 28–14 midway through the third and made what appeared to be a huge fourth-quarter stop to get the ball back. But the Bears were called for an offside penalty that kept the home team's drive alive, and the Red Raiders eventually scored, going on to rally for a 35–28 win.

The 2008 schedule ended with a 4–8 record, just one game ahead of the previous year's 3–9 mark. The difference between the two seasons, though, was tremendous. Baylor won two Big 12 games after going winless in conference play the year before. In 2007 conference opponents outscored them by a combined 244 points. In 2008 that margin dropped to only 58.

The biggest difference, of course, was the quarterback. Griffin was named a Freshman All-American by several media outlets and won the 2008 Freshman of the Year Award. He threw 15 touchdowns to just three interceptions and rushed for 843 yards with 13 more scores on the ground. Baylor had been desperately needing a steady hand at the position for several years. With Griffin, they now had a good one.

How good?

Coach Briles shared those thoughts with Griffin in his end-of-season exit interview: "If you keep doing what you're doing and keep working hard, you'll win the Heisman someday. We're going to get better players around you and start winning more games. And when we do that, there's no reason why you can't be a Heisman Trophy winner. You're that good."

Art Briles truly believed that. He made Robert Griffin believe it, too.

The rest of the world was soon to follow.

27. Fighting For Respect

"Great things only come with great effort."

WHEN ART BRILES first took the Baylor job, he knew he was finally playing with whom he termed "the big boys."

Now, not all the Big 12 schools are in college football's upper echelon. But each year, there are usually a handful ranked in the top 25, and more often than not, one or two competing for the national championship. Of course, nationally, the perception is that the conference contenders typically come down to only Oklahoma and Texas.

But the Sooners and Longhorns don't always finish 1-2 in the Big 12 standings. They've both had down years since Art Briles took over as head coach for the Bears. Still, those two are the biggest competition for programs like Baylor, both on the field from September to December, but also in February when the time comes to sign recruits.

Gaining respect—from anyone—wasn't easy at Baylor, but particularly from the described big boys. And during Briles' first year in Waco, he found himself in the middle of a pair of unique situations against each.

Days before the team's 2008 Big 12 opener against Oklahoma in Waco, Briles caught wind that the Sooners coaching staff had received faxes from Houston, detailing many of Baylor's favorite plays, schemes, and signals. The connection was simple. When Art left the Cougars, he was replaced by Kevin Sumlin, who had been an assistant at OU for head coach Bob Stoops.

The story might have different versions, but he found out his former secretary at Houston, Pam Wright, once a neighbor to the Briles family who oftentimes watched the kids in Stephenville, was instructed to send the faxes over to the Oklahoma offices before the game. Jeff Lebby, a graduate assistant with Baylor at the time, played at Oklahoma before back injuries forced him to hang up his cleats. He still had good friends on the team and within the coaching staff. So the news was bound to get back to Baylor as to what had happened, and it did on the Wednesday before the game. Thoughts of taking the issue to the media or even confronting Stoops or someone else at Oklahoma were discussed, but dismissed.

"It showed me the respect they had for us in our program at that time," Briles said. "I've never really worried about people knowing our signals and our calls. As fast as we play, you might have a good idea about what's going to happen, but it's happening before it has a chance to register. But really, it wasn't a negative thing. Honestly, I just thought, *All right, you boys want to play, let's play. There's two sides to that coin. And we're going to get ours eventually.*"

Later in that first season, the Bears found themselves in a struggle against Texas. Early in the game, freshmen Robert Griffin and Kendall Wright were hurting the Longhorns with big plays, but the more experienced team started to pull away in the second half.

The afternoon was hot in Austin. Emotions were heated, as well.

Late in the third quarter, after Texas had put up yet another touchdown to take a 42–14 lead, Griffin scrambled 63 yards to get Baylor back in scoring position. The Bears then appeared to cut into the deficit with a touchdown pass, but an illegal chop-block penalty wiped out the points—and somehow ignited a fiery exchange that shockingly involved no players.

The Bears went from scoring a touchdown to third-and-24 from the Texas 25. That's when Briles started noticing some hand gestures and movement from the Longhorns sideline. What he saw was a couple of assistant coaches mocking a referee's chop-block signal and pointing toward the Baylor bench. Not sure he was seeing this right, Art called on the headset to his fellow coaches, "Guys look over there. They're not pointing at me, are they? They better not be. Are they really talking to us? Surely, they're not!"

Sure enough, Art was seeing it right. The Texas sideline, including a few assistants who actually recruited Kendal Briles to play for the Longhorns just eight years earlier, didn't like the chop block on one of his defensive players and was getting upset. Art Briles didn't like the scoreboard and didn't like the insinuation that his team was playing dirty. So he didn't just get upset, he lost it.

Art was going crazy, his actions animated toward the Texas sideline. That's when Kendal grabbed him. The conversation looked and sounded like an assistant talking to the head coach. In reality, this was closer to a son talking to his father.

"Coach, you're on national TV," Kendal warned him.

"I know, but do you see what they're—"

"Coach…it's national TV. Be careful."

"You're right. Thank you."

But that didn't stop Art from going ballistic on the headsets. And all the while, he was trying to call plays as the Baylor offense kept losing yards with a sack and then a delay of game. "Why are they talking to me? See who that is over there? Who else is doing it?… By the way, let's run 'X Left 12 Lead Option.'"

Ultimately, Baylor was pushed back to a fourth-and-41 from the Texas 42-yard line. And Art went for it, throwing the ball to Wright, who gained just nine yards. Briles was in no mood to punt. His thoughts centered only on the fact that he was getting embarrassed on the scoreboard and disrespected by the opposite sideline.

Art knows that wasn't his most flattering moment. He likes to consider himself more reserved, even in the most intense situations. But the stage was different now, the national TV exposure constant, just like the pressure. Even though this was exactly where he wanted to be, he was still learning the ropes.

★ ★ ★

Jason Smith getting picked No. 2 overall in the 2008 NFL Draft was a big boost to the Baylor program. His departure, though, also left a big void in the offense. Baylor needed a new left tackle, and they found him in an unusual place: Butte College in Northern California.

But Danny Watkins coming to Baylor from a junior college is the normal part of this story. The fact he was a Canadian who had competed in hockey and rugby growing up, the fact he was already 24 years old when he arrived in Waco, and the fact he had more experience as a firefighter than a football player are all reasons that suggest Baylor was taking a huge risk by offering a scholarship to Watkins before the 2009 season.

However, Briles saw potential. He wasn't the only one, either, as Watkins had other offers, including from California, Hawaii, and Arkansas. He didn't have a lot of playing experience, but his 6'3", 310-pound frame, along with a brute strength and occasional mean streak, was ideal for an offensive lineman.

The first time he spoke with Briles, Watkins wasn't so sure going to Baylor would be a great fit. And the issue had nothing to do with football. "I talked to Coach Briles on the phone for about 30 minutes, and honestly, I don't think I understood half of what he said," Watkins said, referring to Art's southern accent. "And I'm not sure he understood me, either. We repeated each other a lot. From what I could tell, he was a nice guy. I was interested in Baylor. But I didn't know if they'd even understand me. They talk a lot different than Canadians."

Watkins had actually committed to Arkansas after his visit to Fayetteville, but still had another visit left, so he decided to take a "why not" trip to Waco. He first met with Lebby, the assistant offensive line coach at the time, and they hit it off tremendously. Both are big, burly guys with big smiles to match. That was an easy connection. After a few minutes with Lebby, Watkins then sat down with offensive line coach Randy Clements, and once again, they shared several laughs. The recruit from Canada was starting to feel comfortable with moving to Texas.

"And then I met Coach Briles," Watkins said, "and I was blown away. Right then and there I said, 'Get the papers, coach...where do I sign? I want to be a Baylor Bear.' He's the kind of guy I knew I would play hard for. It was a very easy decision for me."

Watkins joined the Baylor squad and immediately jumped into the starting left tackle spot, although there were some learning curves, both with football terminology and even the most common of southern phrases.

During a practice before the 2009 season, Coach Briles had taken several plays to coach Watkins on a specific blocking technique. Finally, the big tackle figured it out and made a block that had everyone excited about his immediate progress.

"Good job, Danny! That dog will hunt."

Watkins immediately looked left and looked right. He kept hearing that phrase and didn't get it. Finally, he tapped his left guard on the shoulder pads and asked, "Where's this dog they keep talking about?"

As it turned out, Watkins was a stellar replacement for Smith. For two years, he was a mainstay at left tackle, giving the offensive line the required nastiness and attitude it sorely needed.

Once against Rice in Houston, Watkins had been dominant all game long, wearing out the Owls' defensive end assigned to face him. During a timeout,

Watkins went to the sideline, and Briles noticed a decent amount of blood had stained his white uniform, both on the jersey and pants.

"Good job, Danny, keep it up.... I know that's not your blood!"

Briles was right; Watkins didn't have a cut on him. The coach was also right on a few other aspects about Watkins, namely his talent. A few games into his junior season, Art told him he had the makings of a first-round draft pick.

"I thought he was crazy. I didn't think of myself like that at first," Watkins said. "But I could tell he was honest with me. He told me the things I needed to do. I just put a lot of faith in him and the coaching staff that they were going to teach me what I needed to know. And they weren't lying."

Watkins was selected 23rd overall in the 2010 draft by the Philadelphia Eagles.

★ ★ ★

Wake Forest was again the first opponent as the 2009 season opened, although this time the game was played in North Carolina on an ABC broadcast. The Bears broke out their all-white uniforms, sporting white helmets for the first time under Briles, along with white jerseys and pants. The look was clean, which fittingly matched a clean performance by the Bears, who stunned the college football world with a road upset over the Demon Deacons.

Griffin was efficient as a runner and passer. He threaded the ball to his receiver Wright, who showed he was ready to become a star. And a freshman named Lanear Sampson caught the first pass of his career, which happened on a throwback touchdown toss from Ernest Smith that gave Baylor a comfortable lead. The Bears would hang on for a 24–21 victory to start the year 1–0.

While a 30–22 home loss to Connecticut was a huge setback, the Baylor program suffered perhaps the toughest loss imaginable against Northwestern State, even though the Bears won the game 68–13. But a season-ending knee injury to Griffin, who was about two series away from getting pulled for the rest of the game, crushed Baylor's hopes of ending its bowl drought, which dated back to 1994.

To make matters worse, senior backup Blake Szymanski, who did have 13 starts under his belt, also suffered a shoulder injury in the second half, forcing the Bears to turn to third-stringer Nick Florence, a redshirt freshman who had barely received any practice snaps.

After Szymanski went down, Florence immediately started to get warm when Coach Briles called him over. The quarterback from Garland, Texas, whose parents both went to Baylor, was nervous about getting in the game but figured the coach was about to give him a motivational boost before he took the field.

"Nick...do you even know the plays?"

Florence chuckled. Coach was serious. The quarterback nodded with a "yes, sir" and ran out there. He might be in over his head. He might be too wound up to be effective. But if anything, Florence knew the plays. He just wasn't so sure he would be calm enough to execute them. He managed to get through that game and played well in his first start the next week against Kent State, as Baylor sloshed around in the rain to win 31–15.

Meanwhile, losing Griffin, who had a torn ACL and needed reconstructive surgery, was a devastating blow, one that took a few weeks for everyone to fully comprehend.

"When I got back to the facility the first time, everyone was crying," said Griffin. "Coach [Briles] was crying. Montgomery, Kendal Briles was crying. Some would say they were crying because their season was over. I didn't look at it that way. I thought they were crying because they look at me like a son to them. And I truly believe coach was hurt."

For that reason, Griffin did his best to balance his time around the team with also keeping his distance. He thought being too visible would remind his teammates about his injury and interrupt their focus on moving forward.

Ultimately, as long as Griffin wasn't on the field, how often he was with the squad probably didn't matter. The Bears started Big 12 play without him and clearly struggled, losing four straight games while scoring a combined 34 points.

The frustration subsided for one day in Columbia, Missouri. The Bears offense, which had yet to post more than 10 points in a conference game, exploded on the Tigers for 40. The light bulb seemingly switched on for Florence, who set a school record with 427 passing yards, throwing three touchdowns and rushing for another.

With Smith offering support on the sideline, taking advantage of his bye week with the Rams and making the easy trek over from St. Louis, the Bears rallied from a 27–16 halftime deficit to upset Missouri 40–32, breaking a 13-game road losing streak against Big 12 opponents.

"We always had faith in Nick," said Wright, who had 10 catches for 149 yards that day. "He just played with a lot of confidence. I think that game really helped him and helped everyone see what he could really do."

Ironically enough, late in the day, with Baylor leading 33–29 and facing a fourth-and-goal from the Missouri 1-yard line, Coach Briles took Florence out of a game he was mastering and inserted the backup Szymanski, who hadn't played in five weeks.

Why? Because of Florence's jersey number, of course.

Just as he did back at Stephenville when he installed a "Hammer Time" formation that included as many oversized blockers as he could manage in one backfield, Briles had a plan to insert 335-pound defensive tackle Phil Taylor into the game as a fullback to open up the hole. The problem? Taylor wore No. 11, as did Florence. Being on the field together would have resulted in a penalty.

So to show just how much faith he had in this play, Briles pulled his record-setting passer and let the backup quarterback, who hadn't taken a snap all game, handle the most important one. The idea worked, as Terrance Ganaway blasted in for a touchdown, giving Baylor a double-digit lead they wouldn't relinquish.

But the game in Missouri proved to be more of an aberration in an otherwise disappointing season. The Bears faltered the next week against Texas, suffered through a blowout at Texas A&M and then dropped a heartbreaker to Texas Tech at Cowboys Stadium in Arlington. Briles decided to start Szymanski in what would be his last game, and he played well enough to keep the Bears close, even throwing into the end zone in the final minutes of the 20–13 loss.

Once again, Baylor finished 4–8, but overall the progress was evident despite the Bears dropping seven of their last eight games.

"We were getting better.... You could see it, but it wasn't showing up in the results," Art said. "We ended that year thinking if we could get Robert back healthy, we were going to really turn the corner. We were getting more confident by the day, and we knew we were getting a lot of players back."

Specifically, a certain quarterback.

28. Goin' Bowling

"Determination determines destination."

ENTERING THE 2010 season, the Baylor Bears hadn't been to a bowl game since 1994.

Robert Griffin wasn't even in kindergarten yet. Art Briles had just won his second consecutive state title in Stephenville. His son Kendal was an 11-year-old ball boy for that same team.

Needless to say, the drought between postseason appearances for the Baylor football program had reached a level of embarrassment, especially considering how many bowl games are played these days. Just 20 years earlier, there had been 19 to finish the 1990 season. In 2010, the bowl schedule included 35 games, meaning Baylor's ultimate goal was to be one of those 70 participating teams.

And they felt as if they had the pieces to make a run, especially with Robert Griffin III returning from a torn ACL injury suffered the previous season. He was at full strength by the start of two-a-day practices in August, although Baylor remained cautious with its star quarterback, whose value was driven home in 2009 when the Bears went 2–1 in his three starts and then 2–7 in the games following his injury. Griffin was held out of all contact drills in the spring. He wore a brace on his right knee for the fall practices and opened the season wearing one, as well.

Still, brace or no brace, Baylor had its leader once again.

"Everyone was so excited to have him back," Briles said. "He's such a freakish athlete. When he's there, you just feel like you've got a chance every game. Even then, he was the most exciting player in America. Him coming back that year created a huge buzz on campus. He was hungry and ready to go. That was exciting."

While Baylor fans weren't sure what to expect from Griffin in 2010, they at least figured he would be there. Not all of them could say the same about

Briles, who had a few sleepless nights following the 2009 season trying to decide if he would even return to the Bears.

Texas Tech had fired Mike Leach as head coach. Ironically enough, his last game occurred against Baylor at Cowboys Stadium, just a few days before he was removed of his duties following his alleged handling of the Adam James injury. Since Briles' arrival, the Bears had posted consecutive 4–8 efforts, but the program's progress was easy to see, especially for Texas Tech officials. Not only did many of them already know Art personally, but the Red Raiders had narrowly escaped Briles' Baylor teams the last two seasons, winning by a touchdown each time.

If any school appreciated what he had done so far, it was Tech. Therefore, when the school's head coaching position became available, Art was contacted unofficially through members of the Red Raiders athletics department.

He never went to Lubbock for an official visit but was told by enough people—and the right people—that he could have the job if he so desired. And indeed it was a desirable job for Briles, who graduated from Tech along with his wife, Jan. Growing up in Rule, which is considered West Texas, Art had followed the Red Raiders. Maybe the term "dream job" is a stretch, but the opportunity was way more attractive to Briles than people realized.

After two years at Baylor, he was happy with where they were headed, but his impatient self was far from satisfied with consecutive losing seasons. He tossed and turned for about four nights wondering if Tech was a better fit for him. He wondered if the fan support at Baylor could ever be strong enough to consistently fill the stadium. He wondered if he could make the same strides with the Red Raiders as he did with the Bears, and if so, would that result in more wins.

At the end of the day, there were several reasons why he stayed, but one in particular.

Robert Griffin III.

"I really thought he was a special player, and one that doesn't come around too often," Briles said. "When I left Houston for Baylor, he was committed to me. He came along with me. And after his freshman year, I told him he could win the Heisman. I believed that. And I thought he could be that good. I just wasn't ready to give up on that."

Texas Tech hired Tommy Tuberville, who had led both Auburn and Ole Miss. The soft spot Art has for Texas Tech will always remain. But he was fully invested in Baylor.

★   ★   ★

The first two games of the 2010 season gave Griffin a chance to get back into the flow once again. Baylor eased by Sam Houston State 34–3 and then dominated Buffalo 34–6 for a 2–0 start.

Up next was a road game at Texas Christian, a former Southwest Conference opponent that had become a consistent powerhouse in the Mountain West Conference and was on the cusp of being considered one of the elite programs in all of college football.

TCU fans have long showed envy over Baylor's invitation to the Big 12 back in 1996. As rivaling private institutions separated by only 85 miles, the Horned Frogs and Bears have developed a personal rivalry, especially for those wearing purple.

On a sweltering sunny afternoon in Fort Worth, TCU got after the Bears in every way, manhandling Baylor 45–10. For the first time in the young season, Griffin looked like a quarterback coming back from an ACL injury. He didn't have much room to run, and when he did, he was bottled up quickly.

"We just got beat by a good team and a program further along than us," Briles said of TCU, whose head coach Gary Patterson was in his 11th year with the Horned Frogs.

TCU had fun whipping up on the Bears that day. Their fans did, as well. Following the game, as the players made a long walk up the stairs toward the locker room, a few of the Frogs' faithful made sure to point out that a team from the Mountain West Conference had just dominated a Big 12 school.

"Good job, Big 12. Nice job. Enjoy that bus ride. Good job, Big 12. It stings, doesn't it?"

The taunts continued, with some fans filming the incident and later posting it on YouTube. While some among the Bears contingent fired back with a shot or two, strength coach Kaz Kazadi couldn't stand for it any longer and had to be restrained from climbing up the cement wall that separates the players from the fans. Baylor officials and even some state troopers tried to calm the situation.

Coach Briles was one of the first ones up the stairs and didn't witness the altercation firsthand. He saw the video and would later use it to his advantage. "That's what makes sports great. You do your talking on the field. That's how I see it," Briles said. "We had an opportunity to keep people from talking and didn't do it. But when it happens, it does increase your awareness and fuel the fire. It lets you understand how others view you. And we knew right then what they thought of us."

The postgame exchange between the TCU fans didn't bother Briles, but a comment he heard Patterson make the following Monday irritated him somewhat. The TCU coach implied Baylor must have been spying on his practices the week before the game, simply because the Bears ran a sprint-option play that Patterson said he had never seen Briles run before. Apparently, the call was one TCU had been working on, as well.

The next week, as TCU prepared for a rival game with Southern Methodist, Patterson closed practices to the media. The insinuation was both laughable and disrespectful to Briles.

"He made a statement without any facts," Briles said. "Where I grew up in West Texas, you don't have to shake hands. You tell someone something, it's done. You mean it. And that's the thing that bothered me. He made a statement without facts. You don't do that—not where I'm from. I'm either right or wrong. I'm not going to have an assumption.

"But another thing, if we spied, we certainly didn't spy very well. We need to get ourselves some new spies."

★   ★   ★

Baylor responded after the TCU loss with a pair of convincing wins over Rice (30–13) and Kansas (55–7) that improved the Bears' record to 4–2 heading into a showdown with Texas Tech at the Cotton Bowl. The stadium is a place that always brings back sad memories for Briles, as it was where he learned that his parents had been killed in a car wreck while driving to watch him play for Houston against SMU.

On the field for pregame warm-ups, with the crowd just starting to file in, Art found a spot on the Baylor bench and did something that was rather rare for him—he reminisced. He allowed himself to go back 34 years and recall the day of October 16, 1976.

"I remember just sitting there and being very emotional," Art said. "Being back at the site and playing against Tech. For a long time, I blocked everything else. I wouldn't let myself be hurt by the day. I finally started accepting the fact that it did happen and this is why I am who I am today because of that. So I can remember walking up the ramp and looking in the stands and standing on the sideline where I was and just rehashing it all."

The trip wasn't Art's first back to the Cotton Bowl since the accident. He actually was there about 11 weeks after the tragedy for the actual Cotton Bowl Classic on January 1, 1977, as a player for the Cougars. And Art watched his son Kendal suit up for Texas in the 2003 Cotton Bowl against LSU, sitting in the stands.

But as a coach, this was his first return. And just before the kickoff against the Red Raiders, tears formed in his eyes, although his sunglasses blocked anyone from ever seeing.

Tech had defeated Baylor by seven points in each of the first two games against Briles' Bears, and on this beautiful October day, the Red Raiders did so again, edging Baylor 45–38 after Griffin threw a desperation pass into the end zone as time expired.

Emotions ran high for Coach Briles again the following weekend in Boulder, Colorado, with Baylor taking on the Buffaloes in a game played on October 16. That date is always difficult for Art, especially a Saturday gameday like this one. Needless to say, it was another teary-eyed pregame for Art, who still wears his father's dog tags.

Over the years, he's tried to make the anniversary of his loss more positive.

"It's always a down day, but it's also a day I feel conversely blessed," he said. "I had a great mother and father and people who loved me and cared for me. They gave me enough instinct and intuition to make it on my own. As much as it hurts, there's a lot of feeling of blessedness."

On the field, Baylor racked up what Art called a "huge win" for the Bears, who needed a pass deflection in the end zone to grab a 31–25 victory over Colorado. That was the first game all season in which the coaches turned Griffin loose with his legs. No longer was he a player returning from an ACL injury. Griffin was back to the "do whatever it takes" phenom that Baylor desperately needed. He ran for 137 yards while tailback Jay Finley rushed for 143 more and had two touchdowns.

"They kept me safe until conference play," Griffin said. "But they took the training wheels off against Colorado and said, 'We've got to go win football games.'" Which is what they did against the Buffaloes, inching Baylor to within one game of becoming bowl eligible and ending the school's 16-year absence from the postseason.

★ ★ ★

Ask Robert Griffin about the most beloved game of his collegiate career, and he quickly fires back the answer. Kendall Wright has the same response, as does Lanear Sampson. All of them came to Baylor during the 2008 season and experienced their share of great Bears memories.

But the Kansas State game in 2010 is the favorite for all of them. Why? Well, it's simple, really. That was the day Baylor football finally got over the proverbial hump.

Beating Kansas State 47–42 on a rainy day at Floyd Casey Stadium was the biggest win for the program in more than a decade. The result had nothing to do with the opponent, although Bill Snyder's Wildcats teams are always challenging, and they were on this day, as well. Mother Nature also played a factor, even stopping the game for 107 minutes because of lightning.

Afterward, Coach Briles quipped about the delay, "Man, it really is that hard to be bowl eligible at Baylor."

But the Bears overcame all obstacles to outlast Kansas State in a wild, back-and-forth affair that included a school-record 250 yards rushing by Finley and a career-high day of passing from Griffin, who threw for 404 yards. The play he remembers most, though, is one that is more likely to be seen on the playground than in a Big 12 stadium.

Griffin was supposed to toss a throwback pass to Wright, but the KSU defenders snuffed out the designed play, forcing the quarterback to keep the ball and roll toward the sideline. That's when Wright improvised and sprinted to Griffin, who then pitched the ball over to his wide receiver. Instinctively, Wright reversed field and came around the edge for a 14-yard run to the 1-yard line, setting up a touchdown on the next snap.

"Once we did that, we just knew it would be our day," Griffin said. "There was something in the air that day."

The fans rushed the field after the win, holding up premade newspaper clippings that read "Bowl Bound."The Bears were 6–2, but more importantly, Art knew the stigma that had plagued Baylor football for years was now gone.

"That was just a monumental task. We got that monkey knocked off our backs," Briles said. "It was like, 'Go jump on someone else.' All the talk about us in recruiting that other schools used, it's gone. They were able to say that we've never been to a bowl in so many years. You couldn't say that anymore."

The next week in Austin, Baylor rode the momentum by beating Texas for the first time on the road since 1991. Early in the fourth quarter, the Bears trailed 19–17 and faced fourth-and-goal from the Texas 1-yard line. Briles knew the smart move was to kick the field goal and grab the lead. That would be the conventional wisdom.

Of course, Art had already proven he was anything but conventional, yet he still asked the coaches in the press box their thoughts.

"Guys, what's the smart thing to do here?"

"Kick the field goal."

"Field goal, coach."

"Let's get the points. Let's get the lead."

Sounded good and logical. Just didn't sound right.

"We didn't come here not to win," coach said. "We're going for it."

Griffin scored on the next play on a quarterback sneak, giving the Bears a 23–19 advantage. They eventually tacked on another score, and Baylor moved to 7–2 after a monumental 30–22 victory over the Longhorns.

But that would prove to be the final win of the season for Baylor. A road loss to Oklahoma State, followed by two home defeats by Texas A&M and Oklahoma, put the Bears in the Texas Bowl against Illinois.

Right from the start, Art didn't like the matchup. He knew teams that could muscle them up front would give his squad problems. Being invited to a bowl was great, and something Baylor hadn't experienced in a long, long time, but because of his competitive nature, Art wanted to win. Plus, he had yet to ever come out on top in a bowl, going 0–3 at Houston. He left for the Baylor job in late 2007, and didn't coach the Cougars in their bowl game against TCU, which they lost, anyway.

But his first bowl victory would have to wait. As predicted, Illinois proved to be too strong, overpowering Baylor 38–14 to give the Bears four straight losses to end the season. A record that started out 7–2, ended at just 7–6.

As a coach, the 2010 season provided the best of both worlds. Art knew he'd satisfied the boosters and alumni by delivering the school's first bowl game since 1994. At the same time, losing four straight to end the year was enough to motivate the players to stay committed and hungry throughout the off-season.

Baylor was getting there. A bowl game was the first major step. But an even bigger stage—literally—was on the horizon.

29. Rising Up

"Win today."

WIDE RECEIVER Kendall Wright was entering his fourth season with the Bears, and he had yet to see it. None of his teammates had ever seen it, either.

Wait, a bowl victory? Or a major award to a Baylor player or coach? Or how about even a win over any Oklahoma school? Every question was valid. Every answer was no.

But on this morning practice day in the middle of August two-a-days, about two weeks before the start of the 2011 season, the senior wide receiver was talking about something else he had yet to witness during his time in Waco. He'd never seen his head coach, Art Briles, without his shirt on.

While that might sound a bit strange coming from a macho football player like Wright, who was hoping a breakout senior season might propel him up the next year's draft boards, he knew how much Coach Briles worked out. He and his teammates could tell that underneath the 54-year-old's usual Under Armour long-sleeved shirts, there was some solid muscle.

"We all knew he was rocked up," Wright said. "He just had never shown us."

So on the practice field one morning, Wright asked the coach when he was going to "show off his guns?" Art laughed it off, his mind more concerned with the practice ahead. Truth be told, he was already worried about playing TCU in their season opener. The Horned Frogs were coming off a 13–0 campaign that included a Rose Bowl win over Wisconsin and a No. 2 national ranking. He remembered the 45–10 loss from the season before and knew the entire country would be watching the game on an ESPN broadcast. Two weeks before the season certainly wasn't too early to start thinking about this opponent.

Turns out the players were, as well.

"Coach, if we beat TCU, will you take your shirt off?"

"Deal."

Briles had done so before while at Houston, ripping off his shirt and show-ing a painted 6 on his chest that had been there through the entire game against Army in 2003. The number symbolized the six-win season that made the Cougars bowl eligible.

Making good on the dare wasn't a big issue to the coach but clearly was to the players, so he figured, why not? Whatever gets them motivated. Actually, Briles already knew he had the perfect motivation for his team heading into the showdown.

The day of the game, which was played on a Friday night, the team gath-ered in its meeting room at the stadium. Usually, coaches and/or players use that time to say a few words of encouragement. Sometimes a video is shown. For this matchup, Art prepared a 2010 highlight reel, showing some of the best plays that occurred during the previous season, which included Baylor's first trip to a bowl game in 16 years.

All of a sudden, the screen simply went black. The video then reappeared with a few lowlights from the TCU game, showing Baylor players fumbling, getting hit, being torched. The final score flashed up: TCU 45, Baylor 10. What followed was the YouTube shot of the players walking into the locker room getting heckled by a few TCU fans, igniting a war of words with strength coach Kaz Kazadi right in the middle.

"I remember everyone getting upset at seeing that," said Robert Griffin. "Then we see Kaz going off on those guys and we all got excited again."

The video ended. The screen went back to black before a graphic reap-peared that read, GO BEAT TCU.

So the Bears went out and did just that. From the very beginning, fans could easily see Baylor's intensity was through the roof. They took the open-ing kickoff and marched down for a quick score—oddly enough on a Wright throwback pass to fellow wide receiver Terrance Williams.

The Frogs were known for having a stingy defense, with the ESPN announcers calling coach Gary Patterson a "defensive mastermind" in the pregame remarks. But Baylor's offense wouldn't be denied. A back-and-forth affair in the first half turned into a Baylor bombing run in the third quar-ter as Griffin launched several deep balls to Wright, Williams, and Lanear Sampson. The Bears were pouring it on against TCU, leading 47–23 late in the third quarter.

And that's when everything changed. With the Floyd Casey Stadium in a complete frenzy, the Horned Frogs suddenly woke up. They stole the momentum, scoring 25 straight points to go up 48–47.

All of the offensive firepower Baylor had shown earlier disappeared while trying to protect the lead. Griffin had fumbled on the previous series, which led to TCU's go-ahead field goal. Now, as they tried to regroup with the ball in their possession, the mindset shifted back into attack mode.

"We weren't thinking about the lead we had just lost," Griffin said. "We were thinking it's time to go win the game."

But two straight incomplete passes from the Bears' own 20-yard line set up a third-and-10 with just over four minutes left in regulation. Baylor has a rather unorthodox play-calling system, in which multiple coaches are sending in signals from the sideline. In this particular situation, Griffin locked eyes with Briles, who called the play himself, despite the lack of faith from his coaches in the booth.

"Guys, what do you think about 'Five-Right Double Pass?'... Hey, 'Five-Right Double Pass?'... Forget ya'll, we're running it. 'Five-Right Double Pass.'"

Griffin was shocked to get the signal, but he could see the demonstrative motions in Coach Briles' hand movements. The play called for Griffin to throw a backward pass to Wright at the line of scrimmage and then dart through the middle, which Baylor expected would be wide open. Instead, the quarterback was somewhat covered, but there was still enough space for Wright to rifle in a pass. Griffin grabbed the offering and then blasted by two defenders for a 15-yard gain and a first down.

"That's not a trick play to us," Griffin said. "We practiced those all the time. So when he called it, I was surprised, but I knew we could execute it."

The Bears continued to drive, and Aaron Jones drilled a 37-yard field goal with 1:04 remaining to give Baylor a 50–48 lead. Shortly thereafter, safety Mike Hicks intercepted a TCU pass in the final seconds to preserve the win.

Let the field be rushed.

The Baylor security guards around the stadium weren't exactly prepared for this. As soon as the seconds ticked off and people started running toward the field, the initial reaction was to stop them. Art's youngest daughter, Staley, was told she couldn't leave the stands, but she ran right past a man in a neon-yellow shirt and yelled, "Tackle me!" She made it through to the field, along with thousands of others, as Baylor celebrated a monumental 50–48 win over a TCU squad that had recently announced its invitation to join the Big 12 the following season.

That victory, coupled with the fireworks from the previous year, proved one thing—the longstanding rivalry was as strong as ever.

Sure enough, the postgame locker room was a wild scene long before Briles entered. The players were dancing, high-fiving and chanting, proud that they had knocked off a team that hadn't lost a regular season game since 2008.

But when Briles walked in and tore off his shirt, the team completely erupted. The players delivered on the field. The coach delivered in the locker room.

And to Wright, the reveal was worth the wait. "Man, he's not your average 50-year-old," he said. "He's pretty jacked up. But that was one of my memorable moments in college, just seeing that scene in the locker room."

★ ★ ★

The win over TCU did more than just give Baylor a respectable victory on national television. Griffin was elevated firmly into the Heisman race. In college football, it's never too early to talk Heisman, and his throwing for 359 yards, five touchdowns, and no interceptions was good enough to land him among the favorites, which included Stanford's Andrew Luck, whom many people figured had the 2011 Heisman locked up unless he got injured.

Griffin helped his cause even more the next day by going up to Dallas to be on set for ESPN's *College GameDay* with Chris Fowler, Lee Corso, and Kirk Herbstreit. And, of course, national exposure for Griffin meant exposure for Baylor.

The Bears ripped through their non-conference schedule to get to 3–0 before meeting Kansas State in Manhattan for the conference opener. But, despite leading by nine in the fourth quarter, Baylor faltered as Griffin threw his first interception of the season on a tipped pass. Wright had two catches that made *SportsCenter's* top 10 plays that day, but the Bears dropped a heartbreaker, 36–35.

A bounce-back win over Iowa State gave Baylor a 4–1 mark heading into its matchup at Texas A&M, a school that would be leaving the Big 12 for the Southeastern Conference the next year. The Bears and Aggies had enjoyed a long rivalry, known as the "Battle of the Brazos," and some fuel was added to the fire in the off-season when Baylor officials threatened legal action against the SEC if A&M left. Baylor initially refused to waive some legal claims and led the charge for the rest of the Big 12 schools that might be left without a conference. As it turned out, the SEC admitted A&M, and the Big 12 ended up on solid ground, but for this game, the actions only increased the bitterness between the two.

Even without the boardroom antics, Art knew playing in front of nearly 90,000 at Kyle Field could be a chore. It most certainly was. The Aggies pulled away in the fourth quarter for a 55–28 win that dropped Baylor to 1–2 in conference play.

In the interviews that followed, Briles' impatience got the best of him. He was waiting outside the locker room for the reporters to finish speaking with Griffin, but after a question about A&M head coach Mike Sherman's post-game conversation with Griffin, Briles had seen and heard enough.

"Is that an A&M question?" he asked. "Where are you from?"

"Coach, I work for the *Bryan–College Station Eagle*."

"Yeah, he doesn't need to answer that. That's okay. Good job. Thanks, Robert."

Briles dismissed his quarterback and then replaced him in the circle of reporters to start his interview.

"Coach, what's wrong with that question? Coach Sherman talked to him after the game. What's wrong with that question?"

"Nothing."

Art then turned to a familiar reporter, David Smoak, a radio host and pro-gramming director at Waco's ESPN 1660 AM, opening the floor for a more Baylor-oriented topic. Even now, Briles knows the offending question wasn't really the issue. There was more to the incident.

Smoak was standing on the field when Briles passed him en route to the locker room. That's when an A&M fan got a few feet from the coach's face and said, "And that's why you'll always be Baylor."

Art turned immediately and fired back, having to be restrained by a couple of Baylor officials. That took place just a few minutes before the press conference exchange in just another example of how competitive juices can sometimes overwhelm even the most steady-handed individuals.

The next week, Baylor went to Stillwater to face an Oklahoma State program that had beaten the Bears in each of the last three years by point differentials of 28, 27, and 27. Unfortunately, this day ended about the same, despite the offense churning out 622 yards. Five turnovers, including three in the red zone, doomed Baylor as they fell 59–24.

Walking off the field, Art glanced up at the scoreboard. He didn't think OSU was five touchdowns better than his squad, but he has always been a coach that deals in reality. The reality was his team just lost by 35 points. The reality was his team was 4–3.

How *realistic* would it be to think his team wouldn't lose another game on the schedule?

★   ★   ★

The 2011 calendar year was big for assistant coach Jeff Lebby, who joined Art Briles' family by marrying the coach's youngest daughter, Staley, that March. Lebby also moved from assistant offensive line coach to running backs coach, which meant he spent the off-season communicating even more with players at his position.

If not for a conversation during the summer with Terrance Ganaway, who knows how things might have turned out for Baylor in 2011? Heading into his senior year, Ganaway wasn't sure he had the desire to go through another season.

His expectations weren't being met at Baylor. Ganaway figured to have had more success on the field by this point in his career. But after expressing his concerns to Lebby, Ganaway realized he didn't have to accept a backup role on this team. He was optimistic he could become a starter.

"He was honest with me and told me that I had the potential to be really good," Ganaway said. "But I had to work for it. I had to take it upon myself to be as good as I could be. I don't think I had done that yet."

Ganaway played for Coach Briles at Houston in 2007, but left the team after his mother passed away from kidney cancer. He felt isolated by the Cougars' new coaching staff, whom he said never knew about his mother's passing. In fact, the only coaches who contacted him were now with Baylor, including Randy Clements and Briles.

"They told me how sorry they were and that I always had a place in their family if I wanted to go," Ganaway said. "I didn't know at first, but I thought about it more and decided I wasn't done playing. That's how I landed at Baylor."

After sitting out in 2008, Ganaway had three years of eligibility, beginning with the 2009 season. In two years, he had rushed for just 495 yards and, after spring ball in 2011, was behind Jarred Salubi for the starting job.

But following his talk with Lebby and other meetings with Briles and Kazadi, Ganaway entered his final season with more focus than ever before, which in turn, started to show on the field. He was averaging nearly 100 rushing yards a game through the team's first seven with 658 total, having already surpassed the production from his first two seasons at Baylor combined.

Heading into the Missouri contest, the Bears were 4–3 after losing two straight. All week long, Briles kept telling Ganaway he was about to have a big game.

"It's going to be a big week for you, G-Way.... A big week. Do you feel it? You should. You're going to have a big night!"

Ganaway just thought his coach was pumping him up again and didn't think about any hidden meanings. But just before kickoff, Briles pulled out black wristbands for the players and coaches to wear as a dedication to their success.

"He said, 'This game is for the person you love the most,'" Ganaway recalled. "'This is the game for someone who laid down the most or sacrificed everything so you could be here today. This is the game we can appreciate everything because none of us would be here without some help.' I took that to heart."

Ganaway rushed for 186 yards and scored twice, breaking free for an 80-yard touchdown as the Bears defeated Missouri 42–39 to jump to 5–3. Once again, Baylor was on the doorstep of becoming bowl eligible. And a road game at Kansas, who was 2–7 overall and 0–6 in the conference, seemed to be a perfect opponent to make that happen once again.

★ ★ ★

With 12:05 remaining in the fourth quarter in Lawrence, Kansas, the scoreboard displayed a shocking sight: Kansas 24, Baylor 3.

Really? This is happening? Baylor had scored more than 40 points in five of eight games to that point, but had only managed a field goal through three quarters on a windy day where nothing seemed to go right. The Bears had produced just 190 yards of offense.

They were about to double that.

The comeback started with a 49-yard scoring run down the sideline by Griffin, which was followed by a defensive stop and a 36-yard touchdown strike to Williams with 7:58 remaining. After getting the ball back again, Griffin then hit Tevin Reese deep for 67 yards to tie things up with 3:32 to play.

Eventually, the game went into overtime, where Reese scored on Baylor's first possession to make it 31–24. Kansas responded with a touchdown, but decided to go for 2 points and the win. Coming through in the clutch, cornerback Joe Williams batted down the ball in the end zone, and Baylor's improbable 31–30 victory sent them to a bowl for the second consecutive year.

"Without a doubt, it's the most phenomenal victory I've ever been involved with," Briles said. "From the standpoint of, 'This can't happen,' but it did. It was all about momentum, belief, and attitude."

Briles did some research and found Baylor became just the second team in 15 years to go on the road and rally from 21 points down in the fourth quarter against a BCS team. "That win showed we were destined to become an extremely dangerous football team," Briles said. "We walked on the edge of the cliff and hung on to survive and get bowl eligible. There's no doubt that's one of the best wins I've ever been associated with."

Seven days later, Baylor topped it.

The Bears had never beaten Oklahoma in 20 tries, dating all the way back to 1901. The Sooners were ranked No. 5 and because of two losses earlier in the day to higher-positioned teams, all OU had to do was win its last three games against Baylor, Iowa State, and Oklahoma State, and the Sooners would be playing for a national title.

But to win a national championship, the ball just has to bounce your way sometimes. That night in Waco, the ball bounced Baylor's way—literally. From the start, the two teams traded big plays with the Bears leading 17–10 at the half. But Oklahoma established the momentum early in the third, regaining the advantage, 24–17, and had Baylor pinned back on its 13-yard line. That's when Griffin fired a pass to Reese over the middle.

"I saw it hit Tevin's hands and go up in the air," Griffin said. "I thought the worst. Tipped balls get picked."

Not this one. Not this night. The ball ricocheted forward about 15 yards and into the waiting hands of a streaking Wright, who never broke stride as he galloped 87 yards for a game-tying touchdown.

"When that happens, you think it might be your night," Briles said.

The lead continued to seesaw until Oklahoma tied the game in the final minute of play, knotting the score at 38–38.

Go win the game or play for overtime? That's what his assistant coaches wondered out loud between possessions. Until then, Art didn't know. He wanted to see how OU head coach Bob Stoops reacted. This was a game of chess to the very end.

So, on first down, the Bears handed off to Ganaway, who got four yards. Oklahoma then called a timeout with 46 seconds to play. That's all Briles needed. "Let's go win the game," he said.

Had Stoops let the clock run, Baylor would've played for overtime. Instead, Art knew he had to score. Griffin did most of the work and got his team to the Sooners' 34-yard line with the clock winding down to under 20 seconds. The Bears just needed a few more yards to get into field-goal range for Aaron Jones.

Instead, Griffin went for it all—the end zone, the lead, the win...and the Heisman.

Throwing across his body, he located Williams in the back right corner of the promised land. Williams was able to free himself from his defender and haul in the strike for a touchdown, one that Baylor fans will remember forever.

Floyd Casey Stadium has never been so loud. To that point, it never had a reason to be.

Griffin went to the sideline where his coach grabbed him by the jersey. He had to get in close to be heard above the deafening fans who were about to see Baylor's first win over Oklahoma.

"Robert, that's why you're my quarterback. That's why you're the best in America. That's why you're going to win the Heisman."

★ ★ ★

Baylor carried that momentum into Cowboys Stadium the next week against Texas Tech, another team Briles had yet to beat in his three previous seasons. But with OU checked off the list, doing the same to the Red Raiders seemed like only a matter of time.

Tech was 5–6 and desperately trying to become bowl eligible themselves in its last regular season game. But even though Griffin suffered a concussion before halftime and didn't play after the break, the Bears couldn't be denied.

While Bryce Petty was listed as the backup quarterback, Art wasn't as comfortable with him in this setting. Sure, the Bears were bowl eligible already, but they had to beat Tech. He had to beat Tech. So at halftime, he asked Nick Florence if he was interested in playing the rest of the game, meaning his redshirt season would be lost.

"Whatever I can do to help the team, I'll do it." he said. "If you need me, I'll play."

"We need you, Nick."

And that's all Florence needed to hear. He played the final two quarters against Tech, and the Bears rolled to a 66–42 victory. Ganaway was amazing, rushing for 246 yards and two touchdowns.

Florence didn't play another snap that year, as Griffin returned the next week. His entire junior season consisted of those two quarters. Still today, he says, "I wouldn't have traded it for anything."

With Griffin back behind center for the following week's outing against Texas, the Bears cruised to a convincing 48–24 win on a rainy day in Waco. Aside from the outcome, the game was convincing mainly to Heisman voters, who watched Griffin torch the Longhorns for 320 passing yards and four combined touchdowns.

After the victory, he was asked by a sideline reporter if he thought he had done enough to win the Heisman. Griffin gave a calculated, yet honest answer: "I could be wrong…but I think Baylor has won its first Heisman tonight." If anything, Griffin knew he'd be one of the finalists, invited to go to New York City the next weekend.

Meanwhile, the Bears had reeled off five straight wins, earning an invitation to the Alamo Bowl against Washington. Just as the year before, Baylor would play indoors and remain in the state. That kept weather from being a factor on gameday, something that's always important to the head coach of a pass-happy offense, and meant the trip would be an easy one for Bears fans, which also proved to be significant as they sold out the Alamodome in San Antonio.

"We were excited about that game and the matchup with Washington," Briles said. "We knew they would be tough and it'd be a wide-open game. But we were on a mission. We had won five straight games and our goal was to finish the season with 10 wins."

Before the Bears could get to No. 10 in the victory column, though, their own No. 10 was headed to New York, where his life would change forever.

30. A Perfect 10

"Don't go chase your dream...catch it!"

HE'S NOT LOST; he's just not exactly sure where he is. He'll find his way before too long, and if not, he'll ask. The kid from Rule, Texas, now a recently turned 56-year-old football coach at Baylor University, is out for a walk on the streets of New York City. And he's pretty easy to spot, wearing a black pullover with a gold *BU* on his chest and a Baylor hat.

Art Briles is soaking up the Big Apple. He's never lived outside of the state of Texas, so New York City is quite a culture shock for this down-home football coach. But he's enjoying the hustle and bustle while trying to pass time before the ceremony.

That's when he sees a text message: "Coach, can you come see me?"

Right then, Art knew something wasn't right. The request was from Robert Griffin III, his quarterback at Baylor who was one of five finalists for the Heisman Trophy, which would be announced in about six hours at the Downtown Athletic Club.

To Art, he was still Robert. To the world, he was RGIII.

And he was now expected to win the award as college football's top player in 2011, tabbed the favorite over the other finalists: Stanford's Andrew Luck, Alabama's Trent Richardson, Wisconsin's Montee Ball, and Louisiana State's Tyrann Mathieu. In fact, Coach Briles just missed having two recruited quarterbacks among the contenders. Houston's Case Keenum was in the Heisman hunt all year and had the Cougars at 12–0 before a loss to Southern Mississippi in the Conference USA Championship Game deflated his stock.

While having two young stars on the Heisman stage would've been quite a feat for Briles, he knew deep down that Griffin was destined for this moment.

He was the quarterback from Copperas Cove, Texas, whom Art and his staff first brought with them to Baylor more than four years earlier. They developed him into a starter as a true freshman and were there when he battled through a knee injury that put him on the shelf as a sophomore.

Now Briles knew his quarterback needed his support once again. He went over to Robert's hotel and met him for lunch. That's when he saw a rare side of the superstar athlete.

"Coach, I'm nervous," he said. "This is a big deal."

Yes, winning the Heisman is a big deal, and it was a big deal to Robert and his family, without a doubt. But he was starting to feel the pressure because he knew this wasn't just a Robert Griffin award. He had been saying all along that this was a Baylor award, and he wanted the trophy for the school. Sure, not winning would've been a huge letdown for himself, but disappointing an entire university was a different story—one that Griffin had no desire to read.

In all his years of coaching, Art hadn't come across a player as "cool, calm, and collected" as Griffin. He had seen him perform at his highest level when the team needed him most, engineering game-winning drives to beat TCU and Oklahoma during the 2011 season, two highly ranked teams.

"I had never really seen Robert act nervous, be nervous, or admit to being nervous," Briles said, "so that really surprised me. You could see how important it was to him. I saw all of those things manifest right in front of me. I felt like my job was to calm him down and to keep him composed and give him confidence, which he very seldom needed."

"Robert, everything that can be done, has been done," Briles told him. "You should be nervous because it's a big deal, but you're going to win it. You've played too well and you've done too good a job for you not to win it."

Those words helped Griffin calm down just enough. Coach Briles always had that effect on him.

Art walked back to his hotel still believing his guy would win this thing. Just a few days earlier, he had sat next to Griffin at the College Football Awards in Florida and saw him accept the Davey O'Brien Award as the nation's best quarterback.

"When he won that, I knew he'd win the Heisman," Art said. "That's for the best quarterback in the country. This is for the best player. And he was the best quarterback and the most dynamic player in the United States. I just knew he'd win."

★ ★ ★

Arriving at the ceremony, Art took his place in the second row with the other head coaches, each sitting right behind their respective players. Watching alongside Les Miles (LSU), Nick Saban (Alabama), David Shaw (Stanford), and Bret Bielema (Wisconsin), Art realized this was perhaps a once-in-a-lifetime opportunity for him, as well.

"It's a sacred place for me," he said. "This event was about Robert, but I knew it was big for me and for Baylor. They showed all the videos of Robert, so it was a great national scene for us."

During the hour-long ceremony, Griffin went to the stage for a customary interview, but unlike the rest of the candidates who fielded questions, the Baylor quarterback was asked to reveal his socks, which had become something of a media-crazed sensation over the course of the season. For Robert, the fun started back in high school when he would wear cartoon-designed socks such as Scooby-Doo or Mickey Mouse. As his image ballooned in college, so too did the interest in his unusual obsession. Every week, Griffin was being asked about his socks, and so he knew on the biggest night of his life, he had better be prepared.

When ESPN host Chris Fowler asked him the expected million-dollar question, Robert simply lifted the legs of his pants to reveal blue Superman socks complete with a red cape dangling from the top of the elastic. The audience broke out in cheers.

Right then and there, the ceremony should've been over. None of the other candidates could compete with that.

Griffin came across the Superman socks about seven weeks earlier but had never worn them. He was waiting for the proper occasion, and once he found out he would be a finalist for the Heisman, he knew that would be the perfect time. Later, he explained the real rationale behind the socks, which he said were mistaken for "everyone thinking I'm calling myself Superman." In reality, they represent something different to him.

"No, I'm just the cape. I just guide the real super men on my team."

With 23 former Heisman Trophy winners lined up along the back of the stage, Art felt even more honored to be associated with such an event. The greatness of players like Archie Griffin, Tony Dorsett, Jim Plunkett, and Vinny Testaverde in one setting like this was beyond belief. All he could wonder at this point was if his quarterback would soon join them, becoming the first in Baylor's history to do so.

Finally, the moment of truth arrived.

Griffin's heart was beating so loud he wondered if anyone could hear it. His face was stoic as he awaited the announcement. Inside, he was a wreck.

Heisman Trophy trustee Carol Pisano opened the card and delivered the magic words: "The 2011 winner of the Heisman Trophy is…Robert Griffin III…RGIII!"

Immediately behind him, Art Briles let out an uncontrollable chuckle. This really happened. The only player whom Art Briles ever told could realistically win the Heisman, just won the Heisman.

After Griffin shook hands with the other four candidates, he turned around and immediately hugged his coach.

"I love you, coach."

"I love you…congratulations!"

Art then snuck back to hug Griffin's parents before the quarterback could get to them. The moment was surreal for everyone.

Meanwhile back in Waco, from the student union to the fraternity and sorority houses to even the nearby restaurants, the campus erupted. Like he had said all along, Robert Griffin didn't just win the Heisman, Baylor won it.

And Robert was especially gracious to the university in his speech:

> Well, now that my socks are out there, I've got nothing to lose, right?
>
> This moment right here is unbelievably believable. It's unbelievable because in the moment, we're all amazed when great things happen. But it's believable because great things don't happen without hard work.
>
> The great coach Art Briles says great things only come with great effort. We've certainly worked for this. That's right, everybody associated with Baylor University has a reason to celebrate tonight. To my teammates, I'd like to say thank you. And as we say: "The hotter the heat, the harder the steel. No pressure, no diamonds. We compete, we win…we are Baylor. Baylor we are, and Baylor we'll always be."
>
> But it's up to us to define what that means, and this Heisman Trophy is only the beginning of that process. To Baylor Nation, I say this is a forever kind of moment, and may we be blessed to have many more like it in the future. God has a plan, and it's our job to fulfill it, and in this moment we have.

> To my dad and my mom, my fiancée, my sisters, my beautiful niece, to my family, to my friends, to my teammates, to Coach Briles and the coaching staff, to the Baylor administration and Ken Starr, the city of Copperas Cove and the city of Waco, and all of Baylor Nation, I say thank you for all your loving support, through the tough times like knee surgeries and glorious moments like this one.
>
> Thank you to the Heisman Trophy Trust and all the Heisman Trophy winners who've given me a chance to be a part of this family.
>
> Last but not least, I want to thank God for giving me all these great people to be in my life. Thank you.

As he watched his quarterback on stage, tears started to form in the eyes of Briles, who wasn't thinking about the first time he met him. He wasn't thinking about the first game in which Robert played, either, or the first time he scored, or the knee injury as a sophomore, or the OU victory just a few weeks before. He was living in the moment—and loving this speech.

For all of Robert Griffin's outstanding performances, Art knew that this right here, in front of the entire nation, was as good as it gets.

"It was an ecstatic, humbling moment without question," Briles said. "He had such poise and such graciousness. Such thankfulness. I thought he did an unbelievable job. Like he said, it was unbelievably believable. But the people who knew him, knew this was destined for Robert."

After the ceremony, Art met back up with Baylor coaches Phillip Montgomery and Randy Clements, the offensive assistants who worked with Briles in Houston when they first recruited Griffin. Still in shock, someone leaned over to Art and asked him why he wasn't showing more excitement.

"Nobody told me how you're supposed to act when your player wins the Heisman," he said. "I didn't read that book. But it was just a thrilling day. I'm so thankful to be a part of it. It was a great day for Robert Griffin and a great day for Baylor."

And with that, the Bears' football program went to a new level. The struggling team that Briles had taken over four seasons earlier wasn't just another molehill on the college football landscape; they were at the top of the sports world mountain on this night, the main attraction. Robert Griffin was on center stage. And Art Briles was right there with him.

★ ★ ★

With bowl preparations beginning on Monday, Art and the coaches flew home right after the Heisman ceremony late on Saturday night. Last year the Bears made it to their first bowl game since 1994. Now they were looking to win one for the first time since 1992. With that in mind, he wanted to be back in Waco to get ready for the initial practice, a practice Robert missed because of his events in New York City.

Art then left Monday afternoon to rejoin Griffin for the Heisman award banquet that evening. Briles had the chance to introduce Robert once more, writing his speech on the plane without any help. Then again, talking about one of his favorite players of all time was easy. "I got to tell them about the Robert that I knew, as a person, as a man, as a leader."

Both the coach and quarterback returned to Waco in time for a Tuesday night practice, where Griffin brought out the trophy for his teammates to see, touch, and take pictures with. He told them what he told the world: "This trophy is for all of us. I couldn't have done it without you guys."

After that, the time had come to really prepare for the bowl game. The Bears were going to San Antonio, looking for a 10th win on the season, something that hadn't happened at Baylor since 1980. While the Heisman festivities might have easily been a distraction, the exact opposite turned out to be true.

"When he came back, we had tremendous energy," Briles said. "Robert had a great week of practice. You could tell it just lifted everyone up even higher. It was just fun knowing we had the Heisman Trophy winner right there practicing with us."

Even better than that was *playing* with the Heisman Trophy winner. The Bears showed up to the Alamodome in San Antonio with a purpose. They weren't just content on making a bowl game, as they were the previous year in Houston. This time they wanted to win, and because of Griffin's award, they were expected to win.

The atmosphere in the stadium was electric, filled with green-and-gold-wearing Baylor fans who were ready for a victory. But they were also fearful, yet understanding that this could be Griffin's last game with the Bears. Although he had one year of eligibility remaining, Griffin was already being projected as a high top 10 pick.

So if this was to be the finale for RGIII at Baylor, his faithful followers at least wanted to see a show. Instead, they got that and much more with one of the wildest bowl games in college football history.

Tennis matches haven't been this back-and-forth as Baylor and Washington traded touchdowns for four quarters. In the first, Griffin produced one of his favorite plays from his collegiate career, handing the ball off to tailback Jarred Salubi, then chasing him to the end zone and throwing a great block that allowed Salubi to score. On the next drive, Griffin broke four tackles in the pocket before scrambling to the right and reaching paydirt on a 24-yard run that gave Baylor a 21–7 lead. After that play, Coach Briles stopped Griffin on the sideline.

"That's why you won the award!... That's a Heisman Trophy play."

But the Huskies would rally for 28 unanswered points in the second quarter alone to lead 35–21 before a late Baylor field goal before halftime cut the deficit to 11.

In the third quarter, the Bears trailed 42–31 with Washington seemingly headed for more when a fumble recovery by Baylor gave the team possession again at its own 11. This time, Griffin didn't have to do anything more than turn and hand the ball off, as Terrance Ganaway would do the rest, scampering up the middle for an 89-yard touchdown that got Baylor back in the game. The run wasn't just the longest of his career, it was also Ganaway's first touchdown of the game, coming with 8:28 left to play in the third.

He would finish with five.

Ganaway kept finding the end zone as Baylor kept putting up points. Unfortunately, though, Washington was matching the Bears score for score, and held the lead, 56–53, at the 9:40 mark of the final quarter. But a little more than a minute later, Ganaway crossed the goal line again to put his team in front for good. After a fourth-down pass attempt by Washington fell incomplete, Ganaway iced the game with a 43-yard run to the end zone.

Baylor 67, Washington 56. For the first time in nearly two decades, the Bears had claimed a bowl victory.

When it was all said and done, Baylor and Washington combined for 123 points, which broke the record for the most points in an NCAA bowl game played in regulation with no overtime. The 1,397 combined yards also set a new mark. While West Virginia actually eclipsed their bowl record for points by a single team, scoring 70 just a few days later, the Bears' nine offensive touchdowns still ranks first in bowl game history.

"I've never been in anything like that before," Briles said. "But it was a huge win for our program. Just very gratifying and a great way to top off a magical season."

The locker room was complete chaos and downright euphoric. Players were chanting, dancing, hugging, and generally reveling in the excitement of the school's exciting bowl win. Art was shaking hands with as many people as he could. Winning locker rooms have always been one of his favorite places to be, so he was savoring this moment. But in the corner of his eye, he saw one of his players off to the side by himself. The young man was crying while his joyous teammates celebrated.

It was Robert Griffin. Right then and there, Art Briles knew. His quarterback was gone.

He didn't say it right away. In fact, Griffin told reporters after the game that he would make the decision in the upcoming days. But when Briles saw Robert's face, the coach was certain he had played his last game at Baylor.

Sure enough, Griffin made the announcement a few days later in a press conference on campus. To this day, Art says he was relieved when Robert finally told him he was going to the NFL. "It was just time," Briles said. "I've always said that if you're going to be a top 10 pick, then you should go, and it was clear to us he would be one of the first picks in the draft, maybe even No. 1. If he had stayed, I always would've worried about him getting hurt or doing something that might have changed his draft status. He was hot right then, and he had to go. There was nothing left for him to do at Baylor."

Before the two parted ways after their conversation about the decision, Art shared a piece of advice with Robert, advice the quarterback has never forgotten.

"Don't go chase your dream...catch it."

31. Big Socks to Fill

"Don't Get Bored...Get Better."

OUTSIDE, THE MARCH afternoon in Waco was beautiful, almost serene, but inside the Allison Indoor Practice Facility, just next door to the football offices and the Baylor practice fields, the music was blaring. There was quite a buzz circulating throughout the building, which also houses a few workouts during the season when the weather is rainy or the Texas heat is sweltering.

The place was energized because Baylor's Pro Day had arrived, when visitors from across the NFL file in, holding stopwatches and clipboards to check out a few of the potential picks in the upcoming draft. In fact, one Robert Griffin III could very well be the No. 1 overall selection. His workout was near flawless, grabbing the attention of every league representative who made the trek down to Waco, including Redskins head coach Mike Shanahan. With Washington holding the No. 2 choice in the draft order after making a bold trade to move up four spots, wide speculation is suggesting that it will take Griffin after Indianapolis drafts Stanford's Andrew Luck.

Griffin put on a show, throwing darts to several graduating seniors, including another projected first-round pick in Kendall Wright. A host of scouts, player personnel reps (including a few general managers), and several media representatives were all on hand to witness the Heisman Trophy winner in action. With every pass completion, the oohs and ahhs seemed to increase in volume, as well. Then came the post-practice interview with the media, which he also aced.

Art Briles said all the right things to the media, as well, stating how proud he was of Griffin and how he'd make a great pro. He also met with the Redskins' brass, but honestly thought his quarterback had done enough to get drafted first overall by the Colts. Deep down, he believed Robert was too special for Indianapolis to pass on him.

Many of the returning Baylor players sat off to the side watching the event, perhaps dreaming of the moment when they would be on the field auditioning in front of NFL scouts from just about every team in the league. Among them was a baby-faced, shaggy-haired kid who didn't look much older than 19, and who had walked in with a hat on and a heavy bag over his shoulder about halfway through the workout.

Nick Florence was the epitome of a student-athlete. Class and football were equally important, which was evidenced by his decision to stay at Baylor his freshman year after he was recruited by former head coach Guy Morriss. When Briles showed up, Florence was told the new staff wanted to "grayshirt" him for his first season, meaning he would not be involved with the football program during his initial semester on campus. He could be a student, but would have to pay his own way and not practice with the team until the spring.

The news was a shock to Florence, whose parents were both Baylor graduates.

"But I didn't want to come to school only for football," Florence said, "so I decided to do it. I didn't want to go anywhere else. And it turned out to be a smart decision for me."

Florence spent most of his career as a backup, although he started seven games in 2009 when Griffin suffered a season-ending ACL injury. His junior campaign was supposed to be a redshirt year until Griffin's concussion against Texas Tech led the coaches to ask him to enter the game at halftime. While Florence was stellar in his two-quarter performance at Cowboys Stadium, that would be the only action he would see all year. Still, he has never shown an ounce of resentment for his 30-minute junior season.

"The team needed me right then," Florence said. "I've never regretted that decision."

So as Griffin was tossing passes around at the Pro Day, reality was setting in with the coaches, administrators, media, and everyone else associated with Baylor football: the person named Robert Griffin, and the character known as RGIII, would never compete on campus again after this workout.

Sure, the ride had been a great one, but what was next? And, more importantly, who was next?

That *who* was standing in the corner wearing a ball cap and holding a backpack, with no idea what kind of a season awaited him as the heir apparent of Baylor's most storied quarterback.

★ ★ ★

For a third time, Coach Briles found himself making a trip to New York on Robert Griffin's behalf. The occasion was the NFL Draft, and he sat right next to his former quarterback in the green room while waiting for the live broadcast to begin.

Just a few months earlier, Briles had accompanied Griffin to the Heisman Trophy presentation, where he was the favorite to win over Luck. Sure enough, Griffin did take home college football's most prestigious award, his counterpart from Stanford being named runner-up for the second straight year.

For this, though, Luck was expected to go No. 1 to the Colts, while Griffin was prepared to hear his name called second by the Redskins. He even wore burgundy and gold socks. And once again there were no surprises, as Griffin became the second Bears player selected No. 2 overall in the Briles era, joining offensive tackle Jason Smith in 2009. And when Kendall Wright went 20th overall to the Titans later that night, Baylor Nation had yet another first-rounder.

While flying back to Texas, Briles received text message after text message congratulating him on two more first-round picks, upping the number to five since he took over as head coach four seasons earlier. Defensive tackle Phil Taylor and guard Danny Watkins had been tabbed with the 21st and 23rd selections, respectively, in 2011.

But this 2012 draft symbolized a true passing of the torch for Briles, who knew there would never be another Robert Griffin to come along. He understood that there was no way any player could adequately fill the shoes (or socks) RGIII had left behind.

In spring practice, Art didn't immediately hand the reins over to Florence, who still had to win the job from Bryce Petty. But as practices wore on, he began to separate himself from the competition.

"I just had this good feeling about him," Briles said. "I just knew he was a guy who, if we're standing on the third floor and we told them someone needs to jump, he's gone before even asking a question. He's got that instinct as a leader and just understands how to get people to go with him."

However, those skills and that image didn't develop overnight. Art even played a hand in forming the perception his teammates would come to have of Florence. Just before the start of two-a-days, Briles called Florence for an impromptu meeting in the weight room. The quarterback wasn't exactly sure what this was about. He wasn't the type of guy to get into trouble. His grades were always good, and football-wise, Florence had more confidence than at any point during his collegiate career. He was ready to take over for RGIII, so what could Coach Briles possibly want to see him about?

His grooming habits, of course.

Over the years, there have been plenty of coaches who harped on their players to maintain a clean-cut image. Keep the hair cut short and the face shaved. On the other hand, Art had proven long ago that he wasn't your average coach. So what did he tell Florence just a few days before practice began?

"Nick, I think you should grow your beard out and grow your hair out. You need to get a little rough on the edges. People look at you as this pretty boy who's perfect and doesn't make mistakes. You need to dirty it up."

Florence wasn't expecting that, but just like he did at halftime of the Tech game the season before, he wasn't about to question his coach. He respected him and knew there was a reason for everything he said and did, so Florence went home that night and talked to his wife, even though he wasn't 100 percent sure Briles was serious. That is, until he received a text message from his coach later in the evening.

"He sent me a picture of Snoop Dogg and Martha Stewart cooking in the kitchen, and the caption said something like, 'Only one of these is a convicted felon.' Obviously, it's not the one everyone thinks it'll be."

So Florence avoided all clippers, razors, and scissors for several months. Once during the year, Briles noticed he had slightly trimmed his bangs, just to keep the hair out of his eyes, prompting the superstitious coach to throw a biblical reference that he knew his quarterback would understand: "You're not going to be like Samson, are you? He cut his hair and he lost his power."

For the most part, Florence kept the shaggy look throughout the season. Whether or not his teammates actually saw him any differently or blocked any better for him is questionable, but there was no doubt as to who was the leader of the Baylor football team in 2012.

★ ★ ★

Art Briles has always stressed the value of looking good and feeling good on the field. He knows if his players are excited about how they're dressed, they'll play with more swagger and more confidence.

In the 2012 season opener against Southern Methodist, the Baylor football team debuted black jerseys and pants to go along with its standard gold helmet. Since Briles came to the school, the Bears had donned an all-white uniform and even an all-gold getup once. Each week, they vary what's worn, often letting the seniors decide.

When the black uniforms were revealed before the season, the players were so stoked to wear them that they paid no attention to the 5:30 PM kickoff on September 2 in Waco and how the dark jerseys might absorb more heat. They wore them anyway.

And they wore out SMU in the process, drubbing the Mustangs 59–24. More important than any jersey color, Florence set the tone of the game and the season with an impressive opening drive that saw him complete all four passes. So fast was the offense's tempo that SMU committed four penalties on the Bears' first possession. Baylor scored early and often, leading 45–3 at one point in the third quarter.

Florence, who received an encouraging text from Griffin before the game, put up RGIII-like numbers with a 21-of-30 passing night for 341 yards, four touchdowns, and no picks.

The next game, against Sam Houston State, the quarterback led Baylor on a second-half comeback, thanks to 312 yards passing with 80 more on the ground. The Bears surged past the Bearkats with 24 fourth-quarter points to win 48–23.

A Friday night victory on national TV against a trending Louisiana-Monroe squad that had shocked Arkansas on the road two weeks earlier put the Bears at 3–0 heading into the conference opener against West Virginia, which just so happened to be the first-ever Big 12 game in Morgantown.

Thanks to Florence and a huge day from wide receiver Terrance Williams, the Bears racked up 63 points…and lost.

In what turned out to be one of the craziest games of the 2012 season, the Mountaineers outscored the Bears 70–63 in a game that rivaled the previous year's Alamo Bowl. Baylor's defense had no answer for quarterback Geno Smith, who at the time appeared to be a clear-cut favorite to win the Heisman Trophy, or receiver Tavon Austin, a player described by Briles later in the year as a legitimate candidate to win the Heisman himself. West Virginia wideout Stedman Bailey also set a Big 12 record with 303 receiving yards.

Remarkably, that milestone lasted for all of two minutes before Williams surpassed the mark with 314 yards on 17 catches. As for Florence, throwing for a school-best 581 yards and five touchdowns and yet still becoming an afterthought seems implausible. But Smith's day included 45-of-51 passing for 656 yards and eight touchdowns, as well as a key third-down throw in the final minutes to keep the Bears off the field.

Briles said he remembers flying home from West Virginia thinking the offense was plenty explosive, and as long as they could correct some things defensively, his team was in good shape. Little did he know that the outcome would be the start of a four-game losing streak.

Florence struggled against Texas Christian the next game during a home loss in which he threw four interceptions. The Bears then fell in a 56–50 heartbreaker to Texas on the road, which was followed by a 35–21 defeat by Iowa State.

For the first time since Briles' second season at Baylor, the Bears found themselves in serious jeopardy of not qualifying for a bowl game. "It was a tough stretch for us," the coach said. "When you're 3–0, and it's now 3–4, you've got to keep the guys believing at all times. But we weren't going to give up. We were going to keep fighting and keep trying."

On the flight to Waco after losing to the Cyclones, Briles already knew of one change he was ready to try. A certain running back who had been eased into the action thus far was about to get his chance to shine.

★   ★   ★

Lache Seastrunk was no stranger to Baylor fans in the Waco area. Having starred at Temple High School just 35 minutes south down Interstate 35, he was one of the top recruits in the country heading into the 2010 prep season. Baylor was never a top contender for his services, and Seastrunk eventually chose Oregon, where he played sparingly as a freshman. But when his name became involved in possible recruiting violations, he chose to leave for a school closer to home.

Thus, Baylor welcomed him into the family in 2011, although Seastrunk had to sit out a season in compliance with NCAA transfer rules. So by 2012 he was ready to play physically, but the Bears coaching staff worried about him being ready to handle the mental grind of learning his assignments, both as a runner and blocker. Sure, he could be dangerous with the ball in his hands, but if he failed on a blitz pickup, Florence could end up wiped out in the process.

So Baylor eased Seastrunk along, and he flashed a nice run here or there, but through seven games, he had just 181 yards on 29 attempts. Sitting at 3–4 with a home game against Kansas on the horizon, the time had come to unleash the "Strunk."

The result was 194 all-purpose yards, of which 103 came on the ground on 17 carries. Seastrunk also had five catches for 91 yards, including a 68-yard touchdown, as the Bears improved to 4–4 with a 41–14 win over the Jayhawks.

Against Oklahoma the next week, Baylor had several chances to take control of the game, but eventually came up short in a 42–34 loss in Norman. While Seastrunk scored three more touchdowns and rushed for 91 yards, the Bears fell back below .500.

But thanks to a team meeting before the game, organized by seniors Lanear Sampson and Chance Casey, combined with a hard-fought battle against the No. 14 team in the country on the road, the Bears remained confident. Briles even lifted their spirits in the postgame locker room, predicting three straight victories to close out the season.

And he knew exactly who remained on the schedule, starting first with No. 1–ranked Kansas State, who came to town with the current Heisman Trophy favorite, quarterback Collin Klein.

Call it confidence. Call it swagger. Call it a hunch. Art thought they would beat the Wildcats, a team he felt stole a game from Baylor the previous season, winning 36–35 despite the Bears seemingly controlling the play start to finish.

Not that it would be easy. In 2012 the Wildcats were mauling people on both sides of the ball. Nevertheless, Briles just knew his team would play well. And he thought that, if somehow Baylor could get out to a big lead, Kansas State's run-oriented, ball-control offense would have a hard time passing its way back into the game.

Bingo.

The Bears scored on their first drive and never looked back, racing to a 28–7 lead in the second quarter. Florence threw two early scores, running back Glasco Martin rushed for three touchdowns, and Seastrunk continued his emergence with 185 yards and two more TDs, including an 80-yard breakaway straight up the middle that saw him avoid three different defenders while showcasing his track-star speed.

"We knew we could win all week," Sampson said. "Coach had us believing it. We didn't just talk about how we could compete with them. We practiced all week like we were going to win that game."

Just as impressive as the Baylor offense, which racked up 580 yards, was the defensive effort led by coordinator Phil Bennett, who was hired before the 2010 season. Bennett, a former head coach at SMU, was once a coordinator at Kansas State under the Wildcats' Bill Snyder, a legendary figure in Manhattan.

Bennett's defense took some criticism after yielding 70 points against West Virginia and another 56 to Texas a few weeks later. But against KSU, Baylor stifled Klein all night.

The signature moment occurred early in the fourth. With Baylor leading 52–24, the Wildcats mounted a 21-play drive that culminated with a first-and-goal from the Bears' 6-yard line. This was normally Klein time as the oversized, run-first quarterback had a knack for finding his own hole from the shotgun formation.

Baylor stopped him on first down as Klein picked up four yards to the 2. On the next snap, he added another yard. But then the Bears tightened up. On third down? Stuffed. Fourth down? Stuffed again.

The defense that couldn't stop West Virginia seemingly all day, just held strong on four straight plays starting from the 6-yard line against the No. 1 team in the country and one of college football's best all-around players that year.

Baylor students and fans rushed the field following the blowout win, one of the most impressive efforts in Briles' five seasons of running the program. With the Bears now at 5–5, they needed just one more victory in the remaining two games to become bowl eligible for the third straight year.

Amid the sea of elation, family and friends were congratulating running backs coach Jeff Lebby when someone reminded him how close they were to the necessary six wins.

"Six wins? Forget that. Eight! We're trying to get eight."

After thrashing the No. 1 team in the country, why not?

★   ★   ★

Baylor now faced Texas Tech at the grandiose Cowboys Stadium in Arlington. About two hours before the game, members of the Red Raiders marching band were roaming the Baylor sideline, and a few of the Tech cheerleaders had moseyed over, as well, all holding out their phones. Usually, there is no reason for one team's traveling party to drift to the other's bench, but then again, there typically isn't a cult hero on hand.

Robert Griffin III, who had just led the Washington Redskins to an impressive Thanksgiving Day win over the Cowboys in this very building two days earlier, stayed in the area to support his Baylor crew, donning the Green and Gold.

He saw a barnburner, as the Bears and Red Raiders played another classic, trading blows throughout the day. Baylor had a shot to win in regulation, but a missed field goal sent the game into overtime, where Martin scored on his team's first possession. Tech then had their chance, but couldn't convert a fourth-down pass attempt, the Bears capturing a dramatic 52–45 win with Griffin and his former teammates storming the field to celebrate. Baylor was now 6–5 and heading to a third-straight bowl game for the first time in the school's long history.

Where they were going was still to be determined. After traveling to Houston and San Antonio the previous two years, the players were hoping to leave the state, perhaps for a sunny locale such as Arizona or California. And the final regular season game would certainly play a major factor in that decision, although Baylor would have to host Oklahoma State, the only Big 12 school Briles had yet to defeat since arriving in Waco.

Senior Day was an emotional one for those like Florence and Williams, who were both enjoying stellar seasons and were ranked among the nation's best. Florence was No. 1 in total offense for most of the year, while Williams finished 2012 as the NCAA leader in receiving yards with 1,832.

Baylor rose to the challenge against an OSU squad that had defeated them by an average of nearly 30 points per game in their four previous meetings. But this year was different. No longer just making stops, Bennett's defense was now scoring points, as linebacker Eddie Lackey returned an interception for a touchdown for the second consecutive game.

In the fourth quarter, Seastrunk then cut loose through the middle for what appeared to be an easy trip down the field. That is, until he cramped up around the 40-yard line with an apparent hamstring injury. He wasn't about to stop, hopping his way to the end zone, still just fast enough, before diving over the goal line. The gut-check 76-yard score gave him 178 yards rushing and his team a convincing two-score lead. Oklahoma State tacked on a late touchdown, but the Bears had their first win over the Cowboys in the Briles era, 41–34.

Afterward, safety Ahmad Dixon used Seastrunk's run as a perfect analogy for Baylor's 2012 resolve.

"His run defined our season," Dixon said. "At the beginning of his run, he was 100 percent. He was going strong, just like our season when we started out 3–0. When we got to the middle of our season, he got to the middle of his run, we had a breaking point. But we kept fighting and kept going, and he kept going. We just found a way. He got to the end zone, and we got to the bowl game."

And not just any bowl. Thanks to a three-game winning streak—all of which came against postseason-bound opponents—Baylor earned an invitation to the Holiday Bowl with a 7–5 record. "The food is going to taste pretty good for the next three weeks," Briles said following the OSU win.

Just as the players wanted, the Bears would be traveling to San Diego, where their opponent, the University of California–Los Angeles, held a distinct geographical advantage. That didn't matter much to Coach Briles, though. He knew UCLA had a storied tradition and would likely have a lot more fans, but he also knew his team was playing as well as anyone.

And leading the charge was Florence, who entered the showdown with a chance to break Griffin's single-season record of 4,293 passing yards. Florence didn't have a huge game, but then again, he didn't need to. While his 188 passing yards marked his second-lowest total of the season, that was still enough for him to surpass Griffin and finish the year with 4,309.

Fortunately, Florence's teammates picked up the slack. After earning just 12 sacks during the regular season, the defense dropped UCLA quarterback Brett Hundley six times. Offensively, Seastrunk and Martin helped Baylor rush for 306 yards.

All in all, the Bears dominated the Bruins by a score of 49–...well, that part is actually still up for debate.

Officially, the scoreboard read 49–26 after UCLA was granted a touchdown as time expired. However, video evidence showed that the team's ball carrier never broke the plane of the goal line. Briles tried to challenge the call, but there was a problem in doing so. "The replay officials were gone," Briles said. "They just left before the game was over, so we couldn't do anything."

UCLA got to keep the score and kick the extra point, cementing the final tally in the record books.

A few months after the season ended, the Baylor players, coaches, and football staff received their shiny, diamond-encrusted rings to commemorate the convincing bowl win over the Bruins. With every minute detail approved by the head coach, the letters BU, formed in green jewels, highlight the top, and on the side of the ring, both teams' helmets are shown. Also proudly displayed in a large font is the score of the game: 49–19, of course.

Art Briles' competitive spirit will never die.

32. Coaching Never Stops

"That's why they call us 'coach.'"

ART BRILES DOESN'T have to look too far outside his office to recognize success. While achievement in sports is usually measured by points, wins, and ultimately championships, it can also be defined by piles of dirt, bricks, and cement.

Briles is still striving to obtain a national title at Baylor, but over his first five seasons in Waco, he has shaped a program that can compete with any team in the nation, both on the field and now in recruiting. Because of that, more than just pride and excitement has been building around the university these days. One of Art's biggest goals when he first took the Baylor job was to bring football back to the campus, Floyd Casey Stadium being located eight miles away.

"You can't have a gameday atmosphere if you're not on your own turf," Briles said.

Just like the team's turnaround on the field, the change didn't happen overnight. But in 2012, Baylor broke ground on a new stadium that sits right off the Brazos River and adjacent to Interstate 35. The projected $250 million landmark, which will have a capacity of about 45,000 with 39 luxury suites, is set to open for the 2014 football season and should be one of the nicest on-campus venues in the nation.

"Baylor is Baylor," said Briles, who is already using the new stadium as a recruiting tool. "That's where the students are. That's where the people come back to now. That's where the football games are going to be. When you add the river and the bridge and all the atmosphere we can have there, it's paramount. It's something Baylor University is really going to embrace."

When asked, he offers his opinions on details about the locker room and weight room and such, but for the most part, Briles sticks to what he does best.

"We'll bring things to him that we feel are important to have his input," Baylor athletics director Ian McCaw says. "But he hasn't been deeply involved in the stadium design. His comment to me was, 'There're other people who can do that better than I can.' Obviously, the things we feel are very important, we'll come to him. That's the sign of a good leader—use your strengths. I don't tell him what play to run on third-and-seven, and he's not going over there and telling them what seat we need to pick out. We're all here to use our strengths."

With so much on his plate these days, Art wouldn't seem to have a lot of time for reflection. Yet despite his keep-moving-forward approach, he still finds a way to honor those from his past—the players and coaches who have "sacrificed body and limb" for him over the years.

From his days coaching in Sweetwater, Texas, beginning in 1980, to the players on the Bears' current roster more than three decades later, the men who have played for him seem to relish the off-the-field stories as much as anything that can be recalled from actual games. They know Briles is trying to build a championship-caliber team at Baylor. They know recruiting is virtually a 365-day-a-year process.

Still, Coach Briles finds a way to surprise his former players with his loyalty, humbleness, and if nothing else, his memory.

★ ★ ★

Former Houston receiver Donnie Avery will forever be grateful to Coach Briles, who wouldn't let him quit the team in 2005 when he wanted to take the easy way out because football, school, and being a father had become overwhelming. So, even now that he's in the NFL, Avery hasn't forgotten the coach who always had his back. And he takes great pride in knowing Art Briles hasn't forgotten, either.

After two promising years with the St. Louis Rams, Avery seemed primed for a breakout in 2010. Unfortunately, a torn ACL in the preseason didn't just shelve him for that campaign, the injury also kept Avery from playing in half of the 2011 games.

He was cut by the Rams and went to the Tennessee Titans, where he made the roster and suited up for the first time with the team in an early October game at Cleveland. Hours before kickoff, Avery received a text message from Coach Briles, one that is now locked in his phone forever.

"Once the man, always the man."

Avery played eight games for the Titans that year, but eventually caught on with the Indianapolis Colts, where he revived his career in 2012 with personal bests in catches and receiving yards, prompting the Kansas City Chiefs to sign him to a three-year, $8.5 million free agent deal before the 2013 season.

Randomly, Briles will fire off motivational texts to Avery, using a number of his catchy phrases. But sometimes on Sunday mornings before games, he'll send a message that he often told Avery during pregame warm-ups during their days together at Houston.

"Can't be stopped. Not today, D.A., not today. You can't be stopped."

When Avery puts on his equipment now in the NFL, the shoulder pads come down right over his chest, just covering a tattoo he received early in his pro career. The tattoo is simple, yet undeniably meaningful.

"Can't be stopped."

★ ★ ★

Art Briles is perhaps the last person who should be described as tech-savvy, although he's definitely functional. Text messages have now become huge in the recruiting world, so he has been forced to keep up. Of course, no one said he had to use emoticons, but every now and then, coach will throw in a smiley face, a picture of a fist, hands clapping, or a thumbs-up sign. More than anything, his text messages are a way to show his former players that he still cares.

While his father, Mike, was an assistant under Art for 12 years, Mitch Copeland was a standout athlete in his own right. As a dominating tackle in the middle of the Yellow Jackets' defense, Mitch was named the Texas Class 4A Defensive Player of the Year in 1994 and claims to have the most starts in Stephenville's history with 46, just edging Jeffrey Thompson (45).

While he had plenty of sacks, tackles for loss, and fumble recoveries, one of his favorite plays occurred in the epic state semifinal win over Waxahachie in 1993, when he chased and tackled the quarterback some 40 yards down the field to save a touchdown. On the next play, the Jackets recovered a fumble, further bolstering the greatness of Copeland's hustle play. Stephenville won the game 22–21 en route to the school's first state title.

These days, Mitch, who like many of the coach's former players calls himself an "Art Briles fan," roots for Baylor as if he went there instead of Abilene Christian University. Immediately after one of the Bears' big victories, Copeland felt the need to send off a text to the coach, letting him know how proud he was to have played for him and how excited he is to watch Baylor grow as a program. Minutes later, Briles responded.

"Thx, Cope…helluva play against Waxahachie."

And that's really nothing unusual. Mike Welch, who played just one season of varsity football for Coach Briles back in 1983 at Sweetwater, was a sophomore then, lining up mostly at defensive back. He wasn't the best practice player in the world but had been dubbed "Light Man" for his ability to shine when the lights were brightest.

In a game against Fort Stockton, Briles referred to the bright lights and then told Welch to take the kickoff back for a touchdown, which he promptly did. Welch went on to become a captain at Baylor, finishing his career in 1990, still 18 years before Briles would arrive in Waco. They remain close to this day and will trade texts back and forth. Every now and then, "Nice return against Fort Stockton," will be included.

In fact, Briles has been known to practice the habit on players he hasn't coached—even to some he has never met.

In January 2011 he showed up in Mobile, Alabama, to check out Baylor linemen Danny Watkins and Phil Taylor during Senior Bowl practices, which are conducted about three months before the NFL Draft. After lunch one day, Art and some of his fellow coaches walked into their hotel and noticed John Elway standing in the lobby alone. The former Broncos quarterback and Pro Football Hall of Famer was staring down at his phone when Art walked by; the coach couldn't resist adding a quick comment.

"Nice drive against Cleveland."

★ ★ ★

Safety B.J. Mercer was a solid role player as a sophomore and junior at Stephenville before becoming a starter and earning all-district honors as a senior.

Never garnering the headlines, he was one of those gritty, core types who laid it on the line weekly for the team and coach he adored.

A member of the 1998 state championship squad, Mercer stayed in Stephenville the following year, playing football at Tarleton State, where he was able to also dabble as a radio DJ. For years, he couldn't hang with Coach Briles in the "who you got on the box?" game where the coach would often challenge his players to name the artist singing the current song on the radio while they worked out in the weight room.

Now, Mercer has about 10 years of DJ experience spanning five different genres, including Briles' favorite, classic rock. But in the early stages of his career, Mercer remembers a day in 2001, not long after his former coach left Stephenville for Texas Tech. In the middle of a crazy on-air shift, Mercer fielded a call from Briles, who was listening online to KCUB (98.3 FM), a small station located in Stephenville.

"Hey, Mo, this is Coach Briles at Tech. I want to make a request."

Surprised his coach still remembered the nickname he used to call him, and stunned he actually found the station online, the website feature having been introduced just two weeks before, Mercer was already reaching to pull Peter Frampton's "Do You Feel Like We Do?" a song he knew was one of Briles' favorites. But the coach caught him off guard again and requested "It's Been Awhile" by Staind. Mercer always knew Briles was good for a subliminal message or two, so he wasn't sure if his former coach was requesting a tune for the folks back in Stephenville, suggesting his recent move to Lubbock and that he would no longer be leading the Yellow Jackets, or if he was simply picking out a song that was recently high on the music charts.

Either way, Mercer was honored by the call and ended up playing Frampton's hit after Briles' request as a subliminal message of his own.

After Mercer got out of the radio business, he became a coach and teacher at Terrell High School, located 40 miles east of Dallas, and later landed in Frisco as their high school's debate coach. He knows the differences between football and debate, of course, but sees plenty of parallels in terms of competition and a determination to come out victorious.

His debate teams, which have qualified at the regional, state, and national levels, wore Under Armour shirts with "We Will Win" on the back, duplicating a banner Mercer saw daily in the Stephenville High School weight room. Another phrase the Yellow Jackets players often used as a rallying cry was

"Work Hard, Dream Big." Mercer said he had that saying on a magnet inside his locker during his football days.

While Mercer recently took another job in Austin, all information needed for the debate and speech teams at Frisco High can still be found at workharddreambig.wikispaces.com, leaving no suspense as to who might have originally set up the website.

While seeing Art Briles' legacy alive on football fields all over the state makes sense, he's apparently had an impact on the success of some debaters in North Texas, as well.

★ ★ ★

Ahmad Dixon was one of the highest-ranked recruits ever to come out of Waco. As just a 17-year-old at Midway High School, he was already on the radar of schools across the country when Art Briles and his staff came to Baylor.

To Dixon, a new coach across town didn't mean much. He had seen other guys come and go and didn't figure anything special was taking place. Plus, he was thinking much bigger, powerhouses such as Texas, Tennessee, Southern California, Alabama, and Auburn. He also wanted to get out of Waco—even more reason not to consider Baylor, whose last bowl appearance occurred in 1994 when Dixon was just barely out of diapers.

In the summer before his junior season, Dixon grew fond of Bears defensive coordinator Brian Norwood, whose son, Levi, was a high school teammate. Norwood's specialty was defensive backs, which also intrigued Dixon. Convinced to come to a Baylor game as a recruit, the program had his full attention after he witnessed Robert Griffin's step-back play against Wake Forest.

But he remembers his conversation with Art Briles even more.

"He told me a few things that day that really stuck with me," Dixon said. "We talked about football and life and family. He had big dreams for the program. He said that Jason Smith would be a first-round pick. He said Robert Griffin, who was a freshman, would be a first-rounder. He said Kendall Wright would be, too."

Dixon didn't know if he was hearing basic coaching rhetoric or if this new guy at Baylor was for real, but once he saw Smith get picked No. 2 overall in the NFL Draft, he began to trust the program more. Dixon then actually committed to Baylor briefly before switching to Tennessee. After the Volunteers had a coaching change of their own, Dixon began to rethink his decision again. Briles was waiting with open arms.

"He never pressured me," Dixon said. "I really never fully de-committed from Baylor. I was just kind of flaky about the process. I got flattered by other schools. But one thing coach always told me was, 'This is a family at Baylor. We're a family.' And when I got on the stage to sign, I really didn't know what I was going to do. But I kept thinking about family and what he said to me. Where I'm from, only a few of my friends have a mom and dad at home. But I'm blessed that my parents are together still, so family is big for me. When I decided to go to Baylor, it was about family.

"And it didn't hurt matters that what Briles had told me about the first-round picks started coming true with Jason. In fact, all of the players he said would go in the first round eventually were drafted in the first round."

As for Dixon himself, Briles predicted he would be the best safety in the country, a status he held in high school.

Early in Dixon's freshman year with the Bears, he got a call from his father, telling him his mother was being rushed to the hospital after suffering an aneurism. Quickly, he went to Coach Briles about the situation, even explaining he had a test that day and didn't know if he could miss.

"A.D., you don't worry about anything, okay?"

"Really, Coach? I have a test today. I don't know if I can miss it. And what about practice and…"

"A.D., you remember when you signed your letter and I said we're about family? Go be with your family. I don't care if it takes you a month, two months, or however long it takes—we're here beside you, no matter what."

Dixon left the coach's office with tears in his eyes. Just like he preached before he signed, Art Briles was true to his word, developing a family atmosphere for his players. Not just within Baylor, but recognizing that players have their own families that need support, as well. Fortunately, his mother's health improved, allowing Dixon to return to the team rather quickly.

Briles was right about the draft picks. He proved to Dixon he was serious about the family atmosphere. The only thing left was making him into the top safety in the country. The problem, though, was that Dixon really hadn't played much safety during his first three years, moving into the "Jack linebacker" role, a hybrid position between safety and linebacker.

Following the 2012 season, Dixon and his parents met with Briles about the possibility of leaving early for the NFL. Briles visited with them in his office during one quiet afternoon in January and didn't hide from the truth.

"I told you that you'd be the No. 1 safety in America, and you've yet to play safety. Now, you know I'm not a man to go against my word. I want you to stay because I promised you that you'd be the best safety here. Honestly, A.D., if you want to leave, that's fine. I'll support you and help you out, no matter what. But if you stay, I'll help you in the film room. We'll go in there and study that safety position together."

When they left, Dixon and his parents still weren't sure about what to do. Less than a week later, he sat alone in his room and remembered all of Briles' previous guarantees that had come to fruition. So he decided to return to Baylor and take coach up on his offer.

Sure enough, a few days into spring practice, Briles called Dixon into the film room, where they broke down tape for nearly three hours. The coach gave him some insight as to what an offensive coordinator sees, giving Dixon a better understanding of the safety position. After they finished, Dixon got in his car and called his father. Sitting in the parking lot of the Baylor athletics facility, tears rolled down his face.

"Dad, this man did exactly what he said he was going to do…again."

★ ★ ★

Before the 2013 NFL Draft, Art Briles fielded a few phones calls from the Dallas area. And no, they weren't all from his oldest daughter, Jancy—but they came from just a few offices down the hallway.

The Cowboys were interested in Baylor wide receiver Terrance Williams, and head coach Jason Garrett made a few calls to Briles, asking everything from his route-running ability to the way he conducts himself off the field.

When the draft finally arrived, the Cowboys considered taking Williams with their first-round pick (31st overall) but passed for a center. On the next day, which holds the next two rounds, Jancy was told by a few people in the building to be prepared for Williams to be a Cowboy. Her dad was calling a few times, as well, in anticipation. But in the second round, they again passed on Williams and took a tight end. No one ever dreamed he would still be around in the third, but when Williams was still on the board when the Cowboys picked again at No. 74, they quickly turned in the card to take him.

Jancy was excited. Her dad was pumped, too. Williams, who grew up in Dallas, was playing for his hometown team. And the Cowboys were elated to get a player that many of their scouts had rated with a first-round grade.

Minutes after the pick, the coaches, scouts, and front-office personnel, including owner and general manager Jerry Jones were celebrating the pick in their War Room when someone in the room phoned Jancy to come over. She hesitantly walked in, unaware how her duties as a public relations assistant could be used at this moment. Instead, she was asked by Garrett to give a quick scouting report.

Caught off guard and already blushing, Jancy quickly regrouped and instantly transformed into the girl who used to jump in the pickup every Saturday morning with her dad to break down film.

"Well, he's a great kid. He's got good speed, good hands, and can stretch the field."

The War Room erupted with applause. It was as if the pick was now validated.

He taught her well.

★ ★ ★

One of the toughest football players Art Briles ever coached was Yellow Jackets middle linebacker Jody Brown. He wasn't the biggest player on the field by any means, but without a doubt, he was always the most intense.

The epitome of a no-nonsense player, Brown wasn't into showboating. He wasn't into celebrating. He just ran sideline to sideline every play, chasing down anyone who wasn't wearing Stephenville's Navy and Gold.

Coach Briles always felt that if Brown had stood a few inches taller than his listed 5'10" height, he could've gone to any Division I school in the country and likely would've played on Sundays. Instead, he attended Division II Abilene Christian and was a two-time All–Lone Star Conference selection.

After college, with Briles having already left for Texas Tech, Brown moved about three and a half hours south to Kerrville and started raising a family. In 2009 his father, Danny, a former Stephenville player in the 1950s and a big supporter of Briles and the Yellow Jackets program, died in a ranching accident at the age of 57.

The next few days were an obvious daze for Brown, who quickly went back to Stephenville with his family, trying to explain to a 10-year-old son what had happened and why. There were several phone calls of love and support, but Brown will always cherish the one from Art Briles the day after the accident.

"Jody Bill…hey, man, how's it going? I just want you to know I'm thinking of you. Is there anything I can do for you? If so, let me know. You're in my thoughts and prayers."

With the funeral still to take place, Brown didn't stop to think about the call right then. He was appreciative, but not in a state of mind to reflect. But afterward, and on his way back to Kerrville, he got a second call from Briles, who again wanted to touch base and ask if there was anything he could do.

"That meant the world to me. He may not realize that, but it did," Brown said. "In my mind, I'm thinking, *What am I to him? He's got a lot bigger fish to fry. And he's calling to check on me?* I had some friends and family who didn't even call me. And here's my high school coach 15 years ago checking on me…twice."

Tragedy hits home for Art, who lost his mother and father when he was 20. No two situations are alike, but the pain is similar. And while he doesn't like to speak of his parents' death, Briles remembers the phone calls of support he received.

He feels their pain because, simply, he's been there.

Jody Brown will always remember Art Briles as the greatest football coach he ever had, but that respect will never compare to how he views Art Briles the person, the man, and the friend. "You can define success any way you want— you take care of your family or you're a good business person," Brown said. "In all of those morals and principals, it carries over to life. With Coach Briles, he goes way beyond Xs and Os. He's influenced lives way beyond football."

★   ★   ★

When Robert Griffin III reflects on his life and athletic career, some of his biggest moments include:

- Competing in the Olympic Trials in 2008
- His first career start at Baylor

- A victory over Oklahoma in 2011
- Winning the Heisman Trophy
- Being drafted No. 2 overall by the Redskins
- Defeating Dallas on Thanksgiving Day at Cowboys Stadium
- Facing the Cowboys again in a do-or-die matchup in the regular season finale with the division title and a playoff berth on the line
- Marrying his college sweetheart

There is a common theme running through all of those events: Art Briles was there. Of course, some of them are a given, considering he was the head coach at Baylor and Griffin was the quarterback. Yet the fact remains, when there has been a significant milestone in Griffin's life, his coach and friend has found a way to make it.

That never was more evident than during his rookie season with the Redskins. Griffin had no clue Briles would be able to attend the game in Arlington. On the field during pregame warm-ups, Griffin came to the sideline and, out of the corner of his eye, saw Briles standing there sporting a Baylor cap and pullover.

"Coach, you're going to make me cry. I've got to play this game. I can't be crying."

If Griffin was truly touched by Briles making the two-hour drive up from Waco, imagine the feeling the quarterback had seeing him on the sideline at FedEx Field in Landover, Maryland, for the Redskins-Cowboys rematch on December 30, 2012.

"I shouldn't have been surprised, but I was," Griffin said. "I know how busy he is, but he finds a way to be there for me. Even if he's not my coach anymore, he still is and always will be."

And that even includes non-football events, too. In July 2013, Griffin married his college sweetheart, Rebecca. Art and Jan made the trip to Colorado as guests. But just minutes before the start of the ceremony, Art was called to the back to chat with the anxious groom. The coach offered a light-hearted joke, mixed in with some encouraging words that helped calm down Robert, who was a bit overwhelmed with excitement and anticipation.

Whether Art Briles is wearing a headset on the sideline or a three-piece suit in the back of a church, coaching never stops.

Afterword:
Praising the Coach

"Give credit where credit is due, unless it is you."

Jason Garrett
Head Coach, Dallas Cowboys
Coach Briles has a great understanding of how to put a winning program together. He's done it on all different levels. The winning culture that he creates is a direct result of the kind of person he is, the kind of coach he is and how he instills his beliefs in his players, coaching, and staff.

He has the unique ability to bring the right people together and then get the absolute most out of each and every one of them. It's what coaching is all about and something that Coach Briles does as well as anyone in the profession.

At both the high school and college levels, this has resulted in amazing turnarounds and the establishment of programs that not only win, but represent everything that is great about football.

Andy Reid
Head Coach, Kansas City Chiefs
I watched Coach Briles closely through Kevin Kolb. When Kevin was a freshman, I caught one of the Houston games on national television. I said to myself: "Who is this kid and who the heck is coaching him?" He was running an offense that presented the defense with every route on the route tree, a QB that could run the option, and most of all a pass/run option within the same play.

I continued to catch every Houston game that I could from that point on. From that first game I saw, I told Tom Heckert, our GM that we were going to draft that QB from Houston when his senior year was up.

When Kevin's senior year was up and he was getting ready for the draft was when I first talked to Coach Briles. It didn't take long into the conversation to know that "creative" is a small adjective to describe Coach Briles' football mind.

We drafted Kevin at Philadelphia in the second round of the 2007 NFL Draft. Coach Briles then visited the Eagles Complex a few times. His love for Kevin as well as his love for the game of football was obvious.

It is not hard to see why Baylor is a force in college football. It is not hard to see why RGIII won the Heisman and was the second overall pick in the 2012 draft. It is not hard to see why Kevin Kolb was our second-round pick a few years back. Coach Art Briles is a great coach—period!

Barry Switzer

Former Head Coach—Oklahoma Sooners, Dallas Cowboys

As a college and professional coach and now a fan, I have witnessed Art Briles' coaching career from Stephenville High School to the University of Houston and now Baylor University. What he accomplished in high school is nearly unprecedented, and now he has proven, in my opinion, to be one of the best collegiate coaches in the game today!

Ronny "Guthrie" Flowers

CEO of Odessa-based Athletic Supply

If you look up "winner" in the dictionary, you will see a picture of Art Briles. He also makes winners out of everyone associated with him. He respects everyone and fears no one.

He is especially fond of his small-town roots which make our relationship special. Art has helped me be successful. Because I was from a smaller community than he was, I could use his help, but there was nothing I could do for him. When Art and I are partners in golf, we tell the "big ones to line up and the little ones to pair up" because of his competitive spirit.

To one of my all-time favorites, Art Briles—Thanks for being my friend.

Mack Brown

Head Coach—Texas Longhorns

When Kendal was being recruited and thought he should be playing for his dad, his parents were so unselfish and let him make his own choice.

That doesn't happen in many homes.

Ken Bailey

Houston-based Attorney/Family Friend

I first met Art Briles in 2003 when I was a member of the University of Houston's Head Football Coach's Selection Committee. After reviewing his past personal history, his determined pursuit of a degree in the shadows of a personal tragedy, and his success as a football coach, I was convinced that he would be my recommendation to be named the head football coach at the University of Houston. Several of the members wanted to go for a "big name" head coach, and I urged them to look at the man and the fact that Art Briles was a winner. One of my great accomplishments was winning the selection committee over to Coach Briles, and he was hired. During the next four years, Coach Briles and I established a strong personal relationship. I advised him on personal and legal matters, including the negotiations of his contract with the University of Houston. I even tried to give him some advice on play selection, but to my knowledge he never took my "Johnny U. to Lenny Moore" first-play-of-the-game advice.

Due to the relationship of lawyer/client, I am not allowed to share or give out the information on my clients, but let me say that when Coach Briles gives his word and seals it with a handshake, it is sealed in stone. This I have witnessed, and I know few men I admired more for his integrity than Coach Art Briles, and that is a fact that I will share with everyone. Coach Briles is a good coach, the best of men, and I am proud to call him my friend. As I like to tell him, "I have love in my heart for him and his family."

Mike Cloud

Childhood Friend

I had the privilege of knowing the Briles family very well in Art's younger days in Abilene. The Dennis Briles family was solid as a rock, full of love, respect, faith, and discipline. Dennis Briles was an outstanding coach who was respected by everyone who knew him from his days in Abilene and Rule. Art and Eddie thought the world of Coach Briles. Art got his "let's get it done" attitude from his dad. After the loss of his father, Art was destined to become the coach he is today. I think Art was just determined to honor his parents in any way he could, and no one was surprised to see him follow in his dad's footsteps.

While Art was coaching at Stephenville, I took my son to watch the Yellow Jackets play 20 or so times. My son got to see, up close, just how high school football is supposed to be played. What Art and his staff did in Stephenville for a dozen years is phenomenal. Art will probably tell you that his father and Bill Yeoman had the most influence on him in how he learned to attack a defense. But most of what you see in Baylor's offense today was created in the mind of Art Briles. He is truly an offensive genius.

Art and Jan are great Christian people and great parents. They have raised three fantastic children, who all lead quality lives. So, without football, Art and Jan have been an unbelievable success. But Art Briles may very well be the single best football coach in the U.S., on any level. At least, he has my vote.

Edwin Young
Senior Pastor, Second Baptist Church, Houston Texas
What a privilege it is to talk about Art Briles, a great friend and one of the most genuine and humble men I know. He is an astute student of football but, more important than that, an inspiring leader. He truly cares for his players and his coaches.

Jeff Reeter and I were visiting with Art in his office one day. He had the Heisman that was presented to Robert Griffin III, and we were taking photographs when a young man came and poked his head in the door. He no longer played at Baylor, but he needed to see his coach. Art left the chairman of the Baylor University Development Council and the pastor of his Houston church to counsel with that former player. It impressed me that Art had his priorities straight. He knew we were okay, but his passion was for making a difference in the life of this young man in a time of need. Art's compassion and interest in those who played for him knows no bounds.

Art and his wife Jan are authentic Christians. He is an excellent communicator. The last time he spoke to our church family, so many people commented on his transparency.

What a man! What a servant! What a friend! What a coach! May God continue to bless Art and his family with His abundant joy.

Dave Campbell
Longtime Editor of Dave Campbell's Texas Football
Several years ago a group of Texas sportswriters was asked to submit ballots ranking football coaches in the state, from one through 25, and they were to

consider coaches regardless of the level at which they had pursued their profession, be it high school, college, or the NFL.

I was among those asked to participate. I remember I put Tom Landry, Darrell Royal, and Gordon Wood in my top three.

I may have put Gordon Wood [who won two state championships at Stamford, seven more at Brownwood] at No. 1 because I have always considered winning crowns at the high school level to be a tougher job than at the other two. The main reason for my thinking: coaches in the NFL can draft players to fill their needs, and college coaches can evaluate and recruit. But high school coaches can only make do with what they inherit and develop.

Keeping that in mind, I had to put Art Briles high on my list. I don't remember exactly how high—I know it was in the top 10, maybe higher.

In that regard, I am reminded of what David Barron [Houston Chronicle] wrote in Texas Football in that magazine's 50th anniversary edition in 2009: "On the high school front, maybe someone will come along to beat Art Briles, who, for my money, accomplished the turnaround of the half-century by enabling Stephenville to eclipse Brownwood, the greatest dynasty in the 1960s and 1970s in Class 4A football."

I think Barron was right. So on second thought, probably Briles should rank in the top 5.

He has been remarkable at all stops, but especially at Baylor. To borrow one of Darrell Royal's old quotes, Briles most definitely did not inherit a warm bed. But once he reached Waco, he certainly warmed it up—warmed it up so much that Baylor Nation now is almost spoiled.

Never before has Baylor won its way to three straight bowl games in a history that reaches back to its first football season in 1899. Over the years, the Bears did win their way to two bowls in a row, but never three.

But now they have. And judging Briles on his track record, who now is to say more is not on the way?

Dary Stone
Board of Regents Chairman, Baylor University

As a regent, chair of the board at Baylor, and parent of a Baylor football player, it has been my privilege to come to know Coach Briles in a deep and personal way. We have fought two Big 12 league realignment battles together, envisioned and financed a new football stadium, and thanks to his great success on the field, worked together to restructure his contract three times! We also shared a dear friend in Bob Perry, whom we lost this spring.

I know Art to be a man of great discipline, character, and humility. My son, Dary Stone Jr., would walk across hot coals barefoot for Coach Briles, which says a lot coming from a walk-on player who uses his feet for a living [kicker]. Baylor aspires to be different and better, particularly as it relates to character and spirituality. Coach Briles is an ideal representative of those values. Baylor is better because of who Art Briles is as a man. I have been blessed to share a love for my son, my university, and my best friend, Bob Perry, with Art. It's easy to love a man who loves what is important to you, and that's why I love Art Briles.

Grant Teaff

Executive Director, AFCA / Former Baylor Head Coach
Having spent a better part of my life playing football, coaching, and now serving coaches through the American Football Coaches Association, I believe I have a very good grasp on what it takes to be a successful football coach. Art Briles is the consummate successful football coach and possesses all the admirable characteristics needed for success. Coach Briles is an organized leader with a passion to teach fundamentals of the game. His offensive and defensive schemes are simple, yet ingenious. It is very clear to me that he cares deeply about his players, his staff, and his university. When adding the facts that he is a strong family man and a man of character and integrity who teaches values and work ethic to his players, it is very easy to see why he has been successful at every place he has ever coached.

I feel very indebted to Coach Briles because of what he has personally done for Baylor University, its football program, and for those of us who have long believed Baylor should be among the elite football programs in America.

Gil Brandt

Former Cowboys Director of Player Personnel / NFL.com Senior Analyst
He goes out of his way to be friendly and make people feel at home. When I go down there to watch practice, he says, "Gil, my office is open. Go make yourself at home." He has a great deal of allegiance to his players.

I remember seeing him on Thanksgiving Day to watch RGIII against the Cowboys. Most coaches would say they couldn't get away. But he practiced in the morning and drove up to see him.

What he has done to raise the level of the rank and file of Baylor is unbelievable. They had no hope. Now they have hope. What he does to build new football offices, the new indoor field house, and now a new system, it's unbelievable.

The university found a real gem in this guy.

Kent Hance
Texas Tech Chancellor

I first met Art Briles at lunch in San Antonio with Ed Whitacre, John Montford, and Coach Mike Leach. Coach Briles had just gone to work as an assistant at Texas Tech, and I really enjoyed meeting him. He was a down-to-earth person, and it was obvious he was a sound citizen. We hit if off well, and I stayed in touch with him on a regular basis. When the University of Houston job came open, I did everything I could to help him, and once he got the job, I introduced him to my friend, the late Bob Perry. Bob and I had dinner with Art one evening, and after that, Art had a new friend and great supporter in Mr. Perry. Bob helped sponsor the Cougar Network and was a big fan of Art Briles because he was a teacher of men and he also won football games.

But the most important thing about Art Briles is that he loves his players and wants them to do well in life. Many of his former players, including All-Pro Wes Welker, always talk about what a great coach and a great friend he has been. I hold Art Briles in the highest distinction and consider him a dear friend and a true patriot who loves God, family, and country. Art is also one great football coach. Baylor is fortunate to have his services.

Bill Parcells
Hall of Fame Football Coach

One of the ways that I judge football coaches is when I watch their team play: Is the philosophy they employ easily recognizable to the trained eye? And has that coach integrated people into their football system who fit and meet the needs of that philosophy? And at several different places, I've seen Coach Briles do that very thing—integrate people into the system who meet his easily identifiable philosophy. And that to me is the mark of a very, very good football coach. And, in my opinion, that's what he is.

Kelan Luker

Former Stephenville QB / Current High School Football Coach

I haven't played for him since 1998, but I think about him every day and still talk about him. I just love the way he carries himself. He's just a special person. It's hard to put into words unless you've met him.

As a player, he trained me to be a champion in my head and my heart. The Xs and Os came later. But I loved the way he respects me as a man. I know not all coaches do that.

Lovie Smith

Former Chicago Bears Head Coach / Big Sandy High School (1973–1976)

Because I know his background and knew he was a coach's son who is a student of the game and came up the ranks like he did, I expect to see his teams play hard and play with fundamentals and fight to the end. That's the way he played. That's what I see when I watch his teams play.

He's on the cutting edge right now with offensive football. Anyone can see that. But what he's done with that program at Baylor is amazing.

Bob Simpson

Texas Rangers majority owner

A humble genius from a small West Texas town, Coach Art Briles may be the best human motivator in collegiate sports. Ask anyone who has played for him, and you will find a lifetime bond and deep friendship.

Many of his students are moving on to the NFL and enjoying tremendous success, and not just RGIII. Any coach saddled with trying to stop Art Briles' offense on any given Saturday has my condolences.

Art Briles is the most likeable and genuine coach I have ever met, as well as being one of the leading football masterminds of our time. Art Briles will always be one of my life's best friends.

Amos Lee

Singer/songwriter

If I ever played football, Art Briles is the kind of man I'd like to play for. He inspires greatness in those around him, and in an age of cronyism and bullheaded bullying, when I watch Baylor, I see a man on the sideline who sees the big picture and wants his players to succeed as men and as athletes.

Tim Tanner

College friend from Lubbock

He and I met when we were students at Texas Tech, wrapping up less-than-stellar academic careers. We worked together at the TG&Y warehouse and just became good friends. I met him about a week before he married Jan. I consider them family to this day.

I was recently at the Baylor Touchdown Club and saw him speaking to people, wanting pictures and autographs. And knowing him from loading trucks to today, it's just amazing. From the deal with his parents and getting his knee blown out, to just put his life together, it's a great story. And he did it on his own. He didn't have a mentor trying to help him. He started from scratch. He amazes me today. I'm so proud of what he's come from and his life.

Drayton McLane

Baylor alum and donor / former owner of the Houston Astros

I have known of Coach Briles since he was coach at the University of Houston during the time I owned the Houston Astros. I have had an opportunity to get to know him much better since he came to Waco as coach of the Baylor Bears. In my view, that was the best decision he has made, but it's been also great for Baylor with the success they have had under his leadership. We have had two Bowl victories, at the Alamo Bowl and the Holiday Bowl.

The best part is the good friendship we have developed and vision that he has for his student-athletes. He also did a great job at articulating how important it was for Baylor's football program to build a stadium on the campus.

What means a great deal to me are Art's high Christian values; his devotion to his family; and the powerful influence he has on the players, the Baylor student body, and Baylor alumni and fans everywhere. I also enjoy having the Ninfa's cheese enchiladas he buys when we have lunch together. We made a deal that he would pay for the enchiladas, and I would help pay for the stadium.

Andre Ware

ESPN college football analyst/Houston Heisman Trophy winner in 1989

There had been coaches that came through Houston before Coach Briles, but it never seemed like it was still home for me when other coaches were there. But when he came in, he made you feel welcome. It was home again for me. He did an excellent job of embracing guys who have been through the program before he got there. And he was one of those guys himself, so he understood.

I think he also understood the culture of Houston and what it took to be successful there. You have to recruit locally and build that way. He knew the state of Texas really well, and you could tell he had always had a plan in place of how to be a head coach. He got to Houston and implemented it right away.

For my job now at ESPN, there are coaches I have to call and talk to about a story or project I'm working on. With some guys, you're waiting and sweating it out just hoping to get an answer back. With Art, he's fantastic. I know he's busy and he's got a full plate. But he always finds time to get back to me in about five minutes.

While my job forces me to be objective, I just root for the guy. When I look at scores on a Saturday, the first score I look for is Houston. And then I'm going to check out where Art is and see how his team did. That's just the relationship we have and I'm so grateful for it.

Bob Glasgow

Former Texas senator / Stephenville-based lawyer

Art Briles is one of the most exceptional individuals I have ever met. As an elected official in Texas, I have had the opportunity to meet with presidents, senators, congressmen, governors, CEOs, and some of the most influential people in the U.S. But none of them are more exceptional than Art Briles.

He is blessed with the type of charisma few people possess, the kind I observed in John Kennedy, Lyndon Johnson, John Connally, and a few others. With this type of charisma, people instantly become dedicated followers of that person. That is the way I and the people in Stephenville are toward Art Briles. The community as a whole instantly became dedicated to Art Briles.

If you want to know what type of person Art Briles is, just ask one of his former players at Stephenville. Or ask a former member of the Stephenville High School Band or Stingerette drill team. Ask an administrator at Stephenville High School or the parents of a student who played football. Ask any member of that Stephenville community. Art Briles is simply a one-of-a-kind person, and those of us who have had the opportunity to know him experienced something very unique. His influence continues to make us better community members, and the students at Stephenville High School will forever be rewarded by the experience of knowing him.

Acknowledgments

THE FIRST TIME I met Art Briles, we were watching basketball, of course. The Baylor men's team was playing in the NIT Championship. As I sat next to him throughout the game, we talked about a wide range of topics, and at one point he said, "Nick, you know your sports, now."

I thought he truly was admiring my knowledge. Maybe he was. But now that I know him better, I can see he was just doing to me what he does to everyone he meets, which is build them up. Art has a way of making each individual feel like the most important person in the room. Out of all the interviews I did for this book, that was the one overriding theme I heard over and over.

I learned quickly this project comes with a lot of responsibility. The more I worked on this, the more I realized how worthy Art is to have his story written. And the fact he allowed me to do it, having never written a book before, is truly an honor I will always cherish.

Just as Art gave me a chance, I am also truly thankful to Triumph Books for this opportunity. I know my publishers were intrigued by the storyline, but they never once blinked, even with my lack of authorial experience. I really enjoyed working with editor Alex Lubertozzi, who not only edited the book but showed extreme patience in designing the photo pages and making sure everyone was happy with the turnout. On my next book—and, yes, a second one is already in the works—I hope for the opportunity to work with Alex again.

Obviously, I didn't quit my job, so to do this in a condensed time frame *and* continue to work meant there would need to be sacrifices made in other areas. Not everyone has a great boss; I realize that. But the best part about Derek Eagleton is that in the 14 years we've worked together, he's been more like a friend than a manager. That was never more apparent than in the three months I spent researching and writing this book. Supportive is not nearly a strong enough adjective to describe his attitude toward this mission. I'll forever be thankful for that.

As for my team members, SEC guys like Ed Cahill, Rowan Kavner, Bryan Broaddus, and David Helman, they may have had to cover a little more, but once again, they never complained—at least not to me. Chris Behm's daily support was often uplifting.

I can't leave out my recently departed Cowboys team members either: Rob Phillips, Josh Ellis, and Blair Eckerle. They're no longer sitting next to me in the office or radio booth, but they've been extremely encouraging.

The same goes for Jaime Aron, an accomplished author in his own right who offered great advice, and Hekma Harrison, who has listened to me speak of this project for at least two years.

Nick Gholson gave me my first job back in 1997 in Wichita Falls, where the Cowboys fortunately decided to spend training camp a year later. In the middle of one hot practice day, Nick told me covering the Cowboys would "expose" me and land me a bigger job someday. About a year later, that very practice field at Valley Ranch would be my place of business for the next 15 years and counting. Knowing how proud of me he was is a great accomplishment to this day.

All of the aforementioned people are more than just coworkers or good friends. I've got some lifelong allies who will always be by my side.

Tony Domenella, who I've known for 20 years, told me he couldn't wait to buy this book. I told him, "You're probably on the free-book list." And he said, "No way. I'm going to the store and I'm buying it. One of my best friends is writing a book? Oh, I'm going to the store and getting it off the shelf."

Drew Myers has inspired me with his passion and drive since our days at Midwestern State University and still does to this day. I look forward to reading his Acknowledgments section in the near future.

There aren't enough pages in this book to fully compliment Chris Fisher. Arguably the greatest person I know, "Fish" has been there for me through it all for the last 19 years. There hasn't been a day that went by where I didn't think he had my back. And I know he feels the same about me.

My mother, Camille Williams, is the most amazing woman on the planet. I know during the months of March and April, when I kept saying, "Nope, still haven't started writing yet," she was getting very nervous. Her husband, Mark, told me the acknowledgments section is the first thing he likes to read in a book, so I guess I shouldn't spoil any of the story here.

My dad, Tim Eatman, a Baylor grad himself, told me when I first got the job with the Cowboys in 1999 that I would write a book someday, so he's not surprised by this at all. He's as proud as a dad can be, but he always knew I had this in me.

His wife, Sharon, my brother, Evan, who has been deployed in Afghanistan, and my Uncle Ronnie—the proudest Baylor alum I know—have all been very supportive.

I know my Aunt Cindy would be so happy for me if she were still with us. She might have been an Arkansas Razorbacks fan at heart, but she loved me even more—if that was possible. But in her last few years, she loved those Baylor Bears, too.

Feels weird to go this long and not talk about my beautiful daughter, Olivia. Right now, we're working on books like *Barbie Goes to School* and the Dr. Seuss collection, but she'll appreciate this over time. Her mother, Josie, has made many sacrifices, but couldn't have been any better. Her backing will always be remembered.

Talk about sacrifices, my roommate, Ryan Marshall, was very helpful, from keeping the house quiet at night to taking care of my dog, Griffin, whose name isn't a coincidence at all.

Unlike many people on this list, Julie Acosta knows exactly where Rule, Texas, is on the map. Growing up in nearby Stamford, she's familiar with the Big Country and was an unexpected source of support through my month of writing.

I know this book is about Coach Briles, but it's been a journey for me, too. I fully realize how special this is, and so there is absolutely no way I could go through this without recognizing the people that mean so much to me.

Again, I know I left off some people. If you're one of those who ever called or texted with, "How's the book coming along?" consider yourself thanked right now. I really did appreciate it.

Now, as for the people who truly assisted me with this specific project, I don't think I have enough room to thank everyone. For all of those I interviewed on the phone, or even met me somewhere for lunch, I will forever be grateful. I won't mention every one of the 83 people with whom I either talked or traded emails, but a few just can't be left out.

Jason Bragg? He was a stud player at Stephenville, and he was a stud player for this project—hands down. Whether it was giving me scrapbooks of old newspaper clippings or relating classic stories, Bragg was truly remarkable.

B.J. Mercer was also very helpful with photos, articles, and tons of stories. Lance Fleming was able to organize a lunch in Abilene with W.T. Stapler and Bill Hart. How he got two complete strangers to drive up for a meeting with another complete stranger speaks volumes for his character, as well as Art Briles'.

Helen Allison, also known as "Mammie," welcomed me to her house in Rule, and I truly enjoyed that visit as much as any of my experiences during this journey. Maybe it was because I finally got to see what this small Texas town was all about, or perhaps it was the buttermilk pie she made. Either way, I loved talking with her.

Art's brother, Eddie Briles, was extremely accommodating and very informative. I had to realize a few times that when the subject came up about Art's parents, we were talking about his parents, too.

Meeting Robert Griffin III in Waco was outstanding. Actually, the entire time I prepped for the interview, I just thought of it as interviewing Coach Briles' quarterback at Baylor. Not until I sat down with him and his eyes glanced down at my blue notebook with a Dallas Cowboys star on the front, did I realize I was also interviewing the current quarterback of the Washington Redskins. But he laughed it off. He's from Texas, so he's seen worse.

Originally, the interview was supposed to be for 20 to 30 minutes. I just knew I was in trouble when I looked down at my recorder, and we'd been talking for 22 minutes and he wasn't out of his freshman year yet. Thankfully, he answered my questions for a full hour. I am very appreciative for not only that, but his willingness to write the foreword.

I have to thank Baylor sports information director Heath Nielsen, who helped me set up a lot of the interviews with Bears coaches and players. I also want to acknowledge Lauren Phillips and Diane Jee McPheeters for their last-second help.

I asked Kurt Daniels to help me copyedit my work, in part because I knew he was good, but mainly out of convenience since he, too, is in the building with me at the Cowboys complex. What I never knew was how dedicated he would be to making this book a success. Not only did he provide the first contact with Triumph Books, he has also worked tireless hours reading my copy, fact checking, and anything else that a true editor does. I've had to make a lot of quick decisions for this book, but asking him to be a part of it has probably been the smartest one I could've ever made. Kurt is a true professional in every sense of the word.

The entire Briles family was amazing, too. Kendal, Staley, Sarah, and Jeff all provided helpful contributions.

Just about every coach will tell you that he can't do anything without his wife. Jan Briles is no exception. She was incredible for me during this process. She's probably the most consistent person I've come across in a long time, which is a blessing, especially when she's consistently helpful, caring, and resourceful.

Jancy Briles. Well, it's pretty obvious I wouldn't have been able to write this book without her. Then again, I wouldn't have wanted to.

She's been more than a friend. I've even joked and called her my "agent" because she was able to get people to call her back in five minutes when I had been trying for a week. I want to thank Jancy for constantly pushing me through these challenging three months, but yet giving me ample words of encouragement along the way. Her dad listens to her. He respects her. And he trusts her. If Jancy didn't think I was capable of writing this book, Art Briles never would've agreed to let me. With that, I'll always be grateful. He didn't just take a chance on me; Jancy did, as well.

As for the coach himself, I won't lie—because his schedule is so demanding, I wasn't sure we would speak often enough to get this book done. But thanks to the end of spring practice, a few pep talks from Jan, and the discovery of tape recorders, Coach Briles wasn't just helpful, he was incredibly gracious with his time and information.

I know some of the topics we discussed are extremely personal and private. For him to sit down and open up to me was a special experience. I am fully aware that he shared more of his feelings about his parents' accident with me than he ever has with his three children. That shows the dedication he has to tell his story. And with that, I don't take this responsibility lightly. It's an honor I will keep for the rest of my life.

One of my favorite memories of this experience occurred in Arlington one day in late April. He drove up on his own for one final sit-down. I had a ton of questions that were all over the map and needed a few hours.

Sitting in a Pappadeaux restaurant, I noticed the TV in the bar area was on ESPN Classic for whatever reason. And the game being shown was Baylor vs. Oklahoma in 2011. He kind of laughed when he saw it, and we watched a play or two and then went to the patio for the interview. But the TV was on out there, as well, and late in the game, he stopped the conversation so we could watch the final drive. I grabbed my recorder and let him go through his entire thought process during each play leading up to the winning touchdown pass from Griffin to Terrance Williams. The irony of that particular game being on at that particular moment while I was talking to that particular person is something I will never forget.

Like everyone else, I received a nickname from the coach, who has called me "Trick" for the last few years—probably because it rhymed. (I guess it could've been worse.)

Obviously, when remembering the great plays in Art's history, I have my share of favorites, but none more so than the "trick" play against Kansas State in 2011 that resulted in a two-yard gain and a first down.

Again, I want to thank Coach Briles for giving me this opportunity to tell his amazing, fascinating story—one of courage, dedication, commitment, faith, love, and a determination to succeed.

It's been a journey. It's been an adventure. But more than anything, it's been an honor.

I'll close with one of my favorite quotes from Art Briles, who at the time was pumping up his Houston team in the locker room before a game against Rice.

"If they wanna talk, let 'em talk. Let's put this shit on paper."

Well, coach, we just did.